M000304633

The *New*

Joy Of Being

Sober

**A BOOK FOR RECOVERING ALCOHOLICS
AND THOSE WHO LOVE THEM**

Jack Mumey

DEACONESS PRESS

Minneapolis, Minnesota

THE NEW JOY OF BEING SOBER © 1994 by Jack Mumey. All rights reserved. No part of this publication may be used or reproduced in any manner whatsoever without written permission, except in the case of brief quotations embodied in critical articles and reviews. For further information, please contact the publisher.

Published by Deaconess Press, 2450 Riverside Avenue South, Minneapolis, MN 55454

Library of Congress Cataloging-in-Publication Data

Mumey, Jack.
    The new joy of being sober : a book for recovering alcoholics and
those who love them / Jack Mumey. -- [Rev. ed.]
        p.   cm.
    Rev. ed. of : The joy of being sober. c1984.
    ISBN 0-925190-31-4 : $11.95
    1. Alcoholism--Treatment.   2. Recovering alcoholics
3. Temperance.   I. Mumey, Jack.   The joy of being sober.
II. Title.
HV5275.M85   1994
362.2'9286--dc20

                                         94-28358
                                           CIP

First printing: August, 1994

Printed in the United States of America
98 97 96 95 94   7 6 5 4 3 2 1

Cover design by The Nancekivell Group
Interior design by Designsmith

Publisher's Note: Deaconess Press publishes books and other materials related to the subjects of physical health, mental health, and chemical dependency. Its publications, including *The New Joy of Being Sober,* do not necessarily reflect the philosophy of Fairview Hospital and Healthcare Services or their treatment programs.

For my children:
Jackson, Tracey, Dana and Dawn.

For Mary Jo:
You had the courage to turn love into action.

Books by Jack Mumey

Age Different Relationships (with Cynthia Tinsley)
Sex and Sobriety
Good Food for a Sober Life (with Dr. Anne Hatcher)
Secrets In The Family
Loving an Alcoholic
Young Alcoholics: A Book for Parents
The Joy of Being Sober

TABLE OF CONTENTS

PREFACE

This book was originally published in 1984. I had carried the manuscript around for two and a half years before that; no publisher would touch it. In fact, it had gotten so yellowed and torn up I became embarrassed to hand it over. Still, hand it over I did to a small regional publisher.

I begged an advance payment of two hundred dollars to buy a new electric typewriter so I could at least prepare a decent rewrite copy. One year later, the book was still not published. Economics being what they were then, the publisher had had to trim his book list. "Sorry," the letter read, "we have had to postpone the publication of your manuscript."

To say I was devastated wouldn't even be close to how I felt. I knew this book could help others entering recovery. I felt that if what I had done made such an impact on me, as sick with alcoholism as I had been, then it could be a helpful tool to others. I remember calling my friend and assigned editor, Jerry Keegan, to ask him, "How can I resurrect this project from the grave?" Jerry told me if we could somehow sell the paperback rights to the manuscript, then maybe his publisher could revive the project.

So Jerry and I began sending letters to every major and minor publisher around the country, trying to generate some interest in my recovery book. The rest is like a Cinderella story. Dr. Marjorie Mack, the fine lady who has served as Medical Director for my Gateway Treatment Center, casually remarked one day that her sister was "in some position or another" at Contemporary Books in Chicago. "Why don't you try her?" Marj asked. "I don't know if she can help, but maybe they would be interested."

I did; they were! They wanted not only the paperback rights, but the whole project. Contemporary bought the project from the publisher I had committed to a year earlier.

Now, almost fifty thousand copies later, I am realizing another dream: that of putting this book into the hands of as many people as possible in a new paperback edition. Thanks to Deaconess Press, you have this copy in your hands now.

Originally, this book had several different working titles. I don't remember them all, but "Joy of Recovery" was the leader for a long time. (The first chapter attests to that title's importance to me, for it bears that name now.) Whatever titles I considered and discarded, however, the idea of joy remained prominent. My editor at Contemporary, Shari Lesser Wenk, kept prodding me for my feelings about recovery and being sober. Thus, *The Joy of Being Sober* as the book title was born, and the feeling of joy has never gone away.

Deaconess' Editor-in-Chief, Ed Wedman, my own Senior Editor, Jack Caravela, and my editor/author wife, Cynthia Tinsley, all debated whether I should write a completely new version of this book. The answer was no. Most of what I wrote almost fifteen years ago hasn't changed. Times have changed. People in my life have changed, as I'm sure they have in your life, too. But the basic premise, the basic joy, has not diminished. Quite the contrary; *The Joy of Being Sober* has grown over the years. This feeling is still so strong in me that I quote from the original preface to this book:

"Now, sober, it is my hope you will discover that there is a permanent method to feeling so good about your life, yourself, and all whose lives you touch through the absence of alcohol and a commitment to lifelong recovery in sobriety."

However, it would have been foolish to just ignore the intervening ten years—they called for added reflections and postscripts to the chapters. Therefore, I have supplemented the chapters with update memos (titled "More Joy") to cast further light on the material in the book, and made other changes when appropriate.

I mentioned changes in my life. In the interest of maintaining continuity between author and reader, I share them with you now. I am now married to one of my former editors and research assistants, Cynthia Tinsley. She is also my coauthor for a series of books on relationships, the first being *Age Different Relationships* (Deaconess Press). She is an added joy in my personal and professional life.

My four children, now grown, continue to be an incredible source of pride, each of them a success in his or her own field. How I managed to father three lawyers and a child development specialist remains a mystery, but my pride knows no bounds. In order of their birth:

My son Jackson and his family live in Plantation, Florida, where he heads a prestigious bar review firm for Florida and several other states. Even that far away, we have managed to spend quality time at the beach with grandkids Megan and Mackenzie.

My oldest daughter, Tracey, is senior partner in her own criminal defense law firm in Englewood, Colorado, and fills a position as a municipal judge for good measure. We breakfast together weekly, by tradition and design.

Dana, one of the twins, is a successful Assistant City Attorney for Aurora, Colorado. For good measure, she also married a lawyer. She and I have worked very hard to learn that, even though we are so much alike, we can agree to disagree and still be friends. It's paying off!

Her twin, Dawn, is not a lawyer; she is an Early Childhood Development Specialist in the Denver Public Schools and a practicing therapist at Gateway. We manage lunch on a regular basis, and our relationship in the workplace is rewarding and a source of pride for me.

I now own Gateway Treatment Center alone. My founding partner and co-owner, Paul Staley, left to reenter managed health care administration.

So my life has changed, of course. The page in this book listing my other books attests to the way my career as an author has flourished—satisfying me and soaring beyond my wildest imagination. I am more grateful than I can say to all the publishers and editors, and especially to the readers who somehow, magically, continue to want to read what I write.

From the original *Joy of Being Sober:*

> *"My mother, Ruth Printz Mumey, would have loved this book and would have been proud of what it meant to our lives. She never knew about it, having died as the result of a tragic automobile accident. She did live, however, to see her only son begin the process of recovery, and it was a source of great joy for her. It meant all the more, I know, because she herself was alcoholic, and the ravages the disease had made upon her played a part in preventing her from coming back from the accident itself. In death, 'Nanna' again inspired a joy to live—sober."*

So there it is. Once again, we shall embark together upon the journey of living your life without alcohol, of understanding the difference between being merely dry and being truly sober. You alone can adapt what you read between the covers of this book to the life you have been granted.

In my practice as a psychotherapist I constantly hear people asking, "Isn't it true that no one can quit drinking unless they really want to?" My answer has remained the same over the years: *Anyone can be given the tools to quit drinking. It is up to each person to pick up those tools and use them.* But the fear of what might come afterward, the apprehension of living a life without alcohol and all that implies, may be the biggest barrier to entering recovery. If there is no obvious payoff to total abstinence, no reward for not drinking, if there is no joy in being sober, then the task remains dark, gloomy, difficult, and maybe even doomed.

The tools in this book can and do work. Adopt them and adapt them to your own personal life. I have traveled this country to promote books, lecture, appear on radio and television—all heady stuff. But I must share with you that the biggest thrill is still when readers come up to me, or write, or call, or communicate through my publisher, that *The Joy of Being Sober* has made a difference in their lives.

Let it make a difference in your life, now. You see, it changed my life for all time.

Jack Mumey
Spring, 1994

From quiet homes and first beginning, Out to the undiscovered ends, There's nothing worth the wear of winning, But laughter and the love of friends.

Hilaire Bellock

1

THE JOY OF RECOVERY

The music assaulted our eardrums, as we were far too close to the mobile sound van and its loudspeakers. I didn't need the music to pump me up—I was already pumped to full throttle and just beginning the cooling down process following the conclusion of a race.

My wife and one of my daughters had never seen me run before. I felt a lot of personal pride when I spied them among the cheering group greeting the runners as we headed for the chutes at the end of the race.

It had been a surprisingly tough race for me, a novice in this challenge between human body and dirt road played out by several hundred persons that Saturday morning. The hill right after the first mile of the scheduled 3.1 mile (five thousand meter) course had been advertised as mild. The hell it was!

Bunches of people were walking up that hill, sipping or splashing water from the paper cups handed us as we rounded the bend. I wasn't about to stop running. You run for the sake of finishing at a sustained pace, and no hill was going to get the best of me if I could help it.

Paul, my running coach, colleague, and friend, kept reminding me, "Don't pay attention to what the others are doing. Just run your own race, at your own speed and stride." Well, I had done just that, saying over and over to myself like a child reading the story *The Little Engine That Could,* "I can make it! I can make it!"

I *had* made it. Up the hill, around the continuing slight incline that made up the next three quarters of the course, then back through the mile and a half to the finish line.

Like I said, it had been a tough race for me. My wife at the time, Mary Jo, my oldest daughter, Tracey, and our houseguests had come out at dawn to see the race. They had since wisely decided to head back to our house to start Saturday morning brunch. But I wanted to stay for the awards ceremony; I had never been part of such an event. Besides, I couldn't run five thousand meters and immediately wolf down a big breakfast.

I visited with others waiting in a large circle by the sound van, talking—as always—about the next race. Racing gets in your blood; you rearrange entire weeks of schedules to make another race somewhere in the state—or the country, for that matter.

The music stopped and the awards ceremony began. There wasn't much to it, really. The announcer began with the first, then second and third place winners in each group, male and female divisions, starting with the youngest participants.

The sponsor of this particular race was the Adolph Coors Brewing Company, and appropriate placcques, beer goblets, steins, and ribbons were the prizes.

I stood and applauded with the rest as each win, place, and show runner walked out of the circle and up to the announcer to shake his hand and receive a well-earned trophy. I remarked to a fellow runner that you can always tell the first-time participants. They're the ones wearing the T-shirt that comes with the entry packet for that day's event. Two races ago I had learned that one doesn't wear the T-shirt to run the race. You wear the shirt, shorts, or prize shoes only *after* the race, as a symbol of having competed and finished.

I was wearing my Bill Rodgers racing shirt. The Indian beadwork headband I always wore when running was still plastered to my forehead, and it was getting darned hot. I had managed to remove my Bone Fone radio that I had worn during the race.

The announcer reached my age category: Male Division, fifty years old plus.

The hell with 'plus!' I'm just fifty—who cares about plus? ran through my mind.

The first-place winner was announced, and he stepped forward to much applause. He was a fine specimen of a guy who had posted a most respectable time for finish. He received a nice wall plaque. And then—my God—they were calling my name for second place!

I walked from the circle up to the man handing out the trophies. He shook my hand with a hearty "Congratulations!" and reached into the trophy box. He took out a beautiful, heavy, pilsner-style beer glass, the kind that held about twenty-four ounces. The Coors logo, so familiar around the country, was emblazoned in red on the goblet. "Thanks," I mumbled, and walked back to the circle to shouts of "Good race!" and "Congrats!"

Second place! My time had been no track burner, but it was plenty respectable. My decision to keep running that hill instead of walking it and then trying for a blaze finish had obviously been right.

And then the enormity of what I had just accomplished hit me.

Less than three years before that race day I had been seated in an alcohol recovery ward of St. Luke's Hospital in Denver, Colorado. There were about forty of us on the ward, and "Doc" Larry Gibson had just dropped a bomb on me in front of God and everyone.

"Jack Mumey, where are you?" he asked.

"Here, Doc." I raised my hand, still shaking from my recent release out of the detox unit.

"Well, Jack, I've got some bad news for you. We just got your neurological data back from University Hospital. You've suffered severe damage to the right hemisphere of your brain—alcoholic impairment—which is why you haven't been walking straight."

Good God! What was this madman saying?

"The damage is severe. You may never walk straight again."

The impact on me was devastating. My career of over twenty-five years in radio and television was down the tubes. I began to cry right there, in that hospital ward room. How the hell could I have let alcohol do this to me? How could I ever go on camera again, read copy, or make sure a simple piece of stage blocking would work? How could I make a living if that brain damage could not be reversed?

I have since learned that the disease of alcoholism can be conquered—not cured, but put into total remission. It happened to me, and some of the ways I have learned to make life abundant and joyous are what this book is all about.

As I crossed the parking lot after the awards ceremony, heading toward my car, I started a slow jog. Some wellwishers saw the red ribbon pinned to my racing number on my shirt and the huge pilsner glass in my right hand, and shouted, "Hey, way to go!" I grinned, raised both arms above my head like Rocky, and shouted back, "Thanks! It's the joy of recovery!"

They didn't know what I meant, but that didn't matter. I knew.

The pilsner glass sits today on our home bar, jammed full of pennies. When it's full, I take them to the bank and start filling it again. That glass is a small, insignificant award in the great scheme of things. But every day of my life of sobriety as a recovering alcoholic is filled with this same joy of living.

What follows in these chapters can help you live your life full of enthusiasm as a winner over the disease of alcoholism. These chapters are tools I lay before you. Pick them up. Use them. They are tried and tested procedures that can help you experience the joy of recovery.

MORE JOY (An Update)

I have never lost the feeling of the joy of recovery. Oh, it does get a little rusty around the edges sometimes when I lose my sense of gratitude for all the wonderful things sobriety has allowed to come into my life. But the enthusiasm, the ride on the pink cloud of sobriety, is amazingly intact after all these years. I can't wait to get to the office in the morning, or to sit at the computer to write. It's during those times I will often remember how I was before. I remember I would make great plans to do something spectacular during the day, only to have my plans, my energy, and my entire sense of direction disappear with that first morning drink of vodka.

My wife Cyn and I started a renovation project in our kitchen while I was working on this writing project. As the painter was taping and preparing the walls and woodwork, we were moving objects out of the kitchen and off the service window ledge between kitchen and dining area. The painter, also recovering, picked up that old pilsner glass full of pennies to move it.

"Be really careful with that, Jerry," I said. "It means a hell of a lot to me."

He had read the first edition of this book years ago and knew this was the trophy glass. "Still keep it around as a reminder, huh?" he asked.

"I keep it around to remind me of two things, Jer. One, it could just as easily contain beer, which is my enemy. Two, the pennies in it remind me of the prosperity sobriety has brought me."

Be like the bee...and do not waste your spring days...gazing on the doings of the eagle. Be like the child rejoicing at the firelight...and let the mother abide. All that you see was...and still is...yours.

Kahlil Gibran

CHANGING YOUR ATTITUDE

"Easy for you to say."

"You don't know how tough it really is."

"Why don't *you* try giving up drinking, and see?"

"What the hell fun is there?"

"Is this what it's going to be like from now on?"

Well, you get the idea. If I listed all the pitiful mournings I've heard from recovering alcoholics, or better yet, from their families, this could be just a book of excuses.

Instead, we are going to discuss three monsters of recovery that can prevent a change in attitude, a change that must take place to help cement the years of your recovery. These three monsters can be called:

The Pity Pot
The Grey Ghost Syndrome
The Sackcloth and Ashes Number

In a way these monsters are all related, for they are bad, bad attitudes that prevent you from "...rejoicing at the firelight..." or realizing that "...all you see was...and still is...yours."

Coming back to the world of the living from the end-of-the-line world of alcoholism does not happen overnight. Quite frankly, no one should expect it to. After all, usually the person afflicted with the disease of alcoholism has spent years perfecting the habits of drunken behavior. We should not, therefore, expect an overnight miracle where suddenly everything is coming up roses. It doesn't happen that way.

What we can do is recognize that our "stinking thinking" from the use of alcohol does not vanish with the booze itself. I have a close friend who never lets himself forget that the old snake of alcohol is always sleeping, always ready to rise up and strike. Mark does this by keeping a perfectly grotesque ceramic statue of a hooded cobra, complete with red beady eyes, staring at him from the dresser opposite his bed. I've told Mark I think that's a bit bizarre, but it works for him. It keeps his attitude on the right track.

If there is to be a serious attempt to adopt a new attitude, it is necessary to review what it is we are changing—alcoholic behavior. Alcoholic behavior and consequent attitudes about life in general come from the abuse of the drug, alcohol. The disease of alcoholism knows no barriers of race, color, creed, sex, or age.

Keep in mind that what you have is a disease, so classified as early as 1782 by Dr. Benjamin Rush. The American Medical Association recognizes it as such and so should you. There are many definitions of alcoholism, but I like to use two examples to demonstrate the range of absurdity that can and does surround the disease. They are:

"Alcoholism is really an outward manifestation of an underlying deep-seated drinking problem," said Dr. Robert Stuckey at a Sunday Symposium on alcoholism sponsored by the AMA. He was, of course, speaking very much with tongue in cheek, for Dr. Stuckey is a very knowledgeable practitioner in the treatment of alcoholics.

"Alcoholism is really a Valium deficiency." This one has been used so often I can't even identify the original source. The unfortunate part is that too many psychiatrists treat alcoholism just that way—with Valium, a drug having the same chemical effect as alcohol, equivalent to dried vodka.

How do we know that alcoholism is a disease? We know because the definition of "disease" in worldwide use is that it is diagnosable, treatable, progressive, and fatal. Alcoholism is all these things.

Alcoholism is diagnosable.

Your doctor has been seeing signs that are clear blueprints of alcohol abuse. The fluid and electrolyte balance in your body has been disturbed. Your cardiovascular functions and carbohydrate metabolism are probably out of whack. You have an elevated blood pressure, and hypertension is clearly linked to alcoholism. Your doctor has seen trauma in your liver indicating that it is fatty; it is not performing its filtering, cleansing functions like it should. He checks the heart again. Alcohol impairs cardiac performance, and the doctor may have detected subacute cardiomyopathy—fatty heart. That's not good, friend.

Alcoholism is treatable.

We cannot cure the disease of alcoholism, but it can be treated. You and I and the rest of the millions of Americans afflicted with this disease will die alcoholics, but we can die sober alcoholics. Treatment programs throughout the world have been designed to operate with the success factors necessary to put the disease into remission. So you can know you can live a fruitful life as a treatable, if not curable, alcoholic.

Alcoholism is progressive.

This characteristic that permits alcoholism to be classified as a disease is, of course, disturbing. It completely shoots down the notion that an alcoholic can quit after one or two drinks. No way! The nature of addiction to alcohol is such that no untreated alcoholic will get better at handling the drug. It's like the Cracker jacks slogan: "The More You Eat, The More You Want." With alcohol it's "The More You Drink, The More You Drink." Relevant to this point in the classification of alcoholism as a disease is the fact that it is a primary disease; that is, it is not the result of something else wrong with you. For example, hypoglycemia (a deficiency of sugar in the blood) is due to alcoholism, not the other way around.

Finally, alcoholism is fatal.

Alcoholism, untreated, unchecked, allowed to run its vicious lifelong course, will kill. It is a fatal disease. Once the liver has ceased to perform its cleansing functions and the heart has been strangled by alcohol, when the anxiety, depression, insomnia and other dysfunctions of the human body have reached their alcoholic peak, the disease will claim its victim.

Cirrhosis of the liver is one of the nation's biggest killers. Those who die of cirrhosis die a painful death. Ninety percent of those claimed will be alcoholics, and ten percent of alcoholics will develop cirrhosis. Sobering thoughts, don't you agree?

So now we've seen the enemy, and it is ours. Alcoholism is a disease. We can begin to change our attitudes, and step one is realizing it's okay to have a disease. That's right. If it's okay to have blonde hair, brown eyes, be a little too short or a little too heavy around the jowls, it's okay to have a disease, a disease you are in the process of treating.

You are not doomed to a life of mediocrity because of this disease. You certainly don't have to keep nurturing the attitudes that stop you from enjoying your recovery.

When the doctor who first treated your alcoholism put you into treatment, you should have put your old attitudes into the same treatment. Unfortunately, you probably didn't, so now is the time to take action. That brings us back to the three monsters I spoke of earlier: The Pity Pot, The Grey Ghost Syndrome, and The Sackcloth and Ashes Number. Remember, they are all related. They can all be treated, even though you may carry them with you for the remainder of your recovery, which means the rest of your life. If you know about these monsters and are willing to talk about them, you can put them into almost permanent remission. Notice I said "almost." Every once in a while, one or the other of these maladies of recovery is going to jump up again, and you will have to be prepared to deal with it.

The Pity Pot

Picture this as a porcelain or other cold, heavy chamber pot that has the miraculous ability to defy physics and expand to several times its normal size. The more you sit on this Pity Pot, the larger the rim grows before your very eyes (or bottom). Without warning you fall into this pot from your perch on the rim. It is very difficult to pull yourself back up to where you are just sitting on the rim again. In fact, sometimes it seems nearly impossible.

There you are on a perfectly beautiful summer Saturday, and you are mowing the lawn. You pause at the completion of your chore to survey the great job of mowing. This time you did the whole job, instead of leaving huge patches like in your drinking days. Your neighbor pops over to borrow some gasoline for his lawn mower. Clutched in the hand not occupied with the empty gas can is, God forbid, a cold can of beer!

It's the coldest, biggest can of beer you've ever seen. They probably used this very can to make that award winning television commercial. Your helpful neighbor, who probably doesn't know you're recovering (see Chapter Thirteen), is holding what must be the ultimate thirst quencher. Every rivulet of moisture has caught the sun; the label gleams brilliantly. The smell is overwhelming. And you, you poor, pitiful thing, *you can't have even one golden delicious sip!*

Poor, poor you. The Pity Pot has beckoned. As you reluctantly hand your neighbor your gas can and watch him take both his can of beer and your can of gas away, you feel the agony. You can't wait to climb on the Pity Pot. The long face appears, accompanied by the deep sigh and the muttered curse.

"What's the matter, hon?" your wife asks from her vantage point in the geranium bed.

"Nothing, dammit!" you growl. "Stop nagging me!"

And into the house you skulk, headed for the Pity Pot. As you climb upon its ever-widening rim, the old support attitudes start in:

"A cold beer always tasted great after mowing the lawn."

"Boy, there's nothing like a cold beer on a hot Saturday." (Substitute whichever of the seven days of the week you drank cold beer—probably all of them.)

"Why can't I have just one cold beer?"

"Hell, I did a good job mowing the lawn. I deserve a reward, don't I?"

By this time you've practically fallen clear into the pot. The only way to stop your descent is a change of attitude led by the key trooper, verbalization.

That's right. You talk about it, right in front of God and your spouse. You learn to say what the problem is. Let's rerun the previous dialogue, this time with a change of attitude:

WIFE: "What's the matter, hon?"

NEW YOU: "I want a cold beer so damn bad I can't stand it!"

WIFE: (understanding) "I know you do."

NEW YOU: (starting personal reinforcement) "I never did this good a job mowing when I was drinking, though."

WIFE: (picking up the cue) "Everything you do now is better, hon."

NEW YOU: (losing it a little) "Yeah, but these hot summer days...that's when beer tasted best."

WIFE: (with pain) "You never stopped with one beer."

NEW YOU: (continuing to reinforce the positive) "God, I guess! I never even stopped with one six pack. The lawn looked like hell for weeks."

WIFE: (planting a kiss instead of a geranium) *"You* looked like hell for weeks!"

NEW YOU: (putting the nail in the coffin) "And the hangovers made Sundays twice as bad as Saturdays."

You exchange hugs and warm fuzzies.

Well, that's gotten you off the Pity Pot. You verbalized your feelings, shared them with another person so you did not have a chance to internalize the anguish of not drinking. You avoided becoming deeply resentful of being in the recovery process.

Turning off the negative attitudes by talking about the positive aspects of not drinking (noticing better performance, improved appearance and feeling better) helps you climb off the Pity Pot before the rim grows until you fall in. I suggest to people who are really hung up on how good a cold can or glass of beer looks to try a simple-picture changing technique I learned from my television directing days.

Try this. First, look at the big, cold can of beer. As you stare at it, start a slow dissolve of that picture into another. Imagine the label on the beer can changing to read, "Premium Blood." That's right, blood. Imagine your name in fancy script on that label. That can of beer is not very appetizing now, is it?

Drinking for you means sure death. For the non-alcoholic, that beer is what it's intended to be, a fine thirst quencher. For you, it is poison. I never could envision what a really gruesome can of poison should look like, so I turned to the blood image. It works, too.

I have clients who have reported that they so effectively envisioned a pitcherful of draft beer turning to blood that they nearly had to leave the affair they were attending. The image was so strong they almost pointed out this transformation to the rest of the assembled guests, all of whom were enjoying their beer.

Well, that reaction may be an extreme. The point is, the imaging and verbalization processes will help you get off the Pity Pot. The other vanguard to this attack is to state simply, "I think I must be on the Pity Pot. I'm feeling kind of sorry for myself."

Once you say this, you'll find the self-pity begins to disappear. You are changing your attitude by learning not to keep feelings bottled up inside, and you change your attitude by giving sight and sound to your feelings. You allow yourself the luxury of stating in a forthright manner both sides of a given situation, with special emphasis on reinforcing what is better now that you are in the recovery process. You'll always find the Pity Pot lurking just around your emotional corner, but you can make sure the rim doesn't grow larger and swallow you up.

The Grey Ghost Syndrome

If you want to walk around like Hamlet's father for the rest of your life, go ahead. I tell my recovering clients to read the story *Winnie the Pooh,* paying very close attention to poor old miserable Eeyore.

"Gosh, Pooh," sighs Eeyore, "it's a blustery day!"

Every day is going to be blustery if you make it so. The idea that the kicks are all gone out of your life because you can't get pie-eyed anymore is ridiculous.

The Grey Ghost Syndrome makes me more angry than anything else in trying to teach the joy of recovery. There are those who simply believe all this world's pleasures revolve around the ability to drink alcohol. Thus, hands shoved firmly into coat pockets, collar turned up against the chill winds of despair, the Grey Ghost shuffles through his or her sobriety. What nonsense! Are you trying to tell me that little kid with the shiny red wagon is looped as she hauls her dolls around the playground? That young couple walking hand in hand sharing a Pepsi is drunk all right—drunk on the joys of just being alive. But the Grey Ghost is comfortable with his dark, foreboding and sullen mood. He's working at becoming a recovering zombie.

"I used to have fun when I was drinking," he mutters.

"What's the use of going to the ball game now?" he intones in deathly low registers.

"I can't possibly enjoy dinner out without booze. I'll be a total bore," says the Grey Ghost.

Ad infinitum. Ad nauseum.

The Grey Ghost Syndrome usually strikes after a session on the Pity Pot when nothing has been done to start the attitude-changing process. The Grey Ghost stalks the streets of his or her life devoid of alcohol and honestly believes that drinking was fun and that life can't be fun now without it. Well, drinking was not fun. Having to call in sick the next day because you suffer that ancient malady of drinkers, "Irish flu," or waking up in a strange city with no idea how you got there—*that was fun?* Hitting your small defenseless youngsters in a fit of drunken anger was fun? I think not, but there are people who absolutely believe the only role left for them is that of the Grey Ghost. You need to count yourself among those absent from that game.

How do you shed the mantle of the Grey Ghost? Well, it's done with mirrors.

When you believe there is no fun left for you because you are sober, and you feel the image of the Grey Ghost creeping into your being, quickly get to a mirror, alone. Look closely at your reflection. The deep-set eyes, bleary from abuse of alcohol, are now clear and focused.

Talk to yourself. Say, "No more sagging jowls, that's good." Pinch your cheeks and watch the red spring to your touch. Say, "Good. Blood circulation is better."

Peer even closer. Notice that the whites of your eyes are now actually white. That awful pale yellow from liver dysfunction has cleared up.

Now move back so you see yourself full-length. Pinch at your waist. You may still have a bulge here and there, your love handles may still be evident, but you say to your image, "Looking good! I'm losing the weight that alcohol was adding. If I keep it up I'm going to be a size smaller."

An image of a confident you will begin to supplant the Grey Ghost. But here's the final kicker. Try to find a picture of yourself taken at a party or family outing during your drinking days. Look at it very closely. Then look again at the image of yourself today, as you are in sobriety. Say out loud, "I'll never look like that again!" Say it and mean it. There's no room for the Grey Ghost in your life of recovery. Oh, he'll keep trying to creep back in now and then, but you'll know how to deal with him (or her).

I named my Grey Ghost. I call him "Ol' Creepy," and whenever I think he's about to pull a number on me, I whip out a Polaroid shot we keep in a drawer downstairs. It's enough to make me cry, seeing how I used to look in my drinking days. It's also enough to banish Ol' Creepy and his despair from my presence. When my family sees me looking at that picture, they know I'm battling with the Grey Ghost Syndrome. And I win!

The Sackcloth and Ashes Number

Finally, we treat with not too loving care the last barrier to changing your attitude. The Sackcloth and Ashes Number can really keep you down in the trenches if you let it. This means, simply stated, that what's done is done. You can't go back and undo all the dismal things you did while in an alcoholic state. It isn't possible to take back the harsh words, abusive behavior, or other actions during your drinking days. The smashed car fenders, broken romances, unbalanced checkbooks, and just plain no-account checks have all been dealt with one way or another. Nothing you can say or do will change that.

Except for one thing. You can tell anyone who will listen that you have said you are sorry, and you've said it for the last time. Alcoholic amnesia, "blackouts" as we call them, are a frequent and distressing malady of alcoholism. What you said and did as a practicing drinker is past now, and should be done with.

It's time to take off your sackcloth, dust off the penitential ashes and get on with seeing to it that your life is full of meaning from here on out. You'll not change what happened before sobriety, and the quickest way to change your attitude is to stop flogging yourself. Give up trying to win the Academy Award for "Best Dramatic Performance."

The Fellowship of Alcoholics Anonymous makes an excellent point when it suggests you "...make amends (for past wrongs), except when to do so would injure them (or yourself) or others." "Them" refers to the people whose lives you may have messed up by your alcoholism. I added "yourself" because somewhere along the line you have to be willing to forgive yourself!

Admitting all your past sins while under John Barleycorn's influence is good for your recovery, up to a point. After that, it simply becomes an easy way out to avoid picking up the pieces of your life and getting on with the important business of joyful recovery.

Therefore, cast off this mantle of ashes. Step out of the sackcloth. Go buy yourself some new clothes. I don't care if it's just a baseball cap, an inexpensive blouse, or a new tie. Just get some new item of clothing for yourself and promptly dub it your "get-rid-of-my-sackcloth" item.

I chose to take a pair of jeans and cut them off (not very expertly, I'll admit). Those jeans became a symbol for me of casting off (or cutting off) the old sins and starting anew. I got a little carried away, because I had gotten hooked on designer jeans, and they're expensive. That was some of my "stinking thinking" about money values creeping back in, so I needed a little help from my wife to keep from buying forty-dollar name-label jeans and whacking the pant legs off. You must constantly guard against the negative habits of the addictive personality.

So, changing your attitude is a key to the secret of enjoying sobriety.

You have to use this tool every day of your life; you have to force yourself to take the smallest of things and make big comparisons.

When you successfully handle a misunderstanding, say to yourself, "How would I have handled that when I was drinking?" When you close a big business deal, say, "Would I have put this together when I was drinking? Would I have made any money?" When you kiss someone goodnight, say to yourself, "Would I have even been allowed this close, smelling like I must have smelled?"

In short, what you were was an actively drinking alcoholic. What you are now, today, is a recovering, joyful, sober alcoholic. There is a difference. Vive la différence!

Get off the Pity Pot. Bury the Grey Ghost. Step out of the Sackcloth.

MORE JOY (An Update)

It's absolutely amazing how easy it is to climb back on the Pity Pot or drape yourself in the Sackcloth and sprinkle yourself liberally with ashes. I still catch myself ready to climb back up to that old pot's rim and plunk myself down. Fortunately, the years of sobriety have also made me aware of what is happening. The process can be stopped.

Here's another new tool for your sobriety toolbox. Tell people what's happening. Give them permission to confront you if they see you start to climb on the Pity Pot or to robe yourself in the Sackcloth. This is a good way to help you snap back to reality and recognize a very old behavior you don't want to crank up again.

Not too long ago I found that old Polaroid picture again. It was still in the kitchen drawer, lost among the other junk I can never remember putting in there. Consequently, I had to move that picture to get to the battery or the garage door key I was positive was way back there in the drawer.

I took the Polaroid into the living room and showed it for the millionth time to Cyn. "Have I ever showed you this?" I asked innocently.

"Not this month. At least not this week," she answered.

The last time I pulled this she handed me a copy of *Age Different Relationships,* a book that we wrote together in 1992-93. There is a wonderful color picture of both of us on the front cover.

"Doesn't look like the same guy to me," said Cyn. "Of course, I suppose you can't see the difference?"

She thinks she's so funny...

Well, every one can master a grief but he that has it.

Shakespeare,
Much Ado About Nothing

3

THE DRY DRUNK SYNDROME

"She talks kinda slurred, but I know she isn't drinking."

"His temper's just as bad as when he was drinking."

"He stormed around the house all weekend, banging doors and generally making everybody else's life hell."

"She still doesn't balance the damn checkbook. That's the way she acted in her drinking days."

Sound familiar? Sure it does. For every sentence like these there are thousands of others uttered by the family and friends of recovering alcoholics. They have sat with me in group therapy when we have each individual talk about a behavior pattern observed in the newly sober person.

Hey—they're talking about you and me! The kind of behavior they describe has been called "The Dry Drunk Syndrome." This malaise can be defined simply as the discomfort experienced by the recovering person when he is no longer drinking. It is the appearance of intoxication and its related behavior without drinking alcohol—the recovering person acts as if he had never stopped drinking. Indeed, the Dry Drunk Syndrome can be a serious roadblock to total recovery.

This erratic behavior doesn't go away in a few weeks or months, either. Some people experience it regularly, just like Christmas. You're going along minding your own business when suddenly, wham!

The dry drunk generally starts with a domestic argument. Simple things in life get to us and get blown all out of proportion. I believe I first heard Dr. Larry Gibson describe these little annoyances as "mouse turds." And that's what they are. We don't worry so much about the recovering person trying to run up Pike's Peak or swim the English Channel. What bears watching is the possibility of stumbling over life's little mouse turds.

I do it all the time—stumble over the damn mouse turds. What other people can handle in the normal course of their daily lives can become unmanageable for me, and probably you, too. The reason is because we were so involved in alcoholic behavior in the past that we had endless excuses for our abominable behavior. We turn to the same kinds of behavior to excuse us now, when we're sober. The alcohol is gone, but the actions of alcoholic behavior aren't. Hence, slamming doors (I'm particularly rough on storm doors because they close nicely and efficiently no matter how hard they're slammed), name calling, and general "let's-blame-it-all-on-you" dialogues are characteristic of a dry drunk.

A close friend of mine who has been in recovery for more than eleven years told me of getting mad at his wife recently and throwing her car keys in a snowbank during a skiing trip.

"That's the same damn stunt I pulled the last time I got drunk," he told me. We laughed over it, remembering that I had told him at the time that he had better do something about his drinking problem. He did, but the old Dry Drunk Syndrome still stalks him on occasion and lays life's little mouse turds in his path.

The dry drunk can occur at any time, any place. It's a convenient method employed by the recovering person to cover his or her actions. If the checkbook doesn't balance, the dry drunker can say, "You know how I am with things like this." She will go on to explain to an exasperated mate that she knows how much she has in her checking account. What difference does it make if the little figures on the bank statement agree or not?

Or the guy who says he can handle criticism about the way he does a particular job, but flies off the handle the first time he gets negative feedback. That's the Dry

Drunk Syndrome at work. It is telling us that we still are not taking responsibility for our actions.

That was one of the key reasons we were forgiven over and over again when we were drinking. No one wanted to blame us, the alcoholic, for what we did, because after all, we weren't responsible for our actions. That's a great comfort and security blanket for life.

Well, that excuse doesn't apply anymore. When we feel things piling up on us, the dry drunk can creep along while we're on the Pity Pot, and *socko!* Another mouse turd lands us in the dust.

As long as the recovering person refuses to accept responsibility for life actions, the Dry Drunk Syndrome will continue to play an important part in slowing the real joy of recovery. So what do you do about it?

Well, one plan that seems to work is to inform the rest of the folks who are important to you about this Dry Drunk Syndrome. Ask them to point out such behavior to you when they see it happen. I know that can be a dangerous weapon, so let's set some ground rules:

1. Don't use the dry drunk as an excuse for all irrational behavior. Some people just have a bad temper, and giving up drinking didn't change that. It's okay to be angry, but call it for what it is. Don't blame a dry drunk for blowing up.

2. Learn to ask for honesty and be willing to hear honesty. "Honey, I'm feeling like I've been grouchy and maybe a little short today. Have I?" Anything less than the absolute truth will only feed into the dry drunk and prolong its agony. Accept an honest answer when you get it.

3. Once again, verbalize. When you know you are in a dry drunk, for Lord's sake, tell someone about it. "George, I didn't mean to snap at you last night. I think I'm in a dry drunk and I probably tripped on a mouse turd or two at the office yesterday."

4. Ask for help. If you had a broken arm, you would ask the doctor to set it. The same is true with this recovery business. Ask for help. "I'm feeling like the whole world's against me. I know it's a dry drunk coming on. C'mon, let's go for a walk, can we?" Asking for help is different from asking someone else to tell you what a jackass you've become in the last twenty-four hours, and it takes the steam out of a full-blown fight. Who will fight with anyone who already admits they are in a foul mood and want help to get back on track?

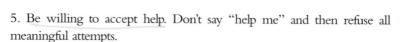

5. Be willing to accept help. Don't say "help me" and then refuse all meaningful attempts.

I have heard clients discuss this last problem over and over—the recovering husband says he wants help to get out of the dry drunk he knows he's in. His wife suggests a picnic.

"Nope."

"How about going for a drive?"

"No way. Every fool in town drives to the hills on Sunday."

"Let's go to a movie."

"What? Spend fourteen bucks to have a bunch of house rabbits running up and down the aisles?"

Every suggestion offered in response to the request for help ends up in the discard pile, and life continues to be a chore for all concerned.

The significant people in the life of the recovering alcoholic do have incredible patience, sometimes bordering on true martyrdom. But even that patience will run out. You have to be willing to take some risks. Run some rapids! Even if you don't care for the initial suggestion to help you through the dry drunk, once you do something you can begin to free yourself from its grip on your mood.

There are some other clues to recognizing the Dry Drunk Syndrome. You will probably begin to make a mental list of your own to use as tools to recognize this syndrome.

One clue is the tendency to be grandiose about everything. When you were on the active drinking list, there were all those "pie-in-the-sky" plans you would brag about. Talking about the big business deal that was just around the corner, the trip abroad for your next anniversary, or the step up the promotional ladder was part of your everyday pattern and lifestyle.

Those same patterns crop up in the dry drunk. They come to the surface easily because they were habit-forming, just like the rest of your alcoholic behavior. They don't belong in your recovery plan, however.

The one sure way I use to keep such patterns in check is to write down all the things I said I was going to do over the past few years. That list goes in one column marked "Promised." In an opposing column I list what actually got done. This column is headed "Delivered." One look at that page nearly always brings my thinking back to earth.

This doesn't mean you should stop dreaming. It only means you need to recognize what you said in alcoholic states can be repeated in a dry drunk state of mind. That's when you have to bridle yourself and start dealing with reality, and you do this by compromise. For instance, the trip abroad you once promised yourself can become a family motor trip you have long delayed.

Not long ago a family sat in my office and told me with tears in their eyes that they had their best time ever on a trip to Disneyland. It was the first trip they had ever made as a sober family, and it was delivery on a promise made many times before, only to be washed away in a tide of booze.

Other recovering persons I know tell me they ask to see their work evaluations after gaining their sobriety. In most cases, seeing the improved nature of their work habits is like a promotion. The positive reinforcement is a tonic without gin for them. Real promotions often come shortly thereafter, but these people don't have to depend upon them; they earn new respect with their recovery plans.

Another compromise is to turn the big business deal into a small but solid victory. Try selling something through the newspaper classified ads—you'll probably make a few bucks and you'll renew your confidence in yourself. It doesn't have to be a big deal to be successful. I wanted to sell a car, and everyone told me it would never bring what I was asking for it. They were right. But after two weeks of haggling on the phone and showing the damn thing, I got close enough to my price to prove I could still handle a big deal. That's compromise.

Another clue for recognizing the dry drunk is what I call the "confetti approach." This is when you throw out so many ideas and thoughts in one conversation that people have a hard time keeping up with what you are trying to say or what point you are trying to make. This confetti approach is a sure sign that the old habits are creeping in, and that a dry drunk is closing in on you.

This confetti number is old thinking from when you were drinking, that you have the answer to everything and that only your opinion counts. It's a hard habit to break, but one way is to ask aloud, "Am I making any sense here?" A little laugh after that question allows enough pause to get you an honest answer and time to organize your thinking into more orderly patterns. Two or three confetti conversations in a row should send you the message, "Hold it, Buster. Here you go again, talking like the great guru. Just like when you were drinking."

See, for every drunken action there's an equivalent sober reaction. All you have to do is label your behavior: "My God! That last statement sounded like something I would say if I were still drinking." Or, "Did that sound like a sober statement? Let me run that by again and see if it makes sense."

Above all, you must guard against overreacting to life's mouse turds. It isn't anyone else's fault that you can never drink again. Your anger, frustration, and grief will boil to the surface in a dry drunk over and over again unless you can identify them.

Did I say "grief?" Yep.

There is a definite grieving process you will go through on your road to recovery. That's why I have stated that The Pity Pot, Grey Ghost, and Sackcloth and Ashes Number are related. They are all part of the grief you experience when you lose your best friend.

"Best friend?" Right again. You grieve over the loss of your friend, alcohol. This emotion is every bit as real as what you would feel over the loss of a relative, a job, or a mate.

The recovering person will go through the same steps of the grieving process as he would over a death. This same sense of loss occurs when drinking is buried forever in your life. Many cases of dealing with recovering alcoholics of both sexes indicate the grief process involved with giving up drinking consists of four general categories: denial, anger, blame, and acceptance.

Denial

Human nature is to deny a tragedy has taken place. On some level we think tragedy always happens to someone else, never to us. Therefore, logic dictates that you couldn't be the alcoholic. Heavy drinker? Sometimes, maybe, but not a true, dyed-in-the-wool alcoholic.

You may see the symptoms of alcoholic behavior, such as:

-Needing a drink the morning after.
-Liking to drink alone.
-Losing time from the job because of drinking.
-Waiting for five o'clock before taking a drink.
-Knowing your moods change drastically when drinking.

However, even faced with these telltale signs of dangerous drinking, you still deny it could happen to you.

There are self-evaluation lists containing fifty to one hundred or more such telltale signs. The real denier can answer every one of them with a "no." If the answers were "yes," you see, then you could begin the grief process and work through the loss.

Anger

After you have faced denial, there is honest-to-God rage that you carry whatever genetic deficiency helped make your system allergic to the chemical, alcohol. "Why can't I drink like everyone else?" "Why does this happen to me? Why can't I be like other people who drink and have a good time?"

This anger has a liberal sprinkling of the question, "Why, why, why?" The best advice for getting through this stage of the grief process is to stop asking "why" in your anger. Move on to the questions "what," "how," and "when." There is just no answer to "why." People do what they want to do in life, and seeking justification by asking "why" is spinning emotional wheels.

You can work the grieving step of anger by asking yourself, "What did I do when I was drinking that caused embarrassment for me and my family? How did I get myself into this financial bind? Wasn't drinking the cause of this trouble?" With this last question, your anger is turned toward your alcoholic behavior instead of toward yourself or others. "When did I lose control over my drinking?" and, "When did my life become unmanageable because of alcohol?" come next.

These are good questions that can help you vent justified anger without the unanswerable "why" clouding up the issue. For good measure, to help you work the grief process you can add the question "where" to this list. "Where did I do my drinking? Where did the money go that I had been saving for a trip?"

By bringing the anger out in the open about what drinking did to you instead of what you *thought* it did for you, you help the grief process work to your benefit.

Blame

The next step in grieving over giving up alcohol is blame. Since logic does not permit the alcoholic to think he is to blame, it becomes natural to assuage the pain by blaming someone else. The list of whom to blame is practically endless. You can count on your spouse, parents, and children being right up there at the top, followed closely by your boss and the company you work for. In group therapy I ask recovering persons to share the reasons they drank. The responses can get pretty ridiculous:

"It was Saturday noon."
"It was Sunday noon."
"I didn't get the raise."
"I got the raise."

"The (insert favorite pro football team) lost the damn game."

"The (repeat above) won the game."

In a 1947 article in *Nation's Business,* one woman claimed to have been cured of her alcoholism by having her mother-in-law removed from the family home. Put a hundred people handing out blame for their drinking in a room, and you'll hear a hundred different responses.

Working through this grief process obviously involves placing some blame somewhere. When you see how ridiculous it is to lay the blame anywhere except where it belongs, you take a step forward in the recovery program upon which you've embarked.

Where does the blame lay? I won't pretend to have the final answers, but there are some exciting things being done in medical research that cast light down a pretty dark tunnel.

The University of Colorado medical research unit has been a leader in research linking hereditary factors to alcoholism. The work indicates that alcoholics have some genetic deficiency in their bodies that may be passed on from generation to generation. Apparently, some generations are hit harder than others.

Boiled down, this research suggests that if you had an alcoholic parent, your chances of inheriting this genetic deficiency are above average. It also means your children could inherit it from you, and their children from them.

So do you want to blame someone or something for your *having* the disease of alcoholism? Doing so makes about as much sense as blaming good old mom and dad for your brown eyes or golden hair. Genetic patterns are handed out in a place beyond your and my comprehension. If you were born, and obviously you were, then there's a good possibility that you received the alcoholic traits along with the rest of the family similarities and frailties. But why blame someone? Just accept these traits as part of the way you were designed.

Blaming yourself for what happened in the past is definitely out. You had very little to do with your alcoholism, in all probability. The best action you took was in going into treatment and/or the fellowship of Alcoholics Anonymous to wean you from alcohol.

Acceptance

Finally, as you work through the grief process as part of the Dry Drunk Syndrome, you end up with acceptance. Alcohol will never again be a part of your life. Accept it. For you to drink even one-half of a glass of wine, or one beer, or an ounce and a half of whiskey will put you right back where you were, no matter how many years you have been sober.

This is a fact of the disease. Accept it. Acceptance may take hours, days, or weeks. However, the recovering person who tries to be that one alcoholic in the world who can take just one more drink and control it is on the road to returning to complete drunkenness. Whatever that genetic deficiency is that makes us alcoholic in the first place never leaves us. That's why the recovering person of thirty-five or forty years duration is just as afraid to test the axiom, "An alcoholic is just one drink away from the next drunk," as a newly recovering person. He knows, and you must accept and know, that this axiom is true.

One way to help you through the grief process during dry drunks is to make a new sacrifice. Dr. Blair Carlson, Medical Director of Kaiser Permanente's Chemical Dependency Program in Denver, has a great plan that he passes along for strengthening the recovering person. Carlson encourages his patients to visit the detox wards of the hospitals on holidays such as Christmas and Easter. When you see the poor devils who are just beginning their recovery, it strengthens your acceptance of the fact that you are an alcoholic. And you can get on the recovery train and ride it the rest of your life.

People who have been on a dry drunk for several days have told me of making such a hospital visit. They found their attitude brightening and their grief over not being able to ever drink again put to a final rest. (More on this in Chapter Thirteen, "Carrying the Message.")

Each Christmas I make this personal sacrifice myself. I give up some time with my family to spend an hour with a suffering alcoholic. By so doing I can arrest any dry drunk I may have felt creeping around.

Grief and the Dry Drunk Syndrome are so tied together that many times hard confrontation with yourself is necessary to snap out of the doldrums. To determine if you've begun the grief process, ask yourself, "Have I allowed myself the freedom to accept that alcohol is dead in my life?" To challenge a dry drunk ask, "Have I been acting like this because I'm really afraid to grow and get on with the joy of recovery?"

Finally, I invented a system that, for lack of a better name, I call "Carpet Squares." This system is really a self-appraisal game I have successfully used with clients in helping them deal with the dry drunk. Imagine yourself standing in front of a full-length mirror covered entirely with those self-adhesive carpet squares.

You may begin by mentally removing any square you like from the mirror.

An elbow appears. Next, select any other square, exposing another part of your body. You keep pulling those squares off, one by one, until the only carpet square left is the one covering the reflection of your face. Now comes the test. Ask yourself, "If I remove this last square, will I like what I see? Will I be willing to look at what others have been looking at for days (or hours) since this dry drunk began?"

Clients have said they imagined themselves pulling off that last square and then quickly shoving it back in place before they had to look at themselves. But it helped them realize they had been in a dry drunk and needed to get out of it in a hurry.

This Carpet Squares exercise came to me when I was laying a large basement floor with those squares for a friend. It had been a rough day, and I was not only on the Pity Pot, but also in the doldrums because this whole remodeling job had not gone right. The carpet had a pattern with lines running through it, and I had been so busy trying to get the job done that I hadn't paid much attention to how I laid the last few squares. When I realized that I had screwed up the flow of the pattern, I had to start backtracking and removing some of the squares.

The surface I was covering was an old vinyl tile floor. It was shiny enough that I could see my image reflected faintly. There I was, swearing up a storm because I had to redo work that I should have done right the first time. "I probably would have done the damn thing right if I was still drinking," I grumbled out loud, typical of someone suffering the Pity Pot/Dry Drunk combination.

I continued pulling up the squares—quite a number of them, because I had made the mistake in following the pattern several yards behind me. Finally, scowling fiercely, I jerked up the last square of the mistake. Staring back at me from the reflective surface was this mean-looking son-of-a-bitch who, instead of being grateful that he could even perform this task, was bitching about it.

One look at myself made me realize that was how I looked to other people. Therefore, I was making them suffer for my actions. That was exactly what I had done as an active alcoholic. This realization snapped me out of my mood, and I wrote a small note to myself on my scratch pad in the toolbox. The note just said, "Carpet Squares."

If you have the guts to pull off that last carpet square and really look at yourself, it will be ego-deflating. That's what you want, to be taken down a peg or two off the high you were getting from being on this dry drunk. You will be clear of mind enough to make some alternate choices in the way you behave, and you will be using the grief process in reverse. You will be allowing yourself the freedom to live life to the fullest.

Recently in a therapy group, a woman in the early stages of her recovery refused to mentally remove that last square and see herself as she appeared to the rest of us. She dropped the group, her recovery program, and went back to drinking. For that unfortunate, the acceptance stage of her grief process, acceptance that she was a recovering alcoholic, was just too great a square for her to lift off the mirror. Rather than face it, she dropped out of her program for recovery and will once again be caught in the alcoholic undertow.

The grief over giving up alcohol is very real, and the family of the recovering person needs to understand that. It's up to you, though, to have enough fortitude to use the tools you have learned to work with through the stages of this process. By working through these stages every time they crop up, you will learn to recognize the telltale signs that let you know you might be heading for a dry drunk.

One other note of caution about the dry drunk: I don't know of anyone in recovery who thinks these drunks are behind them, even after many years of sobriety. Treat them like some immunization program that requires a booster shot every so often.

Remember though, this is a mental "shot." Stay out of the bars, and watch out for those mouse turds!

MORE JOY (An Update)

One of the questions I'm asked regularly is whether this Dry Drunk Syndrome ever goes away. This question is usually preceded by another, whether I really believe there even is such a thing as a dry drunk. The answers, in the order in which I brought up the questions, are "no" and "yes." Now for some explanation.

Friends and colleagues of mine who have been in recovery for many years more than I all talk about how the Dry Drunk Syndrome will suddenly pop up on them, usually when least expected.

Remember, the dry drunk doesn't mean a person is in danger of actually drinking, particularly if they have a long and solid sobriety under their belt. Even though an alcoholic, safe, sober and working a good recovery program, feels secure, we all remember that we are just one drink away from the next drunk. However, this syndrome that I have written about refers to the *behaviors* of drinking.

I can always tell when I am working too hard or not taking care of myself by ignoring my woodshop or forgetting to walk as long and as far as I should. I feel a dry drunk begin to hit when I find myself starting to pick little minuscule fights with my clients. Better yet, I know I'm in trouble when I find myself losing patience with patients, as I refer to it. Recovering friends report the same kinds of weird conditions that hit like a monsoon, quite unexpectedly, but quite severe.

The good news is that as the years of my own recovery have added up, I am much more aware of when these conditions are developing and I, just like everyone else, go back to the basics of H-A-L-T. I don't get too **h**ungry, too **a**ngry, too **l**onely or too **t**ired. (Incidentally, as a therapist I can state that I have never dealt with a client who had relapsed and did not own up to ignoring at least one, and more than likely two, of these H-A-L-T warnings.)

Does the Dry Drunk Syndrome really exist? You bet your bippy it does. If anyone tells you otherwise, my bet would be that the person denying its existence is not recovering and, frankly, might still be arguing that alcoholism is not a disease. Better you accept the reality of the dry drunk, learn to forecast it, and vanquish it.

The wise, for cure, on exercise depend; God never made his work for man to mend.

Chesteron, Epistle to John Dryden

4

THE JOY OF EXERCISE
(JUST DO IT!)

"Do you mean to tell me that riding my ten-speed will make me not want to drink?"

"I didn't like exercise when I was drinking. Why would I want to do it when I'm sober?"

The group of hospital patients was hostile that afternoon as I gave one of my weekly lectures on the "Joy of Recovery." The hostility was perfectly understandable. Here I was, a healthy person, talking to them about what life can be in recovery. They were still trying to begin the grief process over giving up alcohol. I answered the young man who posed the first question.

"No, riding your ten-speed bike isn't going to keep you from wanting to drink," I agreed. "What it will do is help you discharge the built-up adrenaline and nervous energy that accompany these periods of stress and tension related to your recovery."

This chapter is about learning how to help control the body systems as they undergo biological adjustments associated with giving up alcohol. I have answered the second question often in other similar lectures:

"Nobody said you would like to exercise. But it's something you're going to have to do if you want to maintain your sobriety and build a strong bridge to recovery. And you may even learn to like exercise."

The questions for you to think about are: what kind of exercise, how much of it, done under what circumstances, and for how long a period? We'll explore these questions together in these next few pages.

First we need some basic medical facts, which don't require an advanced medical degree to understand. Some people think—mistakenly—that exercise makes you feel better because you get more blood to the brain. The truth is that the flow of blood to your brain is fairly constant, so exercise doesn't affect that flow much one way or the other. However, doctors believe that exercise can possibly drain certain chemicals, such as adrenaline, that accumulate in the brain. These chemicals affect our moods. When substances like adrenaline are metabolized during exercise, then we are stimulated and we feel better.

If you have been sitting in your favorite easy chair in front of the tube all day, you have been building up nervous tension, or stress. Exercise helps to release that stress. I can remember when the only exercise I got on any given day was walking across the room to refill my glass with scotch. Sometimes even that was too much.

Another myth about exercise is the one that says you have to hit it for hours at a time to really do any good. The U.S. Department of Health and Human Services confirms that as little as fifteen to thirty minutes of vigorous exercise three times a week will help the average individual have a healthier heart, eliminate excess weight, and tone up sagging muscles. Another benefit is that you'll sleep better. Now that doesn't sound like a lot of time to devote to your recovery program, does it?

Everyone is calorie conscious these days. Drinking should have brought home that awareness, when you realized that the pounds piled up as quickly as the beer and bourbon bottles.

You added one hundred calories with every little ounce and a half of scotch you drank. Every can of light beer added at least ninety calories, more for the regular variety. Now if you were a pretty good drinker, seven of those ounce-and-a-half scotches per day added seven hundred extra calories to your daily caloric intake. But who ever poured you just one and a half ounces? Even the stingiest of bartenders using an automatic shot dispenser is prone to sweeten your drink, more so if you have been a regular, good customer.

It's realistic to estimate that you were adding closer to fifteen hundred or two thousand extra calories to your bod. And that's just from the booze! We haven't even added the nine potato chips (one hundred calories), the one ounce of cheese nibbles (one hundred calories), or the two plain cookies (one hundred calories) that were consumed along with the alcohol. Do you concede, then, that there is a need to recover from excess caloric binges, too?

"Yeah, but the more I exercise the more I'll eat," cries the skeptic. Not so. As physical activity increases, there is not necessarily a parallel increase in the amount of food you put away. If you combine exercise with calorie reduction, then you have the right combination.

Try to cut about two hundred calories a day from your food rations. One of those inexpensive calorie counter books at most grocery store checkout counters is useful to carry with you in pocket or purse. Two hundred calories less than your normal caloric intake isn't all that much. Now, subtract another three hundred calories from physical activities every day and Voilà! You lose five hundred big ones from your daily diet, and reduce a lot of tension as well as a lot of waistline.

Of course, just like all the ads say, "Before starting this or any other diet, consult your doctor." The stronger a physical program you plan to start, the more important it is for you to have approval from your physician. (Before I became very serious about my running program, I took one of those stress tests that have you on a treadmill while you're hooked up like an octopus in tennies. A treadmill test measures your heart's tolerance to strain for under one hundred and fifty dollars.

Some treadmill tests may run as little as fifty or seventy-five dollars, including the consulting session, the treadmill run itself, and, of course, the diagnostic results and recommendations. Shop around. Many hospitals, in an effort to be more involved in community fitness programs, offer these kinds of services. Also, many of them will sponsor walk-a-thons, fun runs, bike-a-thons, and other fitness activities.

What physical exercise is best for the recovering person? I'm not about to dictate to you. I chose running because my colleague, Paul Staley, started me with a sensible, organized program including built-in rewards that I never thought possible.

Let's look at forms of exercise other than running or jogging that might strike your fancy. They all take effort, remember, but they all help you along the recovery road. Further, you burn calories, so what could be better?

All of these activities are based on what it takes to get rid of one hundred calories. If you think they come off easily, you're wrong. Working off just one hundred calories requires a good deal of effort, so it's obviously a good idea to combine calorie cutting with an exercise program.

Like to swim? Do it! If you swim four hundred yards in nine minutes (that's forty-five yards per minute), you've said goodbye to one hundred calories. Here are some more: fourteen minutes of tennis or twenty-two minutes of bowling will drop one hundred big ones for you. Twenty minutes of golf (not including the time you spend waiting on the foursome ahead of you), or ten minutes of down-hill skiing will also chalk off one hundred calories. And remember, the cardiovascular improvement is much more important than burning calories.

"Isn't there something less, ah, strenuous?" you ask, sheepishly.

Sure there is. Do you like gardening or just lying in bed watching the sun come up? Then this is for you. Messing around out there in the tomatoes or nasturtium beds for twenty minutes, with all that stooping over, clawing, and scratching at the soil, will burn one hundred calories. If you stay in bed for an hour and twenty minutes, in a reclining position, you also eliminate one hundred calories.

However, this exercise program is designed to get you back in the swing of enjoying life, so I'm not personally very big on lying in bed. You probably did enough of that in your drinking days, and not by choice. There are other necessary daily chores that burn the calories, chores you have to do anyway. For example, washing, showering, and shaving all use up one hundred calories when you spend a half hour at it.

If you enjoy the incredible feeling of just being able to walk outside and savor the world in which we live, then do it. When you walk twenty minutes for just 1,500 yards at a comfortable but brisk 2.6 miles per hour, you use one hundred calories for every 1,500 yards you cover.

For me, having definite goals is necessary, and the joy of exercise is in meeting those goals. For around twelve dollars you can buy a little device called a pedometer. The one my oldest daughter gave me for my birthday hangs as close to the center of the body as possible. You adjust the stride lever to the length of your own personal stride, measured from the tip of the toe of one foot to the heel of the opposite foot. As you walk, you'll hear a click-click as the needle on the dial clicks off the distance. You'd be surprised how far you walk in just an hour's time.

The list of activities you can do is pretty long, and I've mentioned just a few that I know work for other recovering alcoholics. Some of the better ones are jazzercise, dancercise, or just plain aerobic workouts. Neighborhood shopping centers are attracting these kinds of dance studios by the hundreds. Men and women can whip into their leotards and tights and be just a few minutes away from a tough but profitable workout. Other activities offer both enjoyment and conditioning benefits. Cross-training from sport to sport is popular, fun, and has the advantage of much diversity. Weights, mountain climbing, even step aerobics are in vogue, with no shortage of videos to help you train. All of these are enormous fun and do much to tone many muscles in the body—muscles you didn't even think you had.

Now to running, the national craze that has so many people hooked, me included. I'm no Jim Fixx or Bill Rodgers, and never want to be. However, setting personal goals for running has helped my own joy of recovery program, and it can work for you. I had never even thought of running while I was drinking. In fact, I was reminded that I used to get pretty worked up wondering how "those dumb runners" could be having fun. It was boring, or so I thought.

Paul started me on a "walk-run" program that we have since incorporated in our treatment of persons in recovery during the early stages of their program. This routine consists of walking for three minutes, light jogging for just one minute, then walking for three more minutes. You continue this cycle for fifteen minutes. That's the way you start. No big deal, but you begin to realize that you can ask more of your heart and lungs than you thought possible.

The first time you run a full three minutes, up from that first one minute, you may feel as if you've run a marathon. That's only the beginning. When you realize that, as a recovering person, you are just beginning to treat your body with any kind of respect, then small victories become big accomplishments.

The amount of time you run is as important as how far. A consistent pattern of your walk-run, expanded from fifteen to twenty minutes, then twenty-five to finally thirty, will make you feel terrific. The real joy of this kind of exercise for recovery is that you are competing only against yourself. The goal is being better this Saturday morning than you were two days ago, going a little longer than you did the last time, finding your lungs expanding more easily and your legs getting stronger.

When Paul told me I was ready to run a consistent half mile without stopping for the walk segment, I was hesitant. So we started measuring off city blocks, discovering that one city block was equal to one-twelfth of a mile. My personal goal was just six blocks, but, oh, they seemed like six miles.

You can average the time you stay on your walk-run program so you will know when you are ready to expand. I started with the basic program I've described, running it three times a week with one day of rest between runs.

For the recovering person, there are some other basics to accept:

1. You will probably tire more easily than your companions.
2. You will be prone to lose interest in your exercise program if you are doing it alone. (This applies to all exercise programs.) It's just another

part of your own resolve not to get too tired, to hungry, or too lonely. When you work on a program with somebody, you can share their enthusiasm. Your own small triumphs will seem like Olympian achievements. Starting an exercise program with someone will help ensure your staying with it long enough to want to continue on your own.

3. You may find your coordination is off during exercise. That is perfectly natural. When you were drinking, you were putting muscles to sleep at the same time you were sedating part of your brain. There seems to be growing evidence that both the right and the left hemispheres of the brain are upset by hard alcohol use. Thus, motor responses and coordination may have been slowed.

Bowling, tennis, golf, even riding a bicycle are all activities that might require extra effort in your recovery. Why is this? How could it happen?

For one thing, competitive sports of any kind bring a certain amount of inner tension, even when you are playing for fun. If you're a sports professional, that tension is even worse. When you were in your drinking prime, some key things were taking place for the benefit of your sport. You were relaxed—to a point—with alcohol, so normal muscle-brain coordination came more freely. You were using booze to block out some normal cautions, so you reached for harder tennis shots even if you missed more than you made. You swam further, unburdened by the realization that you could be overdoing it. You hit the pocket in your bowling games a lot more often because you weren't thinking a whole lot.

So now, in recovery, some of the natural klutziness you may have been hiding all these months or years with alcohol emerges, and you look and act awkward. That's okay. You can probably learn to do it the right way this time.

In learning or polishing up particular skills without drinking, the old natural responses to tension return. You're more cautious and restrained in your sport activity than before. You probably don't and won't take the chances you used to when you were drinking. That's definitely good, because now you can listen to your body sending the clear messages of fatigue that you cheerfully ignored before.

Playing doubles tennis is going to be better for you as you start back on the recovery road. Two games of bowling might be the order of the night instead of three. Riding your bicycle one mile every day may be better for you than trying to ride five, ten, or fifteen miles once or twice a week. Nine holes of golf for awhile will help build the joy of exercise faster than several eighteen-hole games during which nothing seems to go right for you.

Reward yourself for small achievements, even if they were activities you expected to do well. I keep all the old numbers from my races tacked to the study wall, with the times I finished written on them. Everybody entering a race gets a number, but I keep mine to show progress and achievement. They prove that I did something I never dreamed I could in my prime drinking days.

You didn't think twice about keeping piles and piles of bottle caps or "dead soldiers" lying around as a symbol of your ability to put it away with the best of them. Why not collect some small mementos of your exercise program?

I know recovering persons who keep their bowling score sheets or golf or bridge tally cards. They hang them someplace or put them in a private drawer, anywhere where they can be easily accessible to remind them that they are doing something positive now.

When you start winning trophies, when you and your partner nail a tennis doubles victory, that's all the more reason to share your pride. The joy of exercise is that you are coming back to what a life free from the bondage of alcohol can be.

Whatever form of exercise, whatever kind of program you develop for yourself, it's good to keep in mind two things:

1. Your program must provide relaxation. It needs to be done long enough, hard enough, and frequently enough to provide honest-to-God relaxation. Find and use tools to help you stick with your program. I found something that helps me stay out on the running paths long enough to do me some good. I invested in one of those radios that you wear around your neck. There are several different models, most under one hundred dollars. I wear mine even in the races. It helps me relax into my own pace, enjoy nature, and savor the flavor of competition.

2. Your program should provide personal satisfaction. Whatever havoc you wreaked on your body with alcohol, you did to yourself. Therefore, whatever joys you experience in recovery are selfish. And that's okay.

It's enough for me to have run in many three-mile and some six-mile races without suffering any compulsion to do a twenty-six-mile marathon. For you, just seeing some puny muscles increase in size with exercise can be really rewarding. If you're a female, the sagging skin under your eyes will tighten up a little more each time you engage in good, stimulating exercise of some kind. Isn't that a reward for you?

Personal satisfaction for many recovering persons is being able to complete a given task, to be motivated enough to walk a mile (lose sixty calories) or run a two-mile Fun Run (wear your T-shirt proudly!). Finishing is more important to the recovering person than winning. It's more important because when you were drinking, you spent too much of your life starting things you never finished. It doesn't matter in what place you cross the line. What does matter is that you cross it. You will gain many personal rewards.

After six to eight weeks of aerobics, no matter what kind, you should see a marked improvement in your body tone and endurance. Your whole cardiovascular system will be getting stronger. You will find your carotid artery pulse stronger and your breathing more controlled even after four to six weeks of a controlled running program. You'll begin to feel cheated if you don't go more than three miles a day when you run.

Doing something positive for your physical well-being does a whole lot for your personal self-image. Build your body and you'll build your self-image. It works. You don't have to win the Miss Universe contest or the Boston Marathon. It's good enough for your recovery to savor the joy of exercise.

Remember that one of the reasons you need regular exercise is to discharge that adrenaline we talked about in the beginning of this chapter. You need an outlet to help your body restore itself to a true balance. Without alcohol, you are going to regain your appetite. That in itself is enough good reason to exercise, just to keep on top of all the extra calories.

If you sit around and allow tension and stress to build, then you are flirting with danger. It will take effort on your part, but then the whole process of recovery takes more effort than you ever dreamed possible.

Establish a definite pattern for your exercise program. Just as you were in the habit of stopping at the neighborhood pub every day at 5:15 p.m., make it a point to don your exercise gear and hit the workout trail at a regular time and place.

A skeptic asked a recovering friend, a runner, "Honestly now, would you ever think about going back to drinking?"

My friend replied, "What? And screw up my running program? Not on your life!"

That's the joy of exercise. Just do it!

MORE JOY (An Update)

My running career is now over. It crashed and burned in the warm summer of 1990 on the streets of Albuquerque, New Mexico. I was feeling really good. It had been about six weeks since I had run any distance, between recovering from a cold and just not having time to do more than a mile or so in my running program. But this was different. I was in Albuquerque attending a conference of therapists. Instead of eating lunch, I hustled into my running gear, eager to run away from the hotel and around several city blocks. I figured I could probably log three or more miles and work out a little soreness I had been feeling.

It was great. I hit a good stride. My breathing settled in, allowing me to run at a little faster pace than I had been running at home in Denver. I clocked off thirty, forty-five, then finally fifty-five minutes, heading back to the hotel with all my endorphins pumping and me feeling the joy of being sober and able to run more than ever.

I quickly showered, grabbed a couple of pieces of fruit, and headed back for the afternoon sessions. I felt a small twinge of soreness. Not pain, really, and it certainly seemed I had run out whatever was bothering my knee. In spite of the tinge, I felt on top of the world.

During the night my knee felt unusually sore, but it was nothing out of the ordinary for me, especially since I had not been keeping up my miles for awhile. The next morning's session flew by, and I was eager to hit the running path again at noon. One of my colleagues remarked that I seemed to be limping.

"I'll run out the limp," I told him. "It's just a little soreness from yesterday, because I did more miles than I have for a few weeks."

I quickly changed into my gear and hit the pavement. Sure enough, I felt a pain in my left knee. I simply slowed my pace, figuring that I would, indeed, run out the injury.

As I warmed up, the pain began to subside, and as it did, I picked up my pace a little. Finally I was back in stride, feeling very good indeed. I lengthened the amount of time I had run the previous day. I was glad to be back in the saddle again, breathing steadily and hitting a good stride. I was covering better distance with firmer foot placement, since I was wearing a new pair of Etonic shoes that helped correct my tendency to pronate my feet.

What was happening, of course, was that I was running injured. I felt little pain because my natural endorphins (which is short for "endogenous morphine") were deadening the pain. I was, in fact, doped up from my run and couldn't feel the pain.

The next day I prepared to leave for home, first stopping in Santa Fe, where I hoped to run during the noon hour. I hoped to run from the Inn of the Governors to someplace up Canyon Road and back, which would give me four to five miles of running at my usual eight or nine minute per mile pace. But as I sat in the car and drove the fifty short miles to Santa Fe, I knew something was wrong—really wrong.

My knee throbbed, and I could see that it was swelling. Instead of running, I checked into a hotel. I thought I would walk over to the Plaza to shop for something to take home to Cyn, but I could hardly walk. I was becoming scared that something was torn, and it *felt* torn.

It was. I still tried ignoring the pain, and I even tried running when I got back home, but to no avail. It became worse, and finally my sports med doctor strapped me into the MRI. The bad news was that I had torn major stuff in my left knee, so arthroscopic surgery was performed.

I tried running after the surgery, but couldn't. I walked with our golden retriever, Murphy, every morning—even on crutches—hoping that things would get better enough for me to run. But it was over, and I knew it.

The great news is this: I have never missed a day of my four- or five-mile walks with Murphy in the Cherry Creek State Park. We are like the postal service; "Neither rain, snow, nor dark of night..." will keep us from the reservoir. I never lost the joy of exercise. We have literally walked in rainstorms, blizzards, the darkness of early morning (we start at 5:15 a.m. or so), and during the hottest days of summer.

The point is, I could never have done any of this—or even thought of doing it—if I were still drinking. There would be no energy even for walking a short distance, and all good intentions would have gone down the tubes.

When you are feeling tense, tired, or overburdened, there is absolutely nothing like exercise of any kind to relieve that tension. As the good folks at Nike made us all aware in their ad campaign, we have to stop bitching and just do it!

5

REESTABLISHING YOUR MARRIAGE

"I don't even know this man, and I've been married to him for ten years."

"She treats me like some kind of child—just like one of our kids."

"I'll tell you one thing: I'll give this marriage about another two months, maybe just two weeks, and then I'm splitting."

Sounds all too familiar, doesn't it? Anyone who has gone through the pains of marriage counseling has used or heard the above phrases, or at least ones that are similar. My grandmother had a good phrase that worked well for premarital advice: "Marry in haste, repent in leisure."

But it's too late now. You're already married, and your marriage may be more on the rocks than the way you ordered your drinks. The reason is almost too simple, yet true: while you were drinking and spending all that time in bars or with someone else, your spouse was hoping you'd see the light and get sober. When you finally did get sober, your spouse was ready to collect the overdue bill for all the wasted time invested in a marriage that wasn't paying many dividends.

Booze isn't around anymore, so what stands in the way of making this relationship really hum? I'll tell you what stands in the way: you don't know each other, that's what. So much of your married life has been spent with alcohol in the picture that you suddenly sit face to face and wonder, "Who is this person? I don't remember him (her) being interested in that before."

It's always somewhat sad when one of my clients sits in the comfort of the therapy room and admits that he or she has never even had a date without alcohol. That's just the dating process, never mind the years that may have passed in marriage. So there you both are—you now free from alcohol and your spouse loaded for bear (probably your bare hide). After all, you're sober now, aren't you? What's to prevent life from being rosy from here on out? Well, nothing, really, if you both are ready to start at square one.

Your spouse is the person who stood beside and behind you no matter what difficulties your drinking produced. Now maybe you can start being the kind of mate your spouse has envisioned all this time. Lesson one is to acknowledge the debt of gratitude you owe your spouse without giving away all your chips.

It's important for your continued fight back from alcohol to build self-respect. Slowly you'll do that, if you're willing to share the accomplishment of your sobriety with others, namely your mate. Every time you find a way to say "Thank you," you pat yourself on the back, too.

I've found a simple way to do this every day of my life. We hold hands at the dinner table to return thanks. It doesn't matter if you're religious or not, or whether you are Christian, Jew, or Agnostic. You owe a debt of thanks. I happen to believe in God, so while holding my wife's hand I thank God for another day of sobriety. That's all there is to it.

By sharing this debt of gratitude openly with my wife, my God, and anyone else sitting at our table, I keep reinforcing my daily sobriety and strengthening the bonds of our marriage. I'm also saying, "Hey! Join me (by holding hands), and let's all be grateful together for getting well."

Lesson two is to remember you and your spouse got sick together, so you both need to get well together. It's going to be difficult for both of you to try new ways, but it's essential to keep an open mind. This is particularly true of your spouse. This person did so much enabling during your drinking that it's going to be difficult to give up that terrible habit.

By "enabling" I mean what your spouse did for you to enable you to continue drinking—things you could not or would not do for yourself. (The spouse is generally considered to be the most likely enabler. However, the term also applies to all persons who aid and abet an alcoholic in giving up his or her personal responsibilities in life.)

Let's take money as an example of a marital friction point that requires the use of some new tools. Money is a problem in a large majority of marriages even when drinking hasn't been around the house. Add unhealthy doses of alcohol, and you really have a mess.

Now that you're sober, you want the money and checkbook chores and responsibilities back from your spouse. Your spouse isn't quite ready yet to entrust you with those responsibilities. He or she remembers the many months spent staving off the bill collectors, or arguing in vain with the bank about "errors" in your account. How to resolve the dilemma? You install the Two-Month Plan.

THE TWO-MONTH PLAN

This is a simple method that declares a moratorium on any discussions about why you shouldn't get the checkbook back. Rather, this method concentrates on a specific period to prove your reliability.

It's not as degrading as you may think. After all, those alcoholic blackouts after heaving drinking left you unable to account for where your money was or even how you spent it. So why should you be touchy about having to earn your money stripes again with your spouse?

With the Two-Month Plan, you both agree to let you maintain the checkbook for two months. It takes this long to see if you and the bank end up with the same numbers. For two months you pay all the bills, write all the checks, and balance the account. It will help you build a little more confidence in yourself to see that you really can do it right again. Your spouse gets to look over the accounts and the checkbook to confirm your work. If everything is in order at the end of two months, you agree to add two more months to the plan, then finally two more, making a total of six months for you to be at the helm.

The two-month span of time is just about right for you to prove your responsibility. Two months also extends the time your spouse must trust you without making final judgments. Your spouse feels comfortable knowing that not too much damage can happen to the family finances in a two-month period.

At the end of the full six months, you switch roles. You can, and should, look over your spouse's shoulder and watch the action in the checkbook.

However, don't interfere with the immediate decision processes about what or whom should be paid, and how much.

What makes this little trial balloon fly is that it's fun. I have known couples who made a betting game out of seeing who could make the fewest mistakes. The winner would treat for a dinner out. (I hate those people who *never* make checkbook errors.)

It may sound silly, and it requires a lot of bothersome work to put this Two-Month Plan into effect, but it will work. You are probably not as ready to jump in and control family finances as you think. Your spouse is probably nowhere near ready to suddenly turn every chore over to you, being still gunshy about your sobriety and the length of time you've been in recovery.

I've had clients who couldn't wait to finish this Plan—after completing the first stretch, the recovering spouse decided that he or she didn't want control of the checkbook again. But if husband and wife had not been willing to give the plan a try, they would have continued to deal with the same anger and frustration they had when one of them was drinking.

When you stop to think about your marriage, you really may be thinking about how to make up for the lost time that I spoke of earlier. Why not think instead of starting from scratch? Here are five more tools for improving a marriage that I have found helpful. (In fact, I often think these tools would have been handy when many people I know were in the dating stage.) Our clients tell me they help them get more out of their relationship in sobriety.

These aren't listed in any order of priority, just in the progression I have found comfortable to use in helping other people start reestablishing their marriages.

THE "OFF-THE-CROSS" EXERCISE

This is certainly not meant to be sacrilegious, so don't get uptight about it. So many marriages never get off dead center after the drinker has become sober because the spouse (or significant other) never stops "crucifying" the alcoholic for all the past sins he or she has committed. I draw a mental picture for clients in treatment about how their discussions with each other start in their living room and gradually work their way out the front door, down the street, and on up the hill to the top of Mount Calvary. There, the alcoholic, forced to carry his or her own cross all the way, is now compelled to climb on the cross and hang there until the spouse has thoroughly crucified him or her over the unforgotten past.

It won't work—*it just won't work.* While it's true that everyone has been hurt, and hurt deeply, by the actions of the alcoholic, no lasting resolution is gained by this constant rehashing. You all know how the dialogue goes:

> SOBER ONE: "Gee, Myrna looked attractive at the birthday party, didn't she, honey?"
> SPOUSE: (Warming up) "You sure paid attention to her."
> SOBER ONE: (Feeling it coming on) "What's that supposed to mean?"
> SPOUSE: "You know very well what it means." (Here it comes) "That's exactly how you used to fawn over every woman at any party we ever went to."
> SOBER ONE: (Now in full defense mode) "Wait a minute. That's when I was drinking. Gimme a break, will ya?"

And we're off and running. Poor "Sober One" has been innocently dragged up the hill and hung firmly on the cross. He'll stay there, too, unless his spouse is willing to bury the past and get on with the future of their relationship. It's easy to forgive. It's not so easy to forget. As long as you climb on that cross yourself or allow yourself to be put on it, the forgetting will never happen.

So, feel free to invoke The Off-The-Cross Exercise by making direct reference to it. When I see that cross hauled out in a therapy session, I confront the guilty party right away.

"How many times does Charlie need to be put on that cross of yours before he's through paying for his past?" I'll ask.

The mere reference to a cross is often enough to make the couple realize that is exactly what they are doing to each other. They forget that alcohol was the villain in the past, and Charlie was just a willing vessel for the alcohol.

You can do this exercise the same way. When you feel your spouse is about to haul out the cross, or if you feel your recovering person is about to lay some more heavy stuff on you, stop the action. Say, "Hold it! I have the feeling we are about to travel up the hill with the cross again. Is that right?"

While the action may not stop entirely, your attention will be drawn to the fact that the beef is centered around something that happened in the past. Therefore, it is better off buried and forgotten. If the recovering person is never allowed off that cross, there is very little chance that you both can get on with the business of the future. The hurts of the past won't go away easily, but they can be dealt with in a much more constructive fashion with this exercise.

THE TEN-MINUTE DRILL

This is one of the most important and successful tools I know of for putting some new shine back on a relationship. Everyone has a clock with a timer around the house; I recommend using the neat little timer on your oven. You know, the one that makes that horrendous buzz when the biscuits are done. Most everyone has one of those, but if you don't, use something similar. Whatever device you use, it must buzz, squawk, ring, chime, or do something to indicate ten minutes are up.

There are some other ground rules you need to know before employing The Ten-Minute Drill:

1. Turn off the radio.
2. Turn off the TV.
3. Turn off the stereo.
4. Don't have kids or crying babies in the room.
5. Don't have dogs, cats, or other pets that require attention in the room.
6. Don't answer the telephone or the door, if possible.

You should have no distractions of any kind during the period of The Ten-Minute Drill. I know this is hard, but it is not impossible. You'll find after a couple of Ten-Minute Drills that you can plan them during times when these distractions are easiest to control. I had clients who finally settled on a very early Saturday morning to have their drill in quiet and solitude. It worked for them, even with an active household.

You may have guessed by now the purpose of The Ten-Minute Drill. The drill is a device to establish communications involving active listening between the two of you.

Without all those distractions that are a normal part of your everyday world, you must actually listen to what your mate says. This will be a new experience for you. You may have become so lazy in interpersonal communications that you wander around saying, "Have a nice day," "How was work, dear?" and, "What happened at the office today, hon?" You may never (well, almost never) wait for or care about the answer. So, The Ten-Minute Drill.

You set the oven timer for ten minutes, and then in this quiet void you have created, you t-a-l-k. I mean you really, honest-to-God, *talk*. For just ten minutes, that's all. When the buzzer goes off, you quit and hold whatever is brewing until the next Ten-Minute Drill. And there's the hitch; in all the time I have used this drill with people, most report having no desire to quit after ten minutes. They enjoy what's happening, and they rush to reset the buzzer for another ten minutes. But if this happens to you on the first go-round, I suggest that you hold to a limit of two Ten-Minute Drills in the same sitting.

The subject matter doesn't really count for The Ten-Minute Drill. However, a very important point to observe is that if a critical discussion is in progress when the buzzer goes off, you both agree to table the topic until the next drill period. This provides two important elements:

1. It provides an automatic "cooling down" process over the subject.
2. It establishes that the subject is important enough to warrant further discussion.

Some couples tell me that when the buzzer goes off and they are having a worthwhile exchange, they advance the time for thirty minutes and keep going. This can be done with practice, but the basis for sticking to ten-minute segments is to provide safe ground—either party can retreat with honor from the discussion without feeling they have sacrificed all their troops in battle.

As I said earlier, the subject matter doesn't really count. The Ten-Minute Drill is open to all areas. The way I place priority on the subject I want to drill around is to use a refrigerator magnet. When I think of something that has been bugging me or that has never been satisfactorily explored, I make a note and plunk it on the fridge door with the magnet. My wife gets a shot at reading what is on my mind for a discussion. That gives her a chance to think about rejoinders, defenses, explanations, points of view, and counterattacks that will help us solve the nagging question.

The key to this whole process is the openness of it all. That's what's fun about being sober in the first place—you don't have to go about your life in a sneaky fashion. I think a whole book could be done solely on the various ploys, gambits, and strategies that recovering couples have told me they developed during The Ten-Minute Drill. (Don't be bashful. If you try The Drill and it works, write my publisher. He'll nag me until I start a collection of successful Ten-Minute Drill episodes.)

The really beautiful part of The Ten-Minute Drill is that it becomes a habit-forming tool for communication between you and your spouse. The lack of outside distractions makes it some of the most therapeutic time you'll ever spend with each other.

Another guideline: Don't be afraid to say, "Let's save that for the next

Ten-Minute Drill, okay?" This has the effect of telling your partner that you recognize the concern as an important subject, but that the time isn't right for discussion just now. This is particularly important during any sexual activity that may be in the works. You'll kill that mood if you suddenly start something that is better saved for The Ten-Minute Drill. (More about that in the chapter on sexuality.)

A word of caution: Please don't try The Ten-Minute Drill while the two of you are driving in the car or riding bikes or motorcycles. The noise of the machine you are on or in or the distance between you can heighten the intensity of what begins as a quiet little discussion. Then The Ten-Minute Drill can disintegrate into full-fledged shoutin' and hollerin'. Save it. Put it on ice by saying, "Good point, hon—sounds like something we should schedule for The Ten-Minute Drill." Or, "I'm open to kicking that one around. Let's schedule a Ten-Minute Drill. This traffic's already got me on edge."

Your responses will be better than mine. Just don't be afraid to couch the point by:

1. Acknowledging that a problem area exists.
2. Giving it importance by putting it on your agenda.
3. Acknowledging that he/she is obviously bothered enough to bring the subject up in the first place. And,
4. Hoping that you can find a solution amicable to both of you in The Ten-Minute Drill(s).

Try it! You'll like it!

QUALITY TIME

I can't think of a better way to describe what often is missing between the recovering person and his/her spouse. It's Quality Time, the time when the two of you just plain enjoy life together.

We should start by describing what Quality Time isn't. Quality Time is not:

1. Pushing a grocery cart around a supermarket while your spouse thoroughly examines every label on every shelf.
2. Washing dishes.
3. Taking down or putting up storm windows.
4. Putting on or taking off snow tires.
5. Rearranging furniture.

Quality Time can be:

1. Redecorating a room together.
2. Looking in new or used car lots. (Don't go into showrooms unless you are seriously ready to select a new car.)
3. Sharing dinner party preparations.
4. Planting the spring garden.

You get the idea. What is missing is best summed up by the way I hear it at the treatment center—fun!

What happened to the idea of just taking a walk together in the evening? What happened was you were too loaded with booze to even find the front door, or you just didn't want to get that far away from the bottle. You can now. What makes taking a walk fun in sobriety is that you can once again explore the real joy of being together, away from pressures such as telephones and calendars. I suggest you set a goal for your walk, something with a reward at the end so that this painfully new experience of being together doesn't make you so uncomfortable that all the joy of the walk is smothered by anxiety.

I'll give you a goal: ice cream. There's nothing better than suggesting a walk to your local ice cream parlor (as long as it's located at least twenty minutes away). The reward can be a simple Dairy Queen cone or a mammoth sundae loaded with obnoxious weight-producing toppings. It doesn't matter. It's good for you. If you're one of those folks who can't handle sugar in your diet, then make that walk to the supermarket and purchase diet or sugar-free ice cream to take home. Or you can choose a low-fat or nonfat dairy product and help yourself nutritionally as well as in relationship nurturing.

Hold hands while walking. Ah, c'mon now, you can do it. There was a time when you were so close to each other that people had to pry you apart just to take your coats and hang them up. What's all this distance now? There's still a special thrill, whether you're eighteen or eighty, to taking your companion's hand and strolling. *Strolling*, not trying to set a speed record, but setting a brisk yet lazy pace. You might even swing your hands back and forth a little.

Now that's Quality Time. It's different from Ten-Minute Drill time because you shouldn't discuss anything of real importance. What you are doing is just enjoying each other, without pressure.

This is a good time to do some dream planning. You might see a particularly nice garden or patio or sun deck that inspires you to say, "That's what would look nice at our place as soon as we can get to it," or, "That's sort of what I would like to do with our front yard this year."

If you live in an apartment, it's just as much fun to wander past swimming pools, tennis courts, bike paths, and other recreational places that might motivate the two of you to try some activities again as a couple. You may have thought your tennis game was hot when you were drinking. Now you might *really* enjoy a doubles game with your spouse, since there is a better than even chance you will be able to return the ball. If your spouse is a swimmer and you're not, you could still lie around the pool and read while she/he takes a few laps. And the bike paths you pass on your walk to the ice cream reward might just spur you to try biking again.

You don't have to run out and buy eight-hundred dollar Cannondales, either. If you live near a city park there might be a bike rental concession. If you are a parent or grandparent, be bold and ask your kids or grandkids to let you borrow their bikes for a weekend. They've probably abandoned their old-fashioned three-speed models for the high-powered jobbies with eighteen gears anyway. You don't need that for Quality Time riding.

There's a beautiful old hymn that goes something like, "In the rustling grass I can hear Him pass..." I like that, and it has absolutely nothing to do with religious beliefs. It means to me that I can realize the joy of being sober over and over again when my mate and I walk across lush park grounds, hand in hand. I feel good about the world, about her, and about myself.

Like all the other exercises I'm telling you about, you need to plan Quality Time. The Sunday drive is still a nice thing to do. Of course, you have to deal with fluctuating gasoline prices that may make it reasonable one month and prohibitive the next. And we have become a nation of people with important environmental concerns about needless driving. Maybe you can make the Sunday drive work anyway, at least occasionally. It's still a great chance for the two of you to get together.

Above all, Quality Time means the two of you. Does this sound strange, even a little scary? Does the thought of buying a couple of symphony tickets (even though you're not a lover of classical music) terrify you? Most symphony orchestra programs contain program material for everyone. Give it a shot. Add a late supper after the concert, and that's Quality Time.

What about taking in a sporting event together? Here we come to some real diverse opinions. Many spouses don't like or understand a particular sport. I'm no expert on any of them, but I'll give you a couple of examples. There are ways you can turn a sporting event into Quality Time instead of drudgery or a fight-provoking mess. Let's start with football.

The mistake in trying to make a football game a Quality Time event is that you (either sex) probably know more about the game than your spouse. I know females who can tell me more about football than I care to know, so don't think I'm saying that it's only men who know the game or appreciate it. When I see a couple planning to go to a game, I always ask, "Is this what you both decided to do?"

If one squirms or is silent, that is usually an indication it was his or her idea. That's not so good, because Quality Time should not be spent just satisfying only one person's needs. So, before you spend a bundle on a pro game or even a nearby college game, here's a Quality Time tool: go back to high school. That's right, high school. You'll see some outstanding football at a fraction of the cost of either a college or pro game. The really big bonus is that you can leave after a decent interval and not feel bad about it.

Suppose you made a deal with your spouse, who doesn't particularly care about football, to go for just one half of the game. That's your end of the deal. You agree to go, and your spouse will leave when you want to. In the meantime, you can feel pretty comfortable learning about certain parts of the game that you may not understand from your companion .

Unless your kid is playing in the game, local high school contests are ideal to share enthusiasm about a sport. In football, at least, the playing time and action are faster, and the formations, for the most part, are easier to see and understand. I know of a couple that tried this Quality Time tool, and after two weeks you couldn't drag either of them away at halftime. You see, they discovered the power of just being with each other. No one they knew was playing in these games. They were only experimenting with this tool because I had insisted they just give it a try. Now they tell me they are trying for a pro game or two, and they are both becoming pretty hooked on watching the games on television. They are doing something together, in contrast to what was happening when sobriety wasn't in the picture.

You can apply this principle of give and take to any activity. You give a little, your spouse gives a little, and neither of you has to make a binding commitment to go "off the deep end."

Suppose you don't particularly like skiing, whereas your spouse could be left on the top of Pike's Peak and have a ball making it down. Be happy that's what she wants to do. You could be happy with some fine recreational reading or creative sleeping, and when your mate returns from the slopes, the two of you go out to dinner. The whole experience is Quality Time.

Bowling is superior to tennis as a sport that lets you two share time with each other. The skill levels are not so far apart on the bowling lanes as they can be on the tennis courts.

You can even experience Quality Time without being together. For example, if you join a bowling league, I recommend you get on different teams in the same league. Then the competition is not you against your mate, but rather your team against the other. You'll end up bowling against each other several times during the season, but neither of you has to feel that you are out to prove which one of you is better.

There are so many other obvious Quality Time experiences that you can savor. You just need to put forth the effort and not make a big deal out of it. Part of the joy of your sobriety is that nothing has to be the big production it once was. If it rains on the day you were going to have a picnic in the country, then forget it (the rain, I mean, not the picnic). Throw the red and white checker cloth on the floor in the living room, put on a little Streisand, Bernstein, or Indigo Girls, and have the picnic anyway.

There's one other Quality Time event that's really close to my heart, and maybe it'll strike a responsive chord with you, too. I call it "Travel-Teasing." If you haven't been able to afford a very extensive trip lately, you can have more fun by getting travel brochures and maps, sitting on the floor, and spreading the stuff out on the coffee table. It's cheap Quality Time spent daydreaming about what might happen and sharing experiences you remember from trips you made together before.

My sister-in-law is in the travel business. When we are ready to do Travel Teasing, you can count on the fact I will ask her for brochures and other travel stuff to help us out. If and when we ever do get to Europe or Hawaii, she's a cinch to win out and get our business.

THE LAUGHING PLACES

Joel Chandler Harris had the right idea when he had Uncle Remus tell about the Laughing Places. You need them, too, as you struggle to reestablish your marriage. It's been way too long since you and your companion had a really good belly laugh, one that was not brought on by alcohol or the old "life of the party" devices. I'm talking about the ability you must have to laugh at yourself and at each other without hurt feelings. So often in the past, the alcoholic has made someone else the butt of his or her jokes, and it wasn't funny. It just plain hurt. Now you can each have the freedom to laugh at and with each other by using the Laughing Place device.

You might have observed something about your mate that really strikes you as funny. You've started to snicker and your spouse is beginning to say, "What's so damned funny?" He is suspicious because he is playing an old tape of how it used to be in the drinking days. You can stop this from turning into a donnybrook if you will just say, "Hey! Let's go to the Laughing Place, okay?" That's the signal that something has struck you as funny, and you want to share it without hurt feelings.

I know people who tried this and ended up in hysterics over something both thought was funny once they took it to their Laughing Place. Sound silly? Try it. You automatically remove any personal slings and arrows by saying you think your spouse will find what you are about to say funny also. If he or she doesn't think it's funny, then at least you took the chance and it didn't get out of hand.

You can grow old just watching the draperies fade, or you can make every minute that you're together count if you recapture the ability to laugh with each other. I hate to admit this, but one of the best laughing places I know is in bed. I don't know why, but bed seems to be a place for recalling and sharing some outrageous incident that can fill you with laughter. The obvious danger, of course, is that the bedroom as a Laughter Place might come back to haunt you in your attempt to keep that hallowed ground for lovemaking. But if that's where you are comfortable as your Laughing Place, then go for it.

A word of caution to the Significant Other about going to the Laughing Place when it involves a remembered drinking incident. You may be able to laugh about a drinking episode when your mate made a jackass out of himself to the delight of others, but it may still be a painful memory for your sober partner.

Often it takes many months, and sometimes a period of a year or more before the sober person can see the humor in a situation that involved his or her drinking. Your best approach to such an incident is real understanding. For example, "Honey, I just thought of something that I started laughing about. It was when you were drinking. Is it okay to take it to the Laughing Place?"

This doesn't mean you will stifle the guffaw building up inside you, begging to be released. It simply helps you do a little ground-breaking so you are not suddenly hit by a hurtful barrage because what was funny about your spouse's drinking is nothing for him to laugh about.

All too often I will hear a spouse complain about the necessity to "walk on eggshells," fearing that everything said will trigger a torrent of bad words from the recovering person. It just takes a little time to work together on where it's okay to tread. That's what makes the Laughing Place such a super device—it ensures that no one is wearing his or her heart on their sleeve.

WARM FUZZIES

I saved this for the end because I think it has done more to bring couples back together than any other tool, all of which require more skill to use effectively. The Warm Fuzzy is that unsolicited hug, embrace, or plain stand-up cuddly that is freely exchanged and says, "Hey! I love you and care about you." You can always tell recovering folks who have been in treatment together, perhaps at a hospital unit. They will unabashedly exchange Warm Fuzzies, no matter if they are two men or two women. The Warm Fuzzy simply denotes, "We have come through something that almost killed us, and we've done it together."

I rarely attend an AA meeting without exchanging ten minutes of Warm Fuzzies. I think the biggest risk taken is that the spouse who has not been personally involved in treatment may take offense at seeing his or her mate clasped in a warm embrace with a member of the opposite sex. So, to counteract this, the two of you should begin practicing the Warm Fuzzy and allowing it to happen for both of you.

One of the hardest things I do in therapy is to get a couple who have come from very straight-laced, unaffectionate backgrounds to begin exchanging Warm Fuzzies at the end of a session. They are still angry, but I try to get them to give one another a Warm Fuzzy so they can leave the session realizing that they are working on their problems together. There is absolutely nothing like a Warm Fuzzy to make the cares of the day go away. You can use the Warm Fuzzy at any time or place to help get rid of "Old Creepy" (remember your Grey Ghost?). It sure is a tonic when you have something special to celebrate.

I'm sure you have seen those bumper stickers that say "Have you hugged your kid today?" or "Have you hugged your lawyer today?" (I love that one.) Well, it's America's return to the Warm Fuzzy, something that never goes out of style but often gets set aside in the rush and hassle of everyday living.

My old friend Ty Owens is a therapist who has done a tremendous number of crisis interventions—those therapy sessions that become encounters to get a reluctant person into treatment for alcohol abuse. He is a giant of a black man, a former football lineman. Let me tell you, when you get a Warm Fuzzy from Ty, you have been *fuzzied*. People always stop and look at the two of us in a hospital corridor, on the street, or in a restaurant exchanging a Warm Fuzzy. I don't know what they think, and I personally don't care. It's a special greeting between friends. I have seen Ty give a Warm Fuzzy to a little slip of an old lady and to a man who is equal to his own bulk. He doesn't extend his hand for a handshake greeting;

with someone he cares about, you can count on a Warm Fuzzy. And who cares about you more than your own spouse? Who better to exchange frequent and rewarding Warm Fuzzies with than the special person with whom you share your everyday life? There is absolutely nothing sexual about the exchange of Warm Fuzzies when they are shared between persons who are not married. They really don't have much of a sexual connotation, even when you give them to your spouse. They're not meant for that. A Warm Fuzzy effortlessly shared between spouses simply says, "It's good to have you back from the world of the damned."

Trouble just melts away in that fondness of a few moments of holding one another, without words, without the need or pressure to say anything. Just a Warm Fuzzy, a good cup of coffee, and Thou! Eat your heart out, Omar Khayyam.

MORE JOY (An Update)

There is not the slightest doubt in my mind that I am with my life partner now. We will continue to grow and nourish our relationship with as much vitality as can be mustered, considering the busy and hectic schedules we both keep.

Cynthia Tinsley is not only my wife, but also my coauthor for several important relationship books either already published or in the works. Further, she has served as my book editor or several other writing projects. She also manages to put up with me, my moods, my demands and my many projects. Best of all, Cyn is my best friend, my very best friend, and that counts for a lot.

What I have learned, and what I teach the dozens of couples that are doing therapy with me, is to put the emphasis on the relationship, and that will reestablish the marriage. The alcohol that tears away at so many marriages is a grim reaper indeed. It will take all of the recovering person's intuition, ambition, energy and devotion (to name just a few of the necessary qualities) to put it back together again. And it will be different. This is important, because you certainly don't want the marriage to be what it was. After all, alcohol was the great destroyer, and you don't want to go back to that.

Therefore, the couple needs to work on building a new relationship with one another. I feel so strongly about this that I have made it a strong focus of my private practice. Cyn and I have written a book about it, *Recharging Your Relationship* (Deaconess Press), and I use the principles of "Finding The Fun Again" in every way I can; together, my life partner and I are concentrating on what we need to do on a daily basis to build and rebuild the commitment of our relationship.

Sometimes, more often than I care to recall, couples will say to me something like, "Oh, we just want our marriage to be like it was!" They mean that they want their lives to be alcohol-free. I acknowledge their feelings and then quickly tell them that I don't want their lives to be like they were, because that's what brought them to me for therapy in the first place.

Change, risk, and devotion to one another is what this recovery business is all about, especially in the field of all your interpersonal relations. Your marriage is already there; somewhere you probably have a document that states that you are legally married. What I will categorically tell you that you may not have is a relationship; one that is free of alcohol and thus one that is developing with two new people, as we have discussed in this chapter.

So concentrate on building a new relationship with your life partner; don't be an archaeologist and dig around in all the past stuff that you have done wrong, but concentrate on what you are doing on a weekly—even daily—basis, to recharge your relationship and therefore reestablish your marriage, your commitment, and your vision of life together.

He thought he saw a Banker's Clerk descending from the bus. He looked again and found it was A Hippopotamus.

Lewis Carroll

6

REESTABLISHING YOUR CREDIT

Maybe now you'll settle for a banker who looks like a hippopotamus, but chances are when you were in your prime drinking days you had far worse descriptions for those "no-good S.O.B.s" who wouldn't extend you any more credit. I had a few choice descriptions for bankers myself, ranking them right up there with lawyers, insurance agents, and the Asian flu.

Now that sobriety is your way of life, you might find those money lenders and policy writers aren't always wearing black hats after all. As a matter of fact, they can and will help you in your attempt to get back on your feet. However, there is a basic mindset that the recovering person has to deal with to take advantage of the help that is waiting out there. First, understand completely that it was you doing the drinking, not the banker. Second, the banker probably took a chance on you before. You violated the trust placed in you when your payments continued to slip more and more into arrears.

Let's recap briefly how alcoholics treat money in general and their bills specifically. Money is good for just one purpose: to spend, probably in setting up another round of drinks or making sure there's plenty of booze in the house. There may not be enough for the real essentials of life, but you can damn well count on the fact there will always be enough money for cocktail time.

Because money holds no special significance for the alcoholic outside the area of spending, he or she becomes very careless with it. As the intensity of drinking picks up, so does disregard for financial responsibility in the drinker's life. This seems to be due to an avoidance syndrome. If you simply avoid the money problems, the thinking goes, they will go away. We all know thinking like that is nonsense for any mature, clear-headed adult. The difficulty, of course, is that no drinker is clear-headed for very long. The more a person drinks, the less mature he or she becomes, and avoiding money issues only means that the alcoholic delays the inevitable collapse of his or her finances. Like most sick people at some time, the alcoholic turns the blame on the nearest available scapegoat. In this case, the blame goes to the institution that represents money—the bank.

I find bankers to be courteous, helpful, bright, energetic, and underpaid. Of course, the chances are that they have always been like that, and my change from alcoholic to sober behavior made me see them in a new light. You need to see them in a new light, too, because everyone needs a good banker—particularly the recovering person.

Think of this: When you were confronted with bills and creditors while you were drinking, you just took the persistent collection notices and stuffed them further into the desk drawer. That's how they "got paid." Why would anyone want to extend more credit to anyone who had that little regard for the people and companies that gave them credit in the first place?

The answer is, they don't want to. However, you need credit and you probably need to reestablish a solid banking connection again.

I have worked with couples who thought they had hit financial bottom. They also felt that the alcoholic's abusive manner with their bankers had buried them forever in the pit of poverty and despair. In some cases that may be true, but usually bankers, to paraphrase Shaw's character Henry Higgins, "are a marvelous lot." The way you get to know them again is to let them know you, the *new* you. This involves a lot of humility on your part, and you are going to have to add one more character trait to your life in ever-increasing doses—honesty.

Here are some basic rules for reestablishing good relations with your bank. I strongly recommend you think about them, talk them over with a close friend or spouse, and then get busy.

1. Find out if the person who was handling your delinquent account is still with the bank. Contact that person and ask for a personal appointment. If asked what the appointment is for, just say you'd rather visit in person, not over the phone.

2. Sitting across from that bank person, come clean with what's happened in your life. Say that you have been a victim of the disease of alcoholism, and that you have started on the road to recovery. Be sure to say how you are approaching recovery, such as your participation in a treatment program or AA.

3. Don't ask for anything. Tell your banker that you realize you were probably pretty abusive, maybe downright vulgar and hostile, in your dealings with the bank.

4. Apologize for past behavior but don't grovel. You were sick and not responsible for many of the things you said and did.

5. Tell the bank that you wish to reestablish credit, even though past experiences with you may have been disastrous. Remember, the bank stays in business by having customers. They want to have as many people as possible doing business with them. There is, then, a certain amount of hope in thinking the bank needs you, too.

6. Don't argue. You will get a certain amount of lecture time from the banker. I tell our clients who are following these rules to just buck up and take it. Agree that you have been irresponsible in the past. Also be certain to point out that the nature of the disease of alcoholism tends to push everything out of the mind except seeking the chemical high that drinking offers.

7. Offer a testimonial letter from your treatment center, your AA sponsor, or your attending physician. This letter simply states that you have undergone treatment. In the case of your AA sponsor, the letter says you attend meetings regularly and remain motivated to stay sober.

8. Don't ask for the moon. If you need a line of credit from this banker, ask for something modest you know you can pay back quickly and on time. I recommend starting with a simple installment loan of three hundred dollars on a collateral purchase—a small appliance, a lawn mower, or maybe a gas barbecue grill. The important thing is to use your bank

for the financing, at least the first time around. By paying off a small loan on time or, better yet, ahead of time, you will be on the road to reestablishing a higher line of credit.

9. Don't overextend. Make sure your banker is willing to help you keep a tighter rein on your spending. Many times the euphoria and joy of sobriety can trap you into making the same mistakes as before. If you'll use your banker for the financial expertise he or she can offer, you'll find out that person can really be a friend.

10. Get to a bank officer. My philosophy is to go right to the top, if you can. Most banks now insist their officers and other directors on the premises sit out in the open, where they are accessible. It's good therapy for you to introduce yourself to the bank president. You can count on the fact that if he or she doesn't know you, she will go out of her way to ask the loan officer you were working with about you. That's good for your new, sincere image—the image that says, "Sober, I'm worth something to the bank and to myself. Give me another chance."

These ten rules are not set in concrete. Use them as you use the other tools in this book—with modifications to suit your own special circumstances. They have proven successful for many other folks, so they can work for you.

So far, we have assumed that you have a banking connection. What if you don't? Where do you find a banker who will be sympathetic to your miserable past balance sheet? I have three top-drawer pipelines for you:

1. Your lawyer,
2. Any AA groups you have attended, and
3. Your church or temple.

If you have neither a lawyer nor a banker, then ask your employer for his recommendation for both. Your therapist, your family, or your attending physician are also sources for names of bankers who are accessible and interested in helping. At AA, I have heard many a person ask openly if anyone in the fellowship knows of a banker who will help. Five will get you ten there is at least one banker in the meeting, and he or she will surely talk to you. The church or temple you have been attending is another good source. The minister, priest, or rabbi knows his population and is used to handling such matters more regularly than you would suspect.

Now, let's deal with some specific money areas that are difficult for the recovering person to handle, but are a real joy when you know how to conquer them.

THE FINANCIAL STATEMENT

Don't you hate those damn things? The same people who turned you down for all your past pipe dream money schemes must have devised financial statements. They scare me. I don't like seeing all those "Assets" and "Liabilities," "Net Worth" and "Total Indebtedness" columns. So, I overcame my fear of financial statements by taking the blank forms right back to my banker and asking him to help me fill out the first one.

It is time consuming. Once you go through the process, however, you usually discover that you are worth more than you thought. Of even greater importance, you will discover where you stand financially and what sort of game plan you need to establish to meet certain goals.

I'm not expecting bankers who read this to be overjoyed at the prospect of having all their recovering customers come tearing in with their blank financial statements looking for help. But bankers need to understand that the alcoholic may never have dealt with the reality of money before, and needs strong support as an aid to the joy of being sober. Even if the financial statement doesn't look as good as you'd hoped, it is nevertheless an essential part of reestablishing your credit—and besides, it can work for you. When you are finished with your statement, ask for copies. The bank will usually be glad to provide you with at least one copy of your signed and delivered statement. Then, go to the nearest copy machine and make six more copies.

You can use these copies to apply for credit cards and to establish other lines of credit with merchants, automobile agencies, furniture stores, realty firms, and other credit checkers. File one copy of your financial statement for your use a year later, when you update it and resubmit it to your bank. (Now don't blame the bank for making you update it. It's not the bank, but rather the government—both state and federal—that requires such statements as a condition of loaning you money.)

Even if a financial statement is not required because you're seeking such a small amount of money, I highly recommend you ask for and submit one anyway. This is a strong move to reestablish your credit. Even if the statement is bad, it will show that you are sincere in your efforts to start your money life anew in your sobriety. And you may be pleasantly surprised at how your banker can help you show more legitimate assets than perhaps you even knew you had. Your statement may be stronger than you suspected it could be.

If you are buying a house, for example, you are entitled to claim half of the equity or value of the house you now own along with the half of the mortgage burden you must show. However, your equity and your house's value have been steadily rising while your mortgage debt has been diminishing, thus improving your figures on the financial statement.

That's just a small tip of the iceberg that your banker will help you uncover. There are dozens of others, each item helping you to restore confidence that maybe you're worth more than you thought. Hence, in sobriety, the bank may well be interested in taking another chance with you.

I have talked to clients who were terrified about handling a financial statement because they had been through a bankruptcy, probably as a direct result of alcoholism. However, with the help of a banker friend, they filled out a statement showing the bankruptcy but attaching a written statement explaining the nature of the action and the part that alcoholism played. That financial statement was filed away by the bank, protected by the laws of confidentiality. However, the honesty of the approach helped that couple obtain a series of small loans that eventually led to reestablishing a larger line of credit.

By law in most states, a bankruptcy will continue to appear on retail credit bureau reports for ten years. But you can give a good, solidly prepared financial statement to the Retail Credit Bureau in your city, and they will take new facts into consideration. Make a personal appointment with your credit bureau and ask to see your file. They must, by law, show it to you. You, by law, have the right to update and supply additional information that will become part of the credit reporting process. Do it. It's worth it.

Everyone can have a financial statement, even a student still going to college. It's a good way to help cement your sober attitude in the minds of the people you will ask to advance sums of money and credit as you rebuild your new life.

THE CREDIT CARD CRUNCH

These pieces of plastic were a great part of your alcoholic behavior pattern. Now you should view them as part enemy and part friend.

You very possibly don't have any credit cards left. They may have vanished in the wake of your financial woes brought on by drinking. If you still have one or two, then you already have learned that you need to keep them paid and current.

Suppose you want a credit card and know you can't qualify because of previous bad credit? Well, there is a way. Your local savings and loan is probably the best source for obtaining and keeping a credit card such as a VISA or Mastercard. If you deposit funds in an account, many savings and loans, industrial banks, and similar lending institutions will establish a line of credit for you equal to the amount of funds you have on deposit. You will be issued a card that will entitle you to draw against your line of credit. It may not be as flexible as a regular high-line credit card, but it will enable you to carry around some ready credit. Many banks have similar programs, and they are worth investigating.

If you've had bad credit such as that associated with a bankruptcy, you'll probably not get a national credit card until the bankruptcy is purged from your records. It's not that the credit card companies may not be sympathetic to your story; it's just that their computers will almost always kick out your application as soon as the bankruptcy code comes from your local retail credit bureau computer.

You can try writing a personal letter to the credit card company and explaining your plight. My best advice is to get your Retail Credit Bureau account as solid as you can first. Ultimately, the credit card company will still query that source for the final decision on whether to issue you a card.

For your sobriety, the less plastic you have the better. Too much might lead you right back into the same bad habits associated with your drinking days—you could find yourself right back in the soup. So if you get a credit card or two, handle them with care. Share their status of use with your significant other so you don't play old games again. By all means, pay your credit card bills promptly and make certain you are current with your account in the month your card is due for renewal. If you mess up again, you will probably have a most difficult time ever getting anyone to go another round with you.

A simpler form of the extended credit card line is the check guarantee card issued by your particular banking institution. Here again, the financial statement you supply will allow the issuing bank or savings and loan to give you a card that will let you make loans to yourself simply by writing a check in any amount up to your established limit. The lending institution handles your payback schedule, and the monthly payments are usually automatically deducted from your checking account. Periodically, you may apply for increases in the amount of credit on your credit line, and voilá! You have yourself a credit card.

Talk, talk, talk these money issues over with your banking person. Don't be afraid to ask, "What do you think? What's your advice?" This is diametrically opposed to your alcoholic behavior, and it should bring you joy to know that asking someone else's opinion is a worthwhile thing to do.

LET'S TALK ABOUT INSURANCE

I feel strongly about your role as a recovering alcoholic in helping to educate and reeducate some folks about your disease. (You're going to have to if you need whole life insurance policies.) Now, before any insurance people get up in arms while reading this, let me say that I have found many companies to be sympathetic to the situation of the recovering person. I have not, however, found quite as many who are willing to sell you whole life insurance at standard rates.

Here's what I did. You may have a different battle plan and a different method of approaching the situation—all I can share with you is the tool I have used and recommended to others who have used it successfully.

First, you need to reevaluate your insurance position. During your drinking days you may have let some policies lapse, or treatment may have eaten up the borrowing power of some policies. If so, you probably have left yourself and your loved ones woefully underinsured.

It's entirely possible that you didn't even have any life insurance. Now, the depth of your bout with the disease of alcoholism has made you aware of the fatal nature of the disease and the imperative need to be protected with adequate insurance. Age, of course, has a bearing on the scale at which insurance companies rate you, but the really sticky part will come when the medical history is taken for your application.

Like many other groups, insurance companies have been relatively good about recognizing alcoholism as a treatable disease. What's been a little slower has been the realization that the recovering person needs a break for having done something about treating it. That's the rub. Many companies are happy to insure you for almost any amount, but they want to rate you very high up in the high-risk scale. This is understandable. After all, like many other diseases, there is no guarantee that alcoholism will remain in remission. That's where you have to do some really hard, honest selling on your own behalf. The following tools can work if you're willing to put in the legwork required and handle the problem in as honest and forthright a manner as possible.

1. Contact the person or agency that has handled any insurance for you in the past, even if that person doesn't normally handle anything but straight liability policies such as auto and theft. This person or agency will have a referral for you to another person or agency that does handle whole life underwriting.

2. Spend telephone time. Tell the person that you are recovering from alcoholism, and ask what the company's policy is regarding the rating of recovering persons. You want to ask:

A. Can I get whole life coverage?
B. Will I be rated on a standard risk scale?
C. Will I be required to supply past records of treatment?

I think you will find that most agents will be willing to look up company policy, but will not know it right off the top of their head. I was fortunate in having my longtime agent and friend get right to work. He was honest with me by saying, "I don't know the answers to your questions, but I'll get them." Can't ask for more than that.

3. Begin drafting an explanatory letter that will detail treatment of your disease of alcoholism, the length of your sobriety, and the names and places of medical references who could supply further evidence of your state of recovery. If you are recovering through AA alone, explain that in the letter and detail your regular and continuing participation in the program. Be prepared to supply a cover letter from your AA sponsor attesting to your efforts to remain sober. Most sponsors I have known are delighted to be of service in this area.

4. Be prepared to take your case beyond the agent level. Contact the issuing company directly, with a cover and supporting letter from the agent you are dealing with. This will require your agent to locate the name of the top person in the insurance company you are seeking coverage from. Don't hesitate to write to the president of the organization. The key is that you and your agent will have sorted the companies down to the ones that may write insurance for a recovering person at a reasonable rate. I guarantee you will hear from the top person. In one case, a client told me the company president referred him to a competitor who could supply what the client wanted.

5. Make your initial request for insurance at $10,000 or slightly above. Premiums, depending on age, can be high no matter where you are rated. You don't want to get yourself tied up with something too tough to handle.

6. Secure consent forms from your hospital, treatment center, or doctor that will allow them to release information about you to the inquiring company. Time is of the essence; you want to be prepared to strike when the iron is hot. Delays of anything over a few days will possibly lessen your chances to prove that you are serious about your request for help.

7. Ask your friends at any AA meeting how they got their insurance. What you will uncover very quickly will be a recovering agent or two who will be delighted to help you and will speed up the entire process for you. Insurance companies are constantly changing and updating rules for coverage, and new companies will crop up that you have never even heard of before. That doesn't matter—they will be just as reliable as the others. You can count on the fact that any agent that is recovering will have made a thorough check of alcoholism coverage in his or her own search for policies.

8. Contact any hospital patient representative at a hospital that has an alcoholism recovery unit, even if you did not go through that unit. They will have some knowledge of where you might get the information you seek. Often a company that pays for the inpatient or outpatient treatment services will have a direct tie with an underwriting firm, or will be happy to recommend one. (Not all insurance companies provide full or partial coverage for alcoholism. Remember, the company that will cover your medical bills for treatment may or may not have a tie-in with a company that will underwrite life insurance for you, but they are a source that should not be overlooked.)

All these steps I have outlined will take time and energy on your part. The reward is that you will find a source for standard-rated whole life insurance, and it will have been worth the effort. It's just like anything else in your sobriety—you'll discover some real satisfaction in doing responsible chores again. (One final note: Many people I work with have reported that after a year or so of having coverage at a certain rate, they actually received a lower rate from their insurance company).

Dealing with your banker, your lawyer, and your insurance agent can be one of the real joys of your sobriety. You can turn what was once painful, hostile, and embarrassing into long-lasting friendships with people that you once thought were just out to get you.

Give them a chance. Show them the new, recovering you, and the chances are very real they will stand among the first line of defenders of you and your new way of life!

MORE JOY (An Update)

This is not going to be a printed commercial endorsement for the Intuit Company, makers of the personal finance program, Quicken. However, I swear to God I don't know how I would ever have gotten a handle on my personal or private practice finances without this incredibly user-friendly computer program.

One of the things alcoholics do best is to ignore their finances. That is, they overlook the sorry state of their money affairs. Later in my recovery I was able to buy my first personal computer, and several years ago I was introduced to Quicken. Suddenly the whole thing made sense. I write all checks, personal and business, on this program. What used to take me hours, trying to balance a mixed-up checkbook, now takes less than ten minutes—and the thing actually balances!

I am very aware that personal computers are still somewhat expensive. I wouldn't be true to the nature of this book if I urged every reader to go further into debt to buy a computer. However, if you can't afford to own one, maybe you can borrow one or go to one of those places that rents computer time.

Owning the Quicken accounting program requires an investment of less than forty dollars, or you can buy other similar programs for less than one hundred dollars, if you prefer. Simply go to a computer store where you rent the use of the machine by the hour, make a backup diskette of your data, and presto! You could balance any number of accounts in less than thirty minutes, thus helping you know exactly where you are and what you need to do to stay above the red line.

Banks seem to become less personal with every passing year. More and more of them are being purchased by large conglomerates, probably located in another city, that really don't present much of a friendly image. The death of the S&Ls has given a whole new meaning to the word "thrift," because the places you can go to reestablish your credit are now pretty limited. Money is tighter, credit is harder to get, and even credit cards are playing all sorts of interest rate games.

However, there is a new avenue to get a credit card that might appeal to you. It's tied into automatic savings. There are several institutions that will give you a Visa or MasterCard that is strictly tied to the amount of money you put in their savings department.

Want a three hundred, five hundred or one thousand dollar line of credit? Then simply deposit that amount in your savings account at the bank. For every one hundred dollars you deposit over the initial amount (usually three hundred dollars), you gain another one hundred dollars in credit card purchasing power. In the meantime, your savings account is earning some minimal passbook account interest. In addition, you have a credit card, something you may have been denied because of your unworthy past credit.

All in all, the principles I wrote about originally still apply. You can make a new start and you can get credit. Hopefully, you will use that credit in a responsible manner for a change, now that you are in recovery. I still make it a point to have a personal banker and to keep that banker fully appraised of my financial condition.

When I purchased Gateway Treatment Center from my co-founding partner a few years ago, I found myself again with heavy financial burdens. Fortunately, I was able to process those burdens with a clear mind and a considerably better handle on what the real world of finance is all about. You can do it, too. Take real pride in doing simple little chores like balancing a checkbook or two, drawing up a loan amortization schedule, and setting up a monthly budget that you can follow and make work.

It's amazing how the absence of alcohol makes the assets and liabilities side of your financial life something you do not have to fear anymore.

*Children begin by loving their parents. After a time
they judge them. Rarely, if ever, do they forgive them.*

Oscar Wilde,
A Woman of No Importance

7

WHERE WAS I WHEN THE KIDS
WERE GROWING UP?

"I can't believe my Mom actually hears what I'm saying."

"Dad, it's so different... I mean, you can talk and not blow up at me."

"Where were you when I really needed you?"

Good question. Where were you? It's pretty obvious that some of the people in your life thought you had vanished from the face of the earth. You were never sober enough to be of any help when they needed you. If your drinking was even confined to weekend abuse, the chances are pretty good that weekends were when the kids needed things from you, important things like:

1. Your time,
2. Your attention,
3. Your love, and,
4. Your rational judgment for meting out discipline.

That's a pretty good shopping list, one rarely filled due to alcohol's importance in your life. That's behind you now, and you can get on with the business of learning how to be a parent, a grandparent, or an aunt or uncle. If you don't have kids of your own, read this chapter anyway and apply the principles to your dealings with any younger people in your life.

I often think of the trials that beset Hank Ketchum's marvelous cartoon character, Mr. Wilson, in his popular "Dennis The Menace" comic strip. Wilson doesn't have any children, but Dennis lives next door. That's bad enough, for Wilson has to learn to deal with Dennis as if Dennis were his own kid. Maybe you are a recovering grandparent and were told over the years, "We're not bringing little Susan to stay with you anymore, Dad. We can't trust you." I will never forget the pain and tears of a grandmother I saw in my practice. Even in recovery, she was having a very difficult time getting her son and his wife to believe that she was different now, that she was sober and deserved a second chance.

"What can I do?" she asked. "They don't trust me, I guess because they think I'll go back to drinking when they've left my grandson with me."

Well, trust works both ways. The recovering person has the same chance of being trusted as the kids have of being a little different themselves. They haven't always been little dears, you know. Quite frankly, a child living in an alcoholic home learns to manipulate the situation.

Kids have always had the knack of knowing which buttons to push to achieve their personal goals. Parents have helped them find those buttons. The alcoholic parent has practically given the kids a new set of buttons to push every day.

True, the children have gone through incredibly embarrassing times because of alcohol abuse in the home. So think about that, but consider your own situation as you recall those heartbreaking events that occurred because you cared more for booze than booties.

I've lost count of how many times I have heard a youngster say she will no longer have her friends over for a slumber party because she can't count on a parent being sober. That same child will often hook up with a friend whose parents become her surrogate Mom and Dad—she goes to them when she needs comfort, advice, and love. This creates trouble at her own home when her parents, out of petty jealousy, demand the youngster bring her needs to them because, after all, "We are your parents."

The problem is that when alcohol abuse is in the home, no youngster wants to waste time trying to talk issues over with a drinking parent. Kids know that whatever they say on a drinking day or night won't be remembered when the drinking episode is over. So why bother bringing anything up?

You've got to change that. We'll look at some ways that have proven helpful in regaining lost ground between parents, now sober, and their awestruck children. "Awestruck?" you ask. Yep! Kids are perhaps the first to recognize what a big change has occurred from the drinking to the sober parent. So let's set some basic tools on the counter and see how to use them.

TAKE THEM ONE AT A TIME

There is just one of you, and maybe a whole slew of kids. But even if there is just one child, you probably should use this tool. It means dealing with the kids as individuals rather than as a group. If you do have just one, then it means that you will deal with him or her alone—no grandmother, neighbor, or little friend from next door is present.

The kids learned a long time ago there is safety in numbers. Boy, if they can outnumber you they sure are going to try. How many times have you heard the plaintive cry, "But all the other kids are doing it," or "You always let Mary have one of those when she wants it."? See? Safety in numbers.

The joy of your being sober allows you not to knuckle under to the harassment of a whole army of offspring. You need to establish a policy of dealing with each of your children on an individual basis. I am the father of twins, plus two more. I wouldn't trade any of them for the world, but I sure had to learn to deal with them on this one-on-one basis. It's too easy for any recovering person to want to jump right in and meet every child's needs all at once. Don't try it. Invoke the One At A Time rule and make it stick.

Dealing with your children individually is just as important even if the issue at hand is the same for all the kids. You still want to sort out the issue in your mind for each individual. Your brain needs recovery time like the rest of your body, so take everything slow and easy. That's part of the new you. You can dictate a few terms based on your comfort level and make them stick.

ALLOW VENTING

This tool may not be easy for you to use. Like the castor oil you may have been forced to swallow as a child yourself, it may not go down easy.

The tool works because you're saying to your youngster, "I am giving you permission to vent your anger at me. I know you are angry at me, and you hurt." Allowing venting helps you understand the frustrations your young person has kept pent up inside for a long time.

How you allow this venting is the real key to the use of the tool. So, venting is okay when:

1. It is clearly defined as filling a need to blow off steam.
2. It's understood that there is hurt present as well as anger.
3. There is an attempt to resolve that hurt.

You, the now-sober person, control the interview with the youngster. And you bring into play another tool you're about to learn:

REVERTING TO "I" STATEMENTS

To get the interview for venting started, you use the "I" Statement. You say, "I have the feeling there is something troubling you, Susan. Can you help me with why I'm feeling that way?" You clearly state that you are not asking for anything from the other person except help to sort out your feelings. No one has to become defensive. You give permission for venting to start by expressing a desire for help in understanding your child's feelings.

Susan might respond with, "Well, Dad, you might be feeling like something is bugging me because it is. And what's bugging me is you."

Control yourself. Remember you are giving permission to vent feelings and are simply helping that person get started in a clean manner by using the "I" Statement. (It's obvious that the "I" Statement is also very important in reestablishing your marriage, as discussed in Chapter Five. I saved it for here to show you that it can be helpful in all interpersonal communications.)

Every time you employ the "I" Statement you take the monkey off the back of the person with whom you are about to have a dialogue. You give them permission, in a roundabout way, to unload by helping you define your own uneasy feelings. What really happens, of course, is you get a solid clue about what is wrong between you and the other person. Armed with the knowledge of what's wrong, you can proceed to ask:

1. When did this feeling first occur?
2. How do you think it happened?
3. Where did it start? And,
4. What do we want to do about it?

Notice the absence of the word "why." Don't ask why. "Why" only smacks of despair and the "oh-woe-is-me" attitude that you had when you were drinking. Stick with the other tools to conduct the dialogue.

The "I" Statement should be used in any such dealings with your youngsters. Keep it in mind as we examine the other basic tools of dealing—soberly—with your children.

DON'T OVERREACT

Boy, is this an easy trap to get yourself into. When you were drinking it would take days, weeks, or even months to get an opinion or decision out of you. Now, sober, you want to throw all systems to "Go!" and solve all your kids' (and anyone else's) problems in thirty seconds flat. Take some time and stop overreacting.

You can't make up for all the mistakes of the past anyway. The ones you *can* correct can stand the mellowing of a little time. Your kids want everything now, and your newfound sobriety makes you want to jump right in instead of asking yourself, "What's really going on here? What can I do about it?" But by assigning some time frames to problems with your youngster, you can develop a valuable strategy for solving any particular dilemma together. I don't mean to make everything sound like a battle between you and your children, but I am anxious to have you take time to assess everyone's position and point of view before acting on a matter.

Questions such as, "How much time before this has to be done?" and, "Are we able to put this matter on hold until later so we can see what Mom has in mind?" clearly beg for time. Do the begging in a manner that indicates you are not going to forget about the subject; you are just not going to allow either of you to be stampeded into foolish action.

Taking a second look before acting helps you analyze the situation without undue pressure. It's also the main reason for not dealing with your kids in packs, but individually, as previously stated. No stampedes. You don't need that in your sober life.

Overreacting can also make you spend more money and buy more of everything than you probably should. We'll discuss that in more detail under one of the other tools in this chapter—suffice it to say right now that it can and does happen. You become so anxious to prove your sobriety and regain their trust that you go overboard, and in too big a hurry.

Think of overreacting as pushing a red button labelled "in case of emergency only." Once it's pushed, there's very little chance of recalling whatever terror you unleashed because you didn't allow enough time to contemplate the effects of your actions.

BE OKAY WITH CRITICISM

Like other tools of sobriety that bring you joy, you'll find this one a real hummer when you get the hang of it. It seems a little masochistic at the beginning, but you'll get used to it. This is particularly true if you and your youngster are willing to trade criticism. It goes like this:

KID: "Mom, I really want to talk to you." (Notice—talk *to* you, not *with* you.)

MOM: (Using "I" Statement) "I'm feeling like there is something more to this than just wanting to talk. Can you help me with that?"

KID: (Boy, can he.) "Yeah. I think you're smoking too much."

So there's the opening. He wants to criticize you, and you are okay about taking criticism. In your previous drinking state you might have verbally or physically backhanded "the little smart mouth," but not now. Now it's okay for the criticism bit as long as there is a quid pro quo to the whole exchange.

Being okay will mean that you need to take your child's criticism, and only then venture to counter with your own criticism. You might say, "It seems like my smoking upsets you, Kenny."

This gives Kenny a chance to unload about seeing you smoke and to offer a bonafide criticism of the habit. You can very well expect your youngsters to tell you that they wanted to say something about it before, but that you wouldn't have listened then. A not-too-subtle jab at the old drinking days, don't you think?

So you listen to him expound about how your excessive smoking bothers him. Then you are in a position to trade off for something you'd like him to change.

You could say, "Kenny, I think you're right. It even sounds like you might be willing to help me cut down on my smoking. Maybe you could cut down on your snacking between meals." Then the clincher, "Is that what I'm hearing?"

You're gonna love it. When you get the hang of being okay about taking criticism and offering some in return, without anger, you will experience some real joy.

Never, but never, use this tool to explain why you do something ("I'm older, after all"). Rather, handle the criticism as a way to bring more positive interaction between you and your youngster into play. Being okay with criticism is another sign of your healing process. It needs to be encouraged and fostered as a valuable tool in your recovery.

ASK FOR POSITIVE FEEDBACK

This may seem like a variation on the Warm Fuzzy. They are similar, yet different. The Warm Fuzzy is a way to say thank you. Positive Feedback is a tool you can employ to get your kids to tell you what's right with your relationship in addition to what's wrong. If you think this sounds a little like sitting up and begging for strokes and ego soothing, you're right. And there's nothing wrong with that. God knows, everyone has been right in there saying what has been wrong with you. Why not let everyone have a fair shot at helping you feel good about yourself?

When the kids are involved in Positive Feedback there is a double reward. If they can help define what you are doing right in your relationship with them, then they can feel a part of what's right.

"Hey, Kate, that's really great to hear from you. I think I owe a lot of that change to you, too." Then Positive Feedback continues with, "Is there any other area where you see some improvement?"

Who can resist an honest opening like that? It's a chance to share in some credit for improvement in another person. That's fantastic. The use of Positive Feedback as a tool for your continued recovery is valuable because it helps reestablish the fact that sober, you're okay. Not being sober meant you were not okay.

Once established, you can use the tool of seeking Positive Feedback as a way to have your kids help you fight all sorts of problems, such as the Dry Drunk and the Grey Ghost Syndrome. That's when you need Positive Feedback most, when things seem the blackest and the temptation to relapse into drinking is the strongest.

If you couple Positive Feedback with being able to accept criticism, the rewards can be endless in building your relationship with your youngsters. This tool is a way of asking, "How're we doing?" Since you are willing to share the credit, more of it will surely come.

REASSESS CRITICAL SITUATIONS

Often decisions were made by you or by the consensus of you, your spouse, and the youngsters involved, and that was the end to them. This is not always a good idea. It's entirely possible that some new information is available about a certain situation, and if so, you should not feel locked into a previous decision. This is too reminiscent of "You promised!" and, "You can't change your mind now," which you used to hear quite frequently during your drinking days. Well, you *can* change your mind. You can take another look at the situation. By doing so you add another rung to your ladder of credibility. This time, you're no pushover. This time, folks will have to reckon with a sober mind that reserves the right to reevaluate without it being a major catastrophe.

When a client says, "It's not worth the battle for me to back off of a decision I've made," then I think of telling them to look toward winning the war. That requires fighting some battles. If you become too complacent about reassessing a situation, you revert to the alcoholic habit of never making a decision. Call a pow-wow or conference with a single member of the family to talk about changing a decision already made, or at least to look at a new alternative.

This is particularly important when it comes to changes in your financial situation. Maybe you've decided that you can afford to buy a car for your college-bound son. He and you pick out what is safe, classy enough, and affordable. Let's say that he was going to contribute a certain amount to the purchase or the upkeep of the vehicle. Perhaps he had committed funds for the insurance on the car. You have made a decision. Before you can act on it, however, your son tells you that he has lost his job and that he will be unable to carry out his end of the bargain.

A change in plans is clearly called for. If you have to assume this new cost, it may cause undue stress on the family budget and on you personally. Should you go ahead with the purchase anyhow? No. You need to have the courage to make a new assessment of the situation and find a solution that meets both your needs and your son's. For you to forge blindly ahead would be a return to alcoholic behavior patterns—namely, acting without regard for consequences. This won't help you either in your continuing sobriety or in building a trust relationship with your youngsters.

Being locked into a decision means that everyone still has the ability to push the right guilt buttons with you and get whatever they want. They can do this even when new information may be available, such as the loss of a job, which makes a new decision mandatory.

Keep this tool of reassessment handy because you will want to use it frequently, although it will bring loud wails of protest from the aggrieved parties. It will remind everyone that a more mature, stable, and concerned parent is back in the family setting—one who realizes no decision, except the one to remain sober, is set in cement.

Eventually, your children will respect the family's right to change a previous collective decision. Doing so forces all of you to look at alternatives for reaching the given objective. Reassessing also means that as a family unit, you can afford the luxury of being flexible, something that didn't seem to be possible when alcohol abuse was a part of your lives.

SETTING LIMITS

It is imperative that you not turn into a gift or money horse in your sobriety in order to wipe out the guilt you feel for those years of drinking. You will probably be the one to pour on more guilt than anyone else in your family. But let a kid or two throw some fuel onto that fire, and often you'll find you can't reach for your wallet fast enough. That's definitely not the answer. There may be many things you would like to do for and with your children now that you're sober. However, you can have the effect of making *them* drunk with lavish gifts, money, and attention. In effect, you're saying, "Look how I'm trying to make up for what I've been and done in the past."

Setting limits means you recognize, both as an individual in sobriety and as a responsible family member, that you can't buy your way into permanent affection, loyalty, or respect. And, by setting limits you actually increase your chances to help yourself and your children achieve a more complete state of wellness around your recovery.

Letting the sky's-the-limit philosophy into your recovery program means continuing the process of enabling all who are near and dear to you to continue in their own self-centered ways. They, like you, need to be willing to take responsibility for their own actions. If you are the leader in clearly setting limits for your own actions, they will be forced to set limits on their own habits. Some of those habits might be ruinous if not checked.

Setting limits also refers to the physical you, the one who has to learn to say "no" and be comfortable about it. Many times, the euphoria of new-found sobriety will lead you into a real rat race as you try to keep up with all the plans others are making for you. The postponed fishing trips, picnics, bike rides, and other activities with your children can wear you down in a hurry, even if you were not in a state of recovery from alcoholism. The good old precept of not letting yourself get too involved too quickly really holds true.

Guilt may dictate overindulgence in parent-child projects. Avoid this by sitting down with the youngster involved and explaining that you are recovering from a disease. It will take some time before certain mental and physical energy levels are back up where you can cope with demands.

Setting limits means it's okay for you to say that enough is enough, no matter what the particular demand. It does not mean that you won't rise to the occasion later. Setting limits simply means that you need a breather from many things, including being the grand entertainer or family host.

A good way to set limits is to use the phrase, "I think this weekend outing calls for us to set some limits." This puts the process right up front at the beginning. It opens the door for the youngsters to be in on plans for when things will end as well as start. A favorite slogan of AA is "Easy Does It." That's just about the name of the tune, and you need to learn to be comfortable with it.

BE CONSISTENT

Your behavior patterns will vary for quite a while in sobriety. When you deal with the kids, consistency needs to be reinforced. Drinking allowed you to change your mind and the way you did things about as often as you changed your socks—maybe more often. As you recover, you will have a feeling of well-being in knowing that you can do things the same way twice. (Now, don't confuse being consistent with reassessing critical situations, which allows you to change both decisions and promises made.)

Your kids need to learn and respect the fact that your sober behavior with them is going to stay that way—sober. All the taunting, harassing, and temper tantrums are not going to make you drink. You are committed to the joy of being sober, and you're going to stay that way. Being consistent in your behavior will help solidify that resolve. If, for example, you have established a rule with your kids that they need to call you if they are going to be later than agreed, and you'll call them if you're going to be late, then be consistent. You need to observe that rule as long as it applies to the situation. Nothing could be worse for your new life than to have your kids see you try something a couple of times and then drop it, just like you did when drinking.

This does not mean that you are glued forever to a particular action that has become unworkable. When this occurs, it's time for the individual pow-wows and resetting of short-term objectives. It's a general wishy-washy attitude that you want to avoid. When Charles Shultz, the creator of "Charlie Brown," has one of the kids saying to good ol' Charlie, "That's what I like about you, Charlie Brown. You're so wishy-washy," he must be saying that a lack of consistency is a lovable trait in some people. That's not for you, however, because that particular trait was too much of a sign that you had been hitting the juice. You could be counted on to change a policy that was one of yesterday's Ten Commandments.

Being consistent also gives you a way to share many rewards in the form of Warm Fuzzies with your kids. It's a simple tool, really. Your child's responsible behavior earns a reward from you. Irresponsible behavior earns nothing. You stand firm that you won't give in to whatever demands your child may make to get his or her way.

This theory, of course, belongs not to me but to the fine reality therapist, Dr. William Glasser. It's his theory that I use in my own therapy work. If you want more details, Glasser's book, *Reality Therapy,* is a jewel.

The more uncomplicated you make your life of sobriety, the more joy there is in being sober. The more consistent you become in all your relationships, the more you solidify the fact that you are a different person. You are one to be reckoned with, not to be put on hold during family discussions. You should learn to forget how your kids would say, "Wait awhile. Dad'll change his mind." That's how you were when you were drinking. Sober, all who deal with you will have to learn that your behavior patterns will emerge as ones that everyone can count on.

As I said earlier, your behavior patterns may take some wide swings for awhile. Eventually, however, you will find ways to bring each mode of your behavior into clear focus. This will help you and each person with whom you must deal, whether on a short-term close basis or an away-at-college-hit-'em-on-the-phone contact.

REINFORCE WHAT WORKS

When you and your kids discover that a new way of communicating has grown between you, then you can use this tool over and over. You can say such things as, "Hey! Remember how we solved the ski trip problem?" or, "Who can tell me what we did when this came up before?" It works even better when you keep your dialogues on the one-on-one basis I discussed earlier, because it forces the youngster to search his or her memory banks for the way you solved a problem together.

If it worked once, it will work again. That's the philosophy behind the tool, and you can trust it. Each time you bring reinforcement into play, you establish stronger ways to solve problems on a regular basis. It's a thrill to see the many ways you and your kids can get along for a change, if you are willing to work at it. Both parties have to make a commitment to keep reinforcing what works, and also have an equal desire to throw out what didn't work.

That's why I'll play around with a particular furniture design in my home workshop. When I find something that works, I write it down and pin it on the corkboard in the shop. My mistake box reminds me that a lot of trial and error went into building some piece of cabinet work. But once I learn that something works, I'll use it over and over.

You can assess and reassess the success of a particular idea that works for you in your everyday dealings with your kids. You'll need to stick with, use, and shout about the ones that work. Discard and change what doesn't work. It's a good blue-print for you and your kids to keep open in your relationship.

FIND NEW ACTIVITIES

This tool is fun, exciting, and therapeutically helpful to everyone involved. So many times I hear people talk about returning to a particular place like Disney-land, but not really enjoying it. "What do you think was the reason?" I ask. The reply usually can be boiled down to, "It just wasn't the same." And it wasn't. Nothing can really be the same anymore because *you* are different (and three cheers for the difference). So, in an effort to regain family closeness, a revisit to old activities fails more often than not. In sobriety you look, act, and feel so differ-ently about yourself that it may seem as if you shouldn't have attempted the activ-ity in the first place.

Maybe you spent money with reckless abandon then, and now your sobriety causes you to be more prudent. Maybe before you packed everyone off on first class airfare, but now it's better that you all drive. (Driving increases tensions, but does save money.) Maybe the old campground no longer appeals to you because of painful memories. So you search for a new camping place or stay in a cabin for most of the trip.

More than half the fun of new activities is in the planning, and this is an area where you can have real input—maybe for the first time. Your kids, particularly, will want to have your views on what can be done that's new and different.

The reason for finding new activities to share together is so that painful memories of alcoholic behavior do not mar enjoyment of the vacation or the activity. What family members may think of as funny may only be hurtful to you. While it is true that you will eventually have to work through those pains and those griefs, I believe that togetherness activities are not the time.

I had a woman tell me that on a recent family vacation, she tripped, quite by accident, getting off an airplane jetway. Some family members said, "Gee. Noth-ing's changed. Mom's still tripping over things." (She had stumbled during an ear-lier family trip, taken when Mom was still drinking daily.) The kids in her family had come to accept her clumsiness as part of her drinking. This woman told me that she felt so bad after the sober tripping incident that it was several days before she snapped out of her depression.

Using the tool of Finding New Activities certainly doesn't mean giving up flying because you tripped a few times. It does mean that you need to face up to the possibility that old traits might recur and spoil your good times. If so, then a family conference is necessary to agree that when such things do occur, you will deal with them right away. Using the Freedom For Criticism and Warm Fuzzies devices, you will weather them.

Generally, though, it will be more of a challenge to try some altogether different things with your kids. Then, if an incident occurs such as I just described, you all experience it together, sober, and able to treat it as a distinct occurrence and not something laden with grief from the past.

The very idea of sitting down and planning a vacation together can be a real joy. You might split up your vacation times so that each of your kids feels that you are sharing part of your leisure time just with him or her. This isn't as hard as it may seem, and many families in recovery have found their way back to each other by taking shorter, more exclusive trips together.

I learned this firsthand when one of my twin daughters became ill, forcing her to fly home from college. The other twin and I had to drive back from Minnesota with all the luggage. We had a blast! It was the first time in many years we had been alone together. We came to know a lot about each other over that three-day trip. We didn't plan it that way, but since then I have found the one-on-one trip to be a great way to spend some time with my kids.

I take them singly out to lunch or to a game. We have an opportunity to explore some new activity together, such as shopping for a new item of clothing for *me* for a change. In my drinking days, this would not have been possible. In sobriety, it's not only possible, but downright fun.

There are dozens and dozens of other tools you will discover if you search for them. Start with these basic few we have discussed and make your own modifications. You will find a real sense of satisfaction in knowing that you used these guidelines and they worked. Your kids will be stunned to find you are capable of setting a game plan and making it work.

The joy of your children, grandchildren, or other young relatives of yours is a part of your life—a deep part. You don't have to whip yourself into a moral frenzy trying to answer the question posed by this chapter title. You've faced the fact that you were there, at least in body. Now you've got the rest of your life, sober, to be there in the full spirit of what being a parent is all about.

MORE JOY (An Update)

Even though more than ten years have passed since this original chapter was written, the message remains stronger than ever for me. You must separate your kids from the group and treat them individually.

As my private practice has grown over the years, so have my kids. They aren't kids anymore, but young adults with mates, families, careers, and problems, just like other adults. Maintaining separate relationships with them, I've found, is still vital.

I am constantly amazed when clients of mine want to deal with the problems their drinking has caused with their kids, but say, "Oh, we haven't told Christy anything about the drinking (or drugging)…she doesn't need to know." If you think your kids—especially after the age of four or five—don't recognize family dysfunction, then you are an ostrich with your head in the sand.

One of my daughters, Dawn, is an early childhood development specialist, and she has her private practice with me here at the Gateway Treatment Center. Over and over, Dawn will show parents I am treating how their young children have been affected, and, what's better, how the family can work on getting well.

For me, the enjoyment of my adult kids continues. My oldest daughter and I have breakfast once a week. Tracey is a senior partner in her own criminal defense law firm, and a very busy person, but our breakfast visits are a priority with us. Dawn and I see each other weekly, when our practices overlap. We try to have lunch together, but aren't able to as often as we would both like. My other twin daughter, Dana, is an assistant city attorney. We have found a place to meet for lunch that is less than half a mile from both of our offices. Again, the problem is, we don't get to do it as often as we would like.

My son Jackson and his family live in Plantation, Florida. Visits with him and them are limited to trips Cyn and I take there and occasions when his travels bring him to Colorado. He heads the Florida operation for a major bar review program in Florida and several other states, and is himself a law school graduate from Georgetown. (Don't ask me what turned three of my four kids into the law profession, but I'm sure proud of all of them.)

The one other thing that comes through to me about recovery and children is that my kids are still full of surprises when it comes to their memories of my drinking days. Sometimes, not out of spite or anger or anything like that, one of them will remember an incident from the days when I was drinking that I had forgotten.

We were all at a wonderful brunch not long ago when Dawn told the story to her siblings (including Jackson, who was visiting Denver) about "Dad taking our high school graduation pictures with the lens cap still on the camera." I had totally blacked that one out, and as Dawn continued with the story, we all laughed. Yet, beneath the laughter, I felt a sense of pain that I could have screwed up such an important event with a dumb stunt like that.

She was right, of course. I had been using an older 35mm camera that allowed you to see through the viewfinder whether the lens cap was on or off. I shot an entire roll of color film and, of course, never got one picture. That's the bad news. The good news is twofold: one, we all could laugh at that incident, and two, I more than made up for it with excellent color pictures of Dana's law school graduation from the University of Puget Sound in Tacoma, and Dawn's Masters graduation from the University of Denver.

I also got excellent photos of son Jackson at his Regis College graduation, and of my wife Cyn receiving undergraduate and graduate degrees from Regis University. I even took very passable pictures at Tracey's law school graduation from Southern Methodist University. Better than that, I took good pictures of Tracey when she was signing Cyn's and my wedding certificate, after she had married us in her official capacity as a municipal court judge.

Now, have I redeemed myself?

The message I want to leave you with is to listen to your kids—individually, together, I don't care how. Just listen. It's a great part of your recovery, and most rewarding to learn that their love and support for you did not diminish, hardy little devils that they are.

It is a truth universally acknowledged, that a single man in possession of a good fortune must be in want of a wife.

Jane Austen, Pride and Prejudice

Behold her, single in the field, Yon solitary Highland lass!
Wordsworth

THE SINGLES GAME WITHOUT BOOZE

Boy! Have all of us been mean to you. We, those who love you and care about you, have taken away your best friend. (Yes, we helped take away your bottle, your best friend.) How can you possibly meet a member of the opposite sex now?

During the height of your drinking days, you had no trouble at all overcoming that innate shyness, that lack of resolution that was always a part of you until you downed a belt or two. Now, like the Cowardly Lion of "Oz" fame, you are in search of courage. The road is not a yellow brick number, either. It's rough. Your main battleground, the bar, is off limits to you if you want to maintain your sobriety. Still, you want to meet some available personnel on the dating battlefield.

What to do? Where to go? Are you forever doomed to sit in the gloom of your apartment or condo and watch the dust settle on your coffee table?

Must you detour on the way home from work so that the local singles bars will not beckon like some temptress in your path? Are rock concerts now a thing of your past? No, no, and no!

What we will discuss together here is the plight of the sober single. Like in our other chapters, we'll look at some tools that you can try out to help you find added joy in your sobriety while you find companionship. And don't say, "What does he know? He's married." While you're right—I am married—I spend an extraordinary amount of time listening to clients who, in treatment, are facing the same dilemma of single sobriety that you are. I owe the development of many of the following tools to them. And because these tools have worked for others, they can work for you.

In my lecture work, I always look for opportunities to find other singles who are wrestling with these same problems. The wealth of material provided by talking to these groups, exchanging experiences, disregarding what doesn't seem to work and amplifying what does work, provides much of the groundwork for this chapter.

Recovery, as I have told you before, is a program that demands honesty. So I'll level with you—I tried a couple of these ideas myself to see if they worked the way I thought they would, the way that they were presented to me by others. I thought by slipping my wedding ring into my pocket I could pass at a singles gathering and see what was really going on.

It didn't work. The ring left such an indentation on my ring finger that I spent more time denying that I was recently divorced than it was worth. Finally, I came clean and told folks what I was up to—just plain old hard background research. I revealed I was happily married, but asked if I could stay and observe anyhow.

Thus, I can honestly tell you I have tested all but one of these tools myself, and they *do* work. I did not use the advertising tool that we'll discuss later—that was more of a strain on honesty than I felt was called for, but I have seen others use it very effectively, so it's included in my material on the sober single.

Let's begin by asking what you know about yourself as a single person. First, there are over eighteen million of you running around out there, according to the last census. One of every three adults in the United States is single, and about fifty million of you fall within the ages of twenty to fifty-five. So much for the statistics. What they all boil down to anyway is, "Where is the male or female for *me* in all that jungle?"

I am often told that the balance between available men and women is all out of whack here in Denver, but which way the scales supposedly tip depends on whether the client I'm talking to is male or female. I've also heard this in Dallas, and read surveys about New York, Atlanta, San Francisco, and other cities. Alaska may be the exception, where the consensus seems to be that females are in short supply. (However, when I made that statement to a friend of mine recently, he said that he attended an AA meeting in an Alaskan city and met all kinds of single ladies. So take that, statistics. They can work for you or against you, depending on what you want to find.) All I've come to in the way of a conclusion is that the people who really want to find someone to share sobriety with, do.

Most data seem to indicate a common thread or two about the sober single:

1. They are trying to combat loneliness.
2. Their sobriety has fed their insecurity and underlined their fear of rejection.
3. They would like to meet friends of the opposite sex without the enormous sexual pressures of the past.

Fair enough. You can relate to that, can't you? It doesn't really matter whether your sobriety is brand new or several weeks or months old. You need some friends. You want one or two people in your life who are willing to contribute to your continuing sobriety by sharing time without making too many demands, particularly in the sexual area.

With that in mind, let's look at what the missing ingredient in the plight of the sober single is:

BAR COURAGE WITHOUT THE BAR

Boy, howdy! When you were on that bar stool quaffing down a few, you were Superman or Wonder Woman, Robert Redford or Farrah Fawcett. It didn't matter what you were really like. You could let alcohol mask all the imperfections and highlight just the good stuff. That's okay, but now the absence of alcohol forces you to the great and harsh realizations of exactly who and what you are. So you are dealing straight for a change—there are no hidden cards up your sleeve, and it scares you to death.

It shouldn't. Let's see what your goals were for meeting people in bars in the first place; that is, what they were when you were drinking. More than likely, you perched yourself on a bar stool to satisfy fairly immediate needs:

1. Sex,
2. Not wanting to spend the evening alone,
3. Not wanting to spend your own money, and

4. Developing a solid contact place in your life by being one of the establishment's "regulars."

Drinking in that bar gave you courage, albeit false courage. The needs may still be there but, as we discussed earlier, they have changed. Now your needs include combatting loneliness and fear of rejection.

Let's face it. Sober, you will wake up and damn well know who is beside you in bed (if anyone), and how and why that person got there. That can be scary, because it means you need to put a whole lot more effort into the contact in the first place. And to do that, you need some tools to regain bar courage without the bar atmosphere. Here they are:

1. I accept the way I look.
2. There's a lot more to me than just a body.
3. Someone is out there looking for someone like me.
4. I'm in charge of my life because I'm sober.
5. I can make choices as easily as I can be someone else's choice.

With alcohol, you didn't care about those things. Nor did you try to use them as everyday tools in your personal growth. Now you are sober and seriously capable of adding another ingredient to your recipe for finding a companion. That ingredient is that you want to find someone you can count on, someone who will be there when you need him or her.

That shows that you are now ready for some kind of relationship that goes beyond the range of the one-night stand (which, by all accounts, is a very common occurrence in the alcoholic single's life). So, you can afford to take some time to shop around for places where other singles may congregate. You have some items on a shopping list of your own, and you are beginning to feel better about yourself. It takes work, though.

You will never meet anyone staying at home. You will have to force yourself to venture out into public if you are going to test the new waters of the sober single. You can and must carry your bar courage with you wherever you go to meet other people.

Consider this about bar courage: When you drank a few ounces of alcohol—two ounces, to be exact—you sedated part of your brain for one and one-half to four hours. Part of your brain was put to sleep, including the part with good judgment, tension, stress, and many other inhibitors standing in your way to making contacts with members of the opposite sex. The problem was that when the booze wore off, all the inhibitions that were there in the first place returned. You had to have more booze to regain this false courage. And the reality was that you didn't quit with one drink of two ounces of alcohol, but rather had several, and even more than several. Your bar courage came, was nurtured, and vanished when the booze wore off.

As a sober single, you can have your courage with you all the time by recalling that you were not necessarily shy, bashful, awkward, incapable of brilliant conversation, or helpless against any other inhibiting factor without alcohol. It was the alcohol, combined with the desire to meet someone, that allowed you to put everything into full swing and score with a member of the opposite sex. Well, the only thing that's different now is that you have removed the alcohol. The same basic, effervescent, bubbly and brilliant you who has been lurking beneath the surface is still lurking there. You only have to release it.

So, you *can* approach your encounters with potential companions with the same bar courage without being in the bar and without drinking. The basis for this is the belief and understanding that alcohol didn't put any of those neat qualities about your personality in you. It only removed the inhibitors (on a very temporary basis) so you felt free to act. You are *still* free to act. You are even more in command, because you are aware of every subtlety and nuance. And isn't that great?

WHERE TO MEET THE OTHER NON-DRINKERS

Now we get down to the nitty-gritty. You can pick up so many books, magazine articles, newspaper stories, and even pamphlets about this singles game that I sometimes think you could spend most of your time just reading about it and not doing anything about it. I don't want to add to that clutter. What you'll find out on the following pages of this chapter is not a random inventory of meeting places. These are places that I have culled (with the aid of many clients' experiences) into workable, manageable meeting situations. You can and will find a hundred more, and when you do, use them. Keep in mind, however, that most places suggested by many others will have drinking as a part of the package. We'll discuss those pitfalls later.

For better or worse (forgive the expression), here is my list:

1. AA and Al-Anon, Alateen
2. Sports, exercise clubs
3. Church, synagogue
4. Classes
5. Concerts

6. Museums, planetariums, gardens
7. Travel—everyday, short-range
8. Office buildings, the elevator
9. Stores, the supermarket and the "Mom and Pop" variety
10. Advertising

Now let's dissect the list and amplify its richness as a meeting ground for the sober single.

AA, AL-ANON, ALATEEN

There is no question in my mind that regular attendance at your meetings, whether in town or out of town, will acquaint you with other sober singles faster than any other method. At AA, Al-Anon, and Alateen, the game playing was left at the door long ago. You can get right down to an honest confrontation between the sexes, because you have already removed the biggest hurdle. It won't require meeting for "a couple of drinks sometime" before you can begin to find out whether you would enjoy each other's company for an evening or afternoon or Sunday brunch.

Al-Anon, contrary to some popular notions, will contain singles. They are people whose previous relationships were wrecked by alcohol, but who found companionship, warmth, love, and understanding in an Al-Anon group or two and continued coming to keep their personal growth program intact and operating.

The comfort level at AA, Al-Anon, and Alateen is just as high as you want to make it. There's nothing to be afraid of. You all are there with a very common background. Alateens know how to have a great time being drug and alcohol free. Just ask them. Most of the kids I know in Alateen have as many dates and social activities on their calendar as they can handle.

I can honestly say that I have attended many AA meetings and watched people of all ages find each other. You see them come in as singles, and in a few weeks they show up together at a meeting you're attending. An AA therapist friend of mine told me once, "I always start with my sober friends in AA for companionship. There I know I'm starting with most of the ego trips out of the way, and I can look for honest relationships." She's right on target, too, for this lady never seems to lack for true friends of the opposite sex. (In the chapter on finding an AA group, we'll talk more about culling groups of available people.)

Remember, the primary purpose of attendance at any AA meeting is to continue to gain strength in your program of lifelong sobriety. Don't clutter that purpose with other things. The companionship you can find in the groups I've mentioned is centered around your common, number one need: the need to remain sober at all costs. Meeting available new people as you work the main program will be one of the bonuses for the sober single.

SPORTS, EXERCISE CLUBS

Americans never do anything halfway; the phenomenon of wanting to get in shape and stay in shape continues to be a very major rage. With this surge toward taking care of ourselves has come a booming new and growing industry: the sports club/exercise/fitness complex. These places range from storefront shopping center operations to large free-standing buildings. For example, at the World Headquarters of the Manville Corporation, a huge fitness complex—including an indoor pool—is fully staffed and maintained for the employees' benefits. The entire operation is housed right in the building. This is no longer unique. Many such corporations are providing fitness rooms and holistic health programs for their employees. Ones that don't provide their own facilities often make arrangements for their employees to use nearby places. Better ways to spend a lunch hour simply haven't come along.

These exercise rooms, racquetball courts, running tracks, and indoor pools are a regular gold mine for meeting people. Again, alcohol-free people are going to feel right at home in places devoted to building up the body rather than tearing it down. So what if you don't work for a large corporation that has provided you with a membership or place to do all these things? Well, what about the place where you live? Virtually every townhouse, apartment, or condo development offers amenities such as a pool, tennis courts, a rec room, billiards, or video games in either arcade or lounge settings.

Those, of course, are all just facilities. The meeting part comes with your willingness to engage in the activities that are offered. Personally, I think the mixed tennis ladders that match your level of skill with others equally skilled (or in my case, unskilled) provide an excellent way to meet people. There is beginning racquetball, aerobic dancing, and jazzercise exercise classes where many men and women participate.

You already know how I feel about running. Many clubs and condo organizations will hold regular "Fun Runs" of one or two miles, as well as longer 5K or 10K events. Sign up! You'll meet more single folks than you ever thought existed. You'll quickly find a lot of folks who would not be interested in a beer or two, but would rather settle for a great iced tea or Gatorade.

If you're not into much more than a couple of laps in the pool or some easy jogging, that's okay too. Investigate the lounge areas of the athletic club where the video games are. You can hover near one of those, acting as if you never heard of Pac-Man or Asteroids, and the chances are you'll be asked if you want to play a game or two. "Buy you a drink?" can be handled really well in an athletic facility that does sell alcoholic beverages by countering, "As long as it's soft" or some such reply. No hassles, no laboring over long excuses about not wanting a beer. After all, you are in a setting that's conducive to staying smoke-free, and where consuming alcohol is an amenity for the social drinker, not a temptation for the recovering alcoholic.

CHURCH, SYNAGOGUE

More clients have told me about the opportunities to meet single people at their church or temple than I had counted on when researching this. Participation in such interchurch activities as choir or adult Sunday school is supplemented by young adult groups and teaching within the church or temple such crafts or art skills that you may possess. One person told me of starting a film club at his church. Everyone brought popcorn that they popped in a church popper and a microwave. Then the whole group watched a classic movie which they had rented.

This activity is even easier since the advent of videotapes. Films are available for showing in even very small temple and church activity rooms if the necessary player and TV set are available. This young fellow got his group together by having an announcement printed in the church bulletin. A lot of married couples showed up, but so did a surprising number of available singles of both sexes.

The teaching idea came from a lady who said she had decided that it would be fun to share her interest in drawing and sketching with others. She used a church bulletin and flushed out a group of just three who wanted to learn more about it. She was a sixth-grade art teacher, so she simply broadened her teaching level to include adults. Before long the word got around, and eight to ten singles were showing up with their drawing gear to spend a couple of hours near the church, sketching their little hearts out and meeting new people. This teaching example naturally leads to:

CLASSES, ACADEMIC AND CRAFT

While the idea of going back to school may not appeal to you as a full-time proposition, you might consider the absolutely wild array of free or low-cost classes that are both educational in the academic sense and skill-building. Community recreation centers offer classes like "Mr./Ms. Mechanic" for the man or the liberated female who wants to be able to fix her own car, "Beginning Spanish," "Learning Guitar," or "Coed Self-Defense." Photography classes for the beginner and cooking for the male and female gourmet are also very popular.

Again, the common thread—regardless of what the class is about—is helping the sober single to overcome the idea that bar courage is needed to address the question, "What do you like to do?"

Going back to a regular campus in your community is always worthwhile. If you're an older single, then the community college or city college will offer more people your own age. Most of the population at the local four-year liberal arts institution will be right out of high school.

My experience is that many divorced recovering people turn to the educational field to pick up where they left off or to simply try to expand their lives in other ways for the future. Opportunities present themselves handily to meet other people with the same goals. I can guarantee that after one look around, you will definitely not feel too old or out of place in a classroom setting. (I would suggest, however, that you not jump into very heavy loads of any kind of classes if you are new in your sobriety. You will have a tendency to overload yourself, and the pressure can become so intense it outweighs the therapeutic value of going to a class and meeting new people.)

CONCERTS

Today, when you say "concert" to anyone under the age of forty, they may be inclined to think of rock groups, Beach Boy revivals, or Barry Manilow. What I'm really advocating as a proven meeting ground for singles who are sober is a symphonic concert of some kind. If you live in an area that has an orchestra or chorale group that interests you, then by all means attend.

The philosophy here is very simple. If you ask for a single ticket at the box office, they are going to sell you seats where, primarily, other single requests are most often filled.

If your seatmate turns out to be a dud, you still have the beauty of the concert and your show of support for your orchestra. But really, the fun is during the intermission. You can mingle quite casually among the pieces of art in the lobby, or step out for a breath of fresh air. You can space yourself far enough away from any cluster of people so that it's obvious you are attending alone. If the concert provides drinks, as most of them do, make certain you have a soft drink of some kind; make it obvious you are not consuming one of the alcoholic beverages that may be available.

If you are a sober single male, look for the female who is giving these signs of being alone and not being interested in drinking. (Of course, even if the other person *is* drinking, you don't have to. What you want is the chance to meet other people with the same interests as you.) Concerts are just dandy places to do that.

Once again, the initial interest barrier has already been broken. Obviously, the person you approach at a concert is interested in that kind of entertainment. You can simply capitalize on his or her presence at the event. ("The English horns from off-stage really sparked that movement, didn't they?") Actually, concert-going can open up a whole new world for you if you're really into matching intelligence around musical knowledge. (I avoid this game like the plague, but I know singles who really know how to use all the right lines and how to sincerely feel comfortable in striking up a conversation on a specific knowledge base with a stranger.) If you are so inclined, use the program for the evening as a way of learning more about the charmer you have selected.

MUSEUMS

This category of sober single hunting grounds is as broad as the locale in which you reside or are visiting. Art museums and galleries are fine, but there you really need to know your stuff. I advise using them as a base for meeting other singles only if you feel you can really sustain a conversation about the subject at hand.

This said, however, a client once used the "unknowledgeable approach" in an art museum, and it worked fine for her. She just played dumb, even though she was and is a very fine artist herself and was quite familiar with the particular works being displayed. (Her decision to let a gentleman think he was helping her understand the exhibit better was some danger to the honesty part of her recovery program. But she confessed later in the relationship, and all turned out okay.) When she admitted knowing a good deal more about art than she had let on, she also disclosed her disease of alcoholism to the man. She told me in a therapy session later that it was a calculated risk, but it turned out fine.

Her new friend said he was proud of her decision to be in treatment and glad she owned up to the art business, too. He told her he had suspected that one all along, because the "dumb" questions she asked weren't dumb at all. "What gave me away?" she asked. "You asked whether that particular painting was the best in Picasso's Blue Period. Most people who are not well informed about art don't ask questions about an artist's period, but rather what the painting is supposed to mean."

Didn't matter. She struck her prey right in the heart.

Museums of a historical nature are a better hunting ground. Natural history museums, botanical gardens, and Western Americana galleries provide a wealth of small talk topics when you are trying to make an impression on a single you have spotted.

A young friend of mine told me that he had met more ladies than ever at a botanic garden by just wandering around with a houseplant in his hand. He would ask, "Excuse me, do you know if this thing will grow without direct sunlight?" He confided in me sometime later that he had had more fun doing that than all the times he had spent trying to "drink the girls pretty" at a local bar. Ah, the joy of being sober.

History museums offer the same kinds of comfortable openers. "That looks like the wagon hitch my grandmother in Missouri told me about," he says. She replies, "You from Missouri? Funny, I thought you sounded Texan." Write your own dialogue—you get the picture, don't you?

TRAVEL

Too often the newly sober person thinks about getting away for a long time. I don't recommend this, whether you are single or not. The strain and pressures to drink might be stronger away from the safety net of home, so think awhile of shorter trips and more of them instead of one long haul.

We'll deal with jet travel in the chapter devoted to "Flying Without Drinking" later. For now, just consider that you will have opportunities to meet many people when you fly. Your big problem will be to determine their availability—whether they are truly single. I don't have a formula for this, except to say you single ladies will find more single male stewards than men will find unattached female flight attendants. (Don't ask me why—that was the result of my unofficial poll.)

If you are going to fly, make it a short (under a thousand miles) trip if you can, and ask for the middle seat on the plane. You can count on:

1. Being asked to change places so others can sit together, or,
2. Striking up a conversation on both sides of you, which gives you many options.

Train travel has some pitfalls because any socializing is probably going to happen in the club car, even if you're on the Metroliner (where every car is a club car). Watch yourself, and always—but always—keep a visible can of soda pop by you. You don't want to even hint that you are open to buying (or have someone buy you) a drink.

The beauty of a train ride is the length of time you can spend just being able to shop around for other singles. Ski trains are super. So are short-haul excursions, especially if you have a camera slung around your neck. If you're a male, you can look like you know what speed to shoot, and if you're female you can prove you know what you're doing by not having to ask.

My favorite method for the sober single to meet other folks is by bus—more specifically, at the bus stop. That's right, the bus stop. I began to notice as I drove back and forth to the city that almost all the very attractive people, male and female, were waiting for the bus. When a snowstorm allowed me to offer to share my car with some people waiting for a bus, we all started to talk. I listened a lot to the three others in the car, two women and a man, as we headed downtown. The man found out that he and one of the women worked on the same block, and he invited her to lunch with him.

The two ladies, who were roommates, got out of the car first because they had other appointments before going to the office. That left the young man and me. "You can let me off here on the next block if that's okay," he said.

"But I thought you worked farther downtown," I replied.

"No," he said. "Actually, I work out near where you picked us up. But I learned a couple of months ago that if I left my car and rode the bus I could meet a lot of really nice women, and I do."

"But you told that girl you work in her building," I said in my most outraged manner. "How can you start a relationship with a lie?"

"It's not really a lie," he told me. "I do work in her building. I work in many of those downtown buildings. I'm a computer sales rep, but our main office is out south where you picked us up." He went on to tell me that he was totally tired of the singles bar scene. He had decided to devote two mornings a week to walking from his office over to the bus stops near several apartment complexes where he had observed ladies waiting.

"Usually I'll ride the bus down with someone I met waiting for the bus. I'll make some calls that I have, then come on back to the office. It beats the bar scene all to hell."

And not one person had to buy a drink in that whole encounter.

YOUR OWN OFFICE

The following elevator gambit was developed and polished to a fine hone by a middle-aged man in recovery who knew there must be a better way to meet singles than to take a chance on going to a bar. He told me of his drinking days, "I could care less about who was in the building where I worked. But when I sobered up, I began to notice how many really nice people in my age group were riding the elevator with me. I started sort of by accident, saying, 'Floor, please,' to the people on the elevator. It was an automatic elevator, but people got a kick out of it. After a couple of mornings of doing this I knew the floor where one particular lady I liked got off. I pulled my same routine, and when everyone had gotten off the elevator, I went back to the floor where she had gotten off. I spotted her right away, walked up and asked her to have lunch with me."

I asked him if that was successful, and he said the lady had told him, "You don't have to buy me lunch. I would meet you for a drink, though." Our recovering client jumped right in to tell her, "I don't drink anymore, and that's why I can afford to take you to lunch."

This is a good example of the sober single putting his program to work, and realizing some more joy of being sober.

Several other sober singles have told me that they have met more new people in the building where they work just by being sober and able to talk "without acting like idiots." A favorite method of meeting new people is to brown-bag it alone. One woman told me she realized she was stifling her chances of meeting men by always sitting on the building's lunch patio with other people.

"I decided to risk going it alone for awhile to see what would happen. I didn't want to risk losing my girlfriends I had been lunching with, so I hit on a plan. I brought my lunch, but kept it in my oversized purse. When lunchtime came, I begged off, saying I had to go uptown. I did just that. I went uptown three blocks to another building and sat on their plaza—alone. Worked like a charm," she said.

See how inventive you can be?

STORES AND MARKETS

The supermarket continues to be the national racetrack of meeting singles, if you believe all the literature that's written on this subject. I've found a better one, I think. Forget the supermarket and hit the "Mom and Pop" operations; those smaller neighborhood markets and delis beat the big stores and supermarkets all to pieces. You have more time to survey the scene, you can move a lot slower (you have to) through the aisles, and bumping into someone's cart is a lot more accidental than when you try it in a large supermarket.

Hang out a lot around the soft drink aisles and avoid the beer aisles. When you see someone you like who's loading their basket with soft drinks too, you can remark, "Sure is nice to see someone who doesn't need a whole basketful of beer." If that sounds stuffy to you, I challenge you to try it. You can use your own words, but just try the approach. You'll get some answers like, "Yeah, I hate beer. Vodka's my drink." More often than you'd suspect, however, you'll get positive reinforcement about not wanting to drink. As I say, don't take my word for it. Try it out and enjoy the results for yourself.

ADVERTISING

Finally, there's this method of meeting another sober single. I think it has merit, but only if you are open and forthright with the ad you place in the personal column. You should come right out and declare your new sobriety. You're using a hidden box number, or at most a telephone number, so you are pretty well protected. Be prepared! Some eagle-eyed AA folks will pick up on such ads and try to get you to a meeting—and that's great. You may go to some places you may not have known about before. If you want to try your luck on just a one-to-one basis, however, you can stick with answering mail or telephone messages and making your own meeting arrangements with other singles. Again, I stress that you need to be open, honest, and forthright in using this meeting method.

A typical ad can read:

Newly sober and single male (female), age 25, wants to meet person equally free of pressure to drink. I'm just a lot more fun to be with. Interested? Call 555-1234, after six.

How you handle the inquiries is your bag, but you will get responses. A lot of them will ask you how you got your sobriety and how long you've had it. You can take those questions as your comfort level dictates. Basically, the amount of time you've had your sobriety is of no importance to anyone else, so if you like, you can counter such questions by asking the inquirer what makes the length of your sobriety important to him or her. You might discover another single (or someone else) who is looking for encouragement and direction toward sobriety themselves, and who has answered the ad seeking such help.

I feel good about you. Yes, I do! I can see you getting all gussied up and trying some of these new tools for meeting other sober singles, or singles who won't put pressure on you to break your sobriety. I see you riding on planes, waiting at bus stops, and pushing elevator buttons. I see you wondering aloud if brush strokes really can be forged, and if Coleus plants need to be talked to as much as African violets.

I see you trying as hard as you can to select the right mustard and needing help; wondering if you are singing that tenor part too loud; wondering if you did-n't meet him at the Weiss bar mitzvah or see her name on the sign-up sheet for mixed doubles.

Oh, you're doing fine. *Of course* you wonder what that class (or train trip, or symphony) is really going to be like. But I hear you asking, "How's your program coming along? Want to try a meeting on the West Side with me?"

You're single. You're sober. You're leading the good life again.

MORE JOY (An Update)

Where does one begin? In ten years, we have found a scourge among us, an epidemic of such frightening proportions that it gives chills to read the statistics. HIV and the subsequent killer, AIDS, has cast an incredible pall on many of the ways in which men and women meet, date and mate each other.

The basic principles of how and where to meet people without booze remain the same. You still need to muster up the "bar courage without the bar" that I wrote about years ago. And it still works, so take heart.

"One night stands" (now called "hook-ups," by the way) are not on the pri-ority list, but then they never were for the newly sober individual. Singles are much more cautious about the casual relationship. Unfortunately, their younger teenage counterparts seem to be as careless as ever. Many of them spurn the use of condoms and still act as if they are absolutely untouchable by AIDS or any other disaster.

Even though you may not be a devil-may-care dater now that you are sober and single, you can still enjoy the ways and means of meeting new people without drinking, just as I outlined it in this chapter. Some places, like the sushi and karaoke bars, are new on the scene, but the principles remain the same.

Don't ever forget how great you feel to be acting like yourself. You don't need alcohol or some other drug to make you attractive to the person you are trying to interest. Have faith in the real you and keep nurturing that person as the dynamite companion you know you can be.

If anything, putting the brakes on casual dating, practicing safer sex and being a lot more cognizant of the dating history of new people are stronger strokes for the recovery process than before. Now you really will be careful. You will act not only with an alcohol-free brain, but also with a very cautious attitude toward the whole dating scene.

Of course, this doesn't mean that you can't still explore the great marketplace where other available men and women are seeking the right person. You may, however, put more thought into your choice of venue. I still do a lot of guest appearances at churches and church groups of young adults, and I am constantly amazed at the number of attractive and eligible men and women in these groups. So many recovering people bypass this great opportunity to meet someone in a very safe setting.

Most of the churches where I have spoken tell me that being a member of the church is not a prerequisite to belonging to the young adult groups. In fact, I discovered a number of men and women who belonged to a church or—in two cases—a synagogue, but were participating in a particular young adult group because they liked it better than those at their home place of worship.

It was certainly gratifying to know that these churches were promoting the idea of available adults having a safe meeting place. In addition, they offer a world of activities such as theater outings, skiing, hiking, pot lucks, and biking to bring singles together. One church where I spoke had regular travel opportunities that were reserved for their young adults, and they were always booked.

I still watch the personal columns to see what the dating market is looking like. There doesn't seem to be much of a reduction in interest there, and I take that as a healthy sign. (Speaking of signs, the old "What's your (astrological) sign?" line has probably been replaced with "How was your last HIV test?")

I think we call this progress, but it's sad that we are nowhere in sight of a cure for this devastating disease. It definitely makes sobriety—and knowing at all times what you're doing—important premiums in life.

Continental people have sex life; the English have hot water bottles.

George Mikes

9

SEXUALITY AND RECOVERY (DOES RECOVERY TAKE AWAY ALL MY FUN IN BED?)

"I dunno. She says she's interested, but nothing happens."

"It's just not the same. I can't describe it exactly, but it's almost as if he doesn't care about having sex anymore."

"She used to be dynamite in bed, but now that she's sober, well, it's a real drag."

So, like the English in the quote above, you reach for the hot water bottle. Sex is now a drag. You're sober, and all it's gotten you is the feeling that you have no feelings (sexual feelings, anyhow). Well, maybe this chapter will help you understand what taking alcohol out of your sex life has done, and what you might need to do to bring a little pizazz back between the sheets.

The first light of sobriety is not as gruesome as it may seem. You have undergone some physical changes, and your body is naturally wanting a little time to respond to the game plan of your new nonalcoholic life.

Let's consider what this game plan can be, and how simple we can make it.

The first things you need to understand are the effects that alcohol and other drugs have on sex:

1. Use of alcohol simply removes inhibitions.
2. Both alcohol and sex affect the pleasure centers of the brain.
3. Alcohol eventually deadens the senses.
4. Psychological barriers may remain after stopping use of alcohol.

There are other effects, but those four will do to start. If you want highly detailed research on this subject, I refer you to Masters and Johnson, Kinsey, Alex Comfort, and a host of other very knowledgeable researchers who have done the most extensive work in the field.

We do know that the sex drive and the craving for drugs and alcohol seem to come from the same area of the brain, the thalamus. It's encouraging to note that the word "thalamus" is Greek for "bed" or "bedroom." I love it!

We also know that the human brain is conditioned to equate the feelings of being high and sexual pleasure. In fact, researchers have performed laboratory tests that show brain stimulation to drugs and alcohol and "natural" highs to be fairly indistinguishable. That's good news, because it shows you don't need alcohol to feel good. We also have good news for those over the so-called "highly erotic" years. The National Institute on Aging publishes a brochure entitled "Sexuality In Later Life." In that publication the Institute dispels many myths about sex for the elderly. It further proclaims that "…most older people want—and are able to lead—an active, satisfying sex life."

The Institute notes another important point. It says that excessive use of alcohol is "…probably the most widespread drug-related cause of sexual problems." If the use of alcohol causes extensive problems, we are now looking at what the absence of alcohol is doing to our sex lives and the sex lives of the people with whom we are sharing our recovery.

The statements at the beginning of this chapter are typical of those therapists hear daily from clients who are wondering what happened. The answer is pretty plain and simple. In most cases, the absence of drinking has opened the closed-off floodgates of anxiety about your sex life. All the inhibitions you had managed to block have come back to haunt your every move. Those inhibitions about sex and certain acts of sex were probably there all along, but you had managed to camouflage them with booze. Let's start first with the now-sober female to see how she can find a way back.

Here's the formula again:

PAST BEHAVIOR PATTERN: "I have certain inhibitions (fears, taboos) about sex. I take enough alcohol into my system, and I lose those fears. Take alcohol away (gain sobriety), and my fears (taboos, inhibitions) return."

NEW FORMULA: "Since I already had some fears and inhibitions about sex, I obviously had to learn them (from others, from bad experiences). Anything I learned, I can unlearn. Alcohol only prevented me from unlearning."

If you stop to remember, the chances are very real that most of your sexual experiences have involved alcohol in one form or another. This begins with the adolescent fumbling around in the back seat of the car, and continues right through the much-overrated wedding night. If you have been married to or lived with an alcoholic, then you are pretty used to sex being a legalized form of rape and very little more.

Now you begin sober sexual relations, and what happens? Nothing, that's what. You have high expectations, and they lead to failure. Suddenly, you hear terms like "frigid" and "dysfunctionate" applied to you as you try to pick up where you left off before achieving sobriety.

Well, you are not dysfunctionate by nature. You had to learn it. Sex therapists apply the term "dysfunctionate" to a female who cannot achieve orgasm. Maybe that just happened to you in sobriety. When you were drinking, you may well have experienced multiple orgasms, having achieved a state of relaxation of your fears. Everything was just peachy. Sober, you suddenly become a bundle of nerves. You may even begin to hate the thought of having sex, because it will most certainly lead to failure to achieve orgasm. This failure to reach orgasm can leave you in a state of frustration and discouragement.

It's safe to say that most of this failure is caused by you thinking "failure." Your old alcoholic ways tell you that you need a couple of belts to bring this off. Nonsense. You need a reevaluation of what the sexual needs of your life are. I believe strongly that they are:

1. The need to share with someone.
2. The need to care about someone before, during, and after.
3. The need to trust.

Sex therapists have determined that ninety-five percent of a female's orgasmic dysfunction is mental. If you ever read the story of *The Little Engine That Could*, then you've got the idea. "I think I can, I think I can" becomes "I knew I could! I knew I could!"

There are three other major reasons for female dysfunction, according to specialists in the field. Those reasons are:

1. A low sex drive (lack of libido).
2. Painful intercourse (if it hurts, why do it?).
3. Vaginismus (clamping down of the vaginal walls, making penetration difficult and painful).

It is estimated that more than one quarter of all female alcoholics suffer from vaginismus, an outward "and visible sign of inner and spiritual uptightness," as Dr. Alex Comfort so aptly phrases it. If physical problems are ruled out by a doctor you trust, it is time to reassess your sexual needs.

The same recommended tool for new sexual relationships apply to recovering males as well as females: recognizing the need to share, care, and trust. Before we discuss this tool in detail, however, let's examine the major reasons for male dysfunction. Again, these reasons are pretty well agreed upon by sex therapists, at least the ones I have been privileged to study under.

There are four primary reasons the sober male (and probably even the still-drinking male) fails to perform. They are:

1. Premature ejaculation.
2. Ejaculation incompetence (lack of ability to achieve orgasm).
3. Primary impotence.
4. Secondary impotence.

I want to add one that I believe may not have been given as much importance as I believe it should for the recovering male alcoholic, and that is alcoholic neuritis. Many men I have worked with have reported an inability to feel anything. The degenerative process of alcohol on the nervous system causes this. The prognosis is good or guarded, depending upon complete abstinence from alcohol and the extent to which toxic damage was done by drinking in the first place. It does get better, but it can temporarily add to the feeling of being unable to perform. Time and the total abstinence from all alcohol increase the restoration of the feeling process.

Now to detail, briefly, what seems to cause the four major reasons for male dysfunction:

Premature ejaculation is probably the most common and prominent problem.

A man ejaculates before even beginning to satisfy his partner, leaving her with nothing but frustration. This dysfunction sometimes appears to have its roots in a man's experience with prostitutes, when the order was, "Hurry up and get it over with, honey." This is a deep-set block. Depending upon the age that a man first encounters it, premature ejaculation can grow stronger as the use of more and more alcohol sets the block deeper and deeper. The second reason for premature ejaculation may be more easily accepted. It is the experience a man had as a teenager, when the fear of discovery caused him to hurry sex. I once worked with a man who had had several experiences when he had to bail out of a girl's bedroom window because they heard her parents returning to the house. It took him a long time and a lot of therapy to remove that sexual block.

Ejaculation incompetency is said to be caused primarily by the fear of having a child. It is often coupled with religious or other taboos from a man's upbringing. (This is the old belief that almost anything was okay as long as a man didn't ejaculate inside a woman.) While drinking, he didn't care. Now sober, the old taboos come flooding back, and he becomes dysfunctionate.

Number three, primary impotence, seems to be a little more clinical, and oriented in some basic pathology but the use of alcohol and drugs is the number one reason given by the experts as the reason for primary impotence. (Disease, such as diabetes, is also a major cause, and treatment can help there.) When a man's anxiety gets so high and he develops such an intolerance to that anxiety, he will fail to perform. A major part of that anxiety lies in the pressure put upon the male to perform. Other anxieties, many of them very deep-seated, can cause mammoth psychological roadblocks that cause some men to become impotent, and their sobriety only makes them more completely aware of this. Patience, time, and continued understanding by all parties concerned can ease this trauma. Once understood through some pretty heavy-duty psychotherapy by skilled sex therapists, the chances for eliminating this roadblock are favorable.

Sexual deviation from heterosexuality and certain religious beliefs can also cause primary impotence. The homosexual and lesbian may perform completely while practicing their sexual preferences with members of the same sex, and be totally dysfunctionate in a heterosexual situation. Understandable. However, the figures show that fewer than fifty percent of homosexual or lesbian relationships survive sobriety. The absence of alcohol may make one of the two partners very much aware of their homosexual behavior and unable or unwilling to continue the practice.

Religious upbringing in the stricter faiths can and does influence this primary impotence in certain men. Again, the key is that alcohol abuse has smothered these feelings and the guilt that went with them. When the alcohol is out of the picture, as you have heard me say before, the guilt comes flooding back and must be dealt with.

Secondary impotence as a major cause of male dysfunction is another name for the inability to maintain an erection. If it happens more than twenty-five percent of the time, it is considered a dysfunction and not just a fluke. The reasons behind it are much the same as for primary impotence.

I want to keep tying all this in to your joy of being sober, but this whole chapter up till now has been pretty discouraging, hasn't it? There's not much joy in finding out that your sobriety is causing you to wonder if you'll ever again be great in bed, or even if you'll ever again get back to basics. Sure you will. And better than ever.

You must begin to look at sex in the context of sharing, caring, and trusting. At least, I've found those tools to be helpful in dealing with others afflicted with the problems mentioned above. If you consider that sexual relations which were prompted by, heightened by, and fulfilled by alcohol made for a pretty dismal relationship to start with, you'll agree that the recovering one and his or her companion may need to start all over. They need to ask themselves, "What do I really want from this person, and what am I willing to give?"

Before, sex was a "take" situation only. The hangovers and fights that ensued before, during, and after sexual combat steadily reduced it to just that—combat. So get out of the war. Make love! You do this by sharing, caring, and trusting.

SHARING

It's an overworked word, but I'm using it anyhow because it's a tool of our trade and I'm comfortable with it. Sharing is the concept of communication that goes beyond telling. You *tell* small children what to do. You *share* your feelings of love, tenderness, and concern with them. I had a client once who became extremely irate with me because he wanted me to just tell him something instead of sharing it. After a few weeks of therapy, I noticed him saying in group, "I want to share something with you all." Later I asked him why he didn't just *tell* the group. "Because," he said, and not at all timidly, "the way I feel has to be *shared.*"

Same thing with your lover. He or she needs to be a part—an integral part—of the lovemaking process. That's different from simply being the object of your sexual desires. It calls for sharing your feelings with someone. You want to let a very special person know what's going on with you, how you feel, and what you are afraid of, if anything, at the moment. It is the sharing of tenderness, hopes, fears, and triumphs that leads to desire. Strong desire will lead, in all probability, to very rewarding sex.

Let me state right here that you will get no technique training from this chapter. Sharing is not a technique; it is a tool for recovery. It means, "I care so very much about you that I'm anxious to just hold you for awhile, and have you listen to what's going on with me." Through your willingness to share who you are, you demonstrate your willingness to let sex be a further expression of what you are, what you want to continue to be, and the place you wish to occupy in your very special person's life.

Using the tool of sharing, you express the strong point that your lover is an integral part of your life and your recovery. You could not even think of just "having sex" without it being an expression of the joy you feel in just being with him or her. It is a way of saying, "Making love *with* you, not *to* you, is no longer an act of my selfish gratification." Which leads us naturally to:

CARING

The need to care about someone before sex, during sex, and after sex is essential if, in recovery, you are going to make progress toward a lasting sobriety. Before, sexual encounters were "wham, bam, thank you ma'am" kinds of things that only satisfied your lust but did not meet your emotional needs. The one-night stand takes care of the moment but seldom has anything to do with caring.

Sobriety, and the joy of it, means that you have a sincere concern for meeting the needs of your partner as well as your own. Sexual encounters become a matter of what you can do for each other instead of what you can do for yourself. Caring means finding the meaning of the word "tenderness" again. It means being gentle, kind, and concerned for your love partner, rather than playing the old "grab, feel, hit and run" games of the past.

You no longer have wine and mixed drinks to ply her with before dinner. You do still have soft music, candlelight, dinner out, and a small lunch in front of the fire on a rainy Saturday afternoon. In short, you have all the elements of good sex without needing the alcohol. Believe it. The best thing you have to offer him or her is a sober you. The sober you shows how you care by taking a little extra time before, a lot of time during, and even more time after sex.

The tool of caring, properly used, increases the joy of your sexuality. It is a way of saying, "You are someone so special to me that when we have spent our physical desires, I still want to be right here with you." The sadness of hearing a woman say that her mate won't even take five minutes to hold her after sexual intercourse is all too depressing. It doesn't have to be that way. That's the way it was when you were drinking and you only cared about satisfying yourself.

I remember a female client telling me that after her lover had made love, rolled over, and gone to sleep, she became furious. "You sonofabitch!" she roared. "I just made love with you, and you can't stay awake even five minutes to hold me?" Understandable anger. No caring, no sharing. Just taking, and taking, and taking.

So, caring for someone requires your expression of that feeling after the various acts of sexual gratification. You don't have to jump right up and run for the shower. That old habit is the equivalent of saying, "There must be something dirty or unclean about this." Take time to hold your mate. The holding, dearly, of one body against the other is such a Warm Fuzzy. It says something of the dignity you ascribe to the person you have just shared the ultimate experience with. You are worth everything you think you are. Your sobriety now allows you the freedom to express your feelings of your mate's worth by caring for her/his feelings, fears, and needs. Which leads to:

TRUST

You want to feel that you can trust the person to whom you have given the gift of your body. In sobriety, this gift becomes even more precious than it ever was in drunkenness. "Can I trust you?" used to mean, "Can I be sure you will be faithful to me?" Now, the word "trust" means "I want to know that you are with me, beside me, encouraging me, and helping me as never before to remain sober." As a token of that trust, you become willing to share your body with that special person. Does that make sense to you?

So much of your sexual activity before was not willingness, but rather a reward. Or it might have been something that was expected, like a payoff for an evening out or what you had to do if you went away for a day or two. And there was little or no trust in either the sex or the relationship. The trust lasted as long as the alcohol lasted. That was the sum total of many commitments.

Now, trust is earned and not expected. It's given after very careful examination of the other elements of sharing and caring that make up this new triumvirate of your sexuality in recovery. But you need to trust that very special someone in your life, because you will be very fragile for quite awhile. Time will help heal the sexual wounds that were caused by alcohol abuse, but the element of trust will have to be an immediate and continuous process.

Your word didn't mean very much during your alcoholic days. You could not be trusted, therefore you didn't expect much trust from anyone else. All that's changed now, and you need to be trusted as much as you need to trust. Trust, like the other tools, is a mutually sought-after and shared experience, and one that you may never have used very much before.

When you practice the use of these tools of sharing, caring, and trust, the other elements of a satisfying sexual relationship will begin to grow. Recovery, after all, does not relegate you to a life of celibacy, nor was it ever intended to. It is a state in which new values around your sexuality replace some old, very bad habits.

Exploring one another's sexual needs and meeting those needs is twice as satisfying in recovery because *you remember them.* You don't have to wake up and wonder who that person is beside you. You know, and you invited him or her to be there by choice. The sexual fantasies that came pickled in alcohol are replaced by loving, sharing, caring, and trusting in and with the person in your bed.

You certainly have the same capacities for making love as before. Your sex drive may even be considerably greater than it was when you were drinking, because honest feelings have replaced false ones. More than ever, this is the time in your recovery program when you can reach out and touch someone and make it really count. Sobriety allows you the latitude to know the sexual experience.

It doesn't have to happen in bed, either. You can feel it riding side by side in a car, walking hand in hand, or even just sitting side by side watching television. It is a very different feeling from sexual arousal caused by stimulation with alcohol. It is real and lasting, an emotion upon which you can build and rebuild.

Like everything else connected with your sober life, you can make this feeling more secure by savoring the rare moments. For couples straining at the bit to get it on with the intensity of previous experiences, I say "Mellow out. Take it easy." Savor the joy of your sex life by starting over with new guidelines, as we have discussed. If you care about someone, you'll put their needs ahead of yours. By so doing, your needs will continue to be met more fully than you ever thought possible.

If you want to settle for the hot water bottle, then you can have it. Not me. Recovery and sobriety are destined to put the fun back in bed, and maybe a few other places, too.

MORE JOY (An Update)

I have felt so strongly about the link between sex and sobriety that I finally wrote an entire book about it, and I guess my Deaconess Press publishers will won't object to a brief plug. The title is *Sex and Sobriety* (Simon & Schuster). In it I have detailed what I believe to be more than basics concerning the problems that occur with recovery and your own sexual feelings.

The more I have worked with recovering people as a therapist, the more I see this one topic as a particularly worrisome one. I am often concerned about the flip manner many clients present when I ask them about their sex lives. "Oh, it's just as good as ever," they say, and then quickly change the subject.

This, of course, doesn't help one damn bit. It seems that they don't even want to try sometimes, because their sexual activities have been so closely connected with drinking. Take one away and the other vanishes, or so it seems. My point is, it's important to continue to talk through the problem. There are solutions available; trust me.

The important points of this chapter remain the caring, sharing, and trust elements that I wrote about. Over and over, it becomes clear that we are operating in a society today in which trust is something pretty fragile. I believe it to be of paramount importance to the sex and sobriety issue. The trust that can be built and nurtured between two people is the cornerstone of a great sex life. Think of all the ways that trust was threatened, broken, even destroyed while you were using alcohol. Then you can look at sex and the recovery process as a new opportunity to build a brand-new trust account. This trust will enhance your sex life in a new and wonderful way, free from the confines and false promises that your drinking encouraged.

I remember a female client, new in recovery, who told me during one of our sessions, "I wonder whatever made people think sex would be no good without drinking. It's terrific!"

So God created man in his own image, in the image of God created he him; male and female created he them.

Genesis

If God made us in His image, we have certainly returned the compliment.

Voltaire

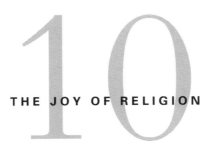

THE JOY OF RELIGION

Saying "Hello" to your God again is not as hard as it may seem at first glance. It's just as easy as when you were drinking and said "Goodbye." ("Who, me?") Yes, you. You did it. You walked away from your God, beating your chest and crying up and down the aisles like some modern-day Job, "Why me? Why can't I drink like everyone else? Why am I different?" We knew whose fault it was, didn't we? It was God's. Sure enough, you were damned with the disease of alcoholism because your God didn't love you quite enough, so you walked away. ("Galloped" might have been a better description.)

Either way, you got up from your pew seat and caught a cab. It could have been in the city's finest cathedral or temple. It might have been in a little clapboard-sided church at the far end of the farmland. It might have been in an inner-city storefront church. It doesn't matter. You got up and stumbled out and away from the whole idea that there even was a God. But that was the old alcoholic you. Now there is the sober, joyous person who has timidly tested the waters of returning to the fellowship of your church or temple and doesn't know quite how to do it. It's easy: you walk in.

There is shame, you believe, in standing in the church parlor or the fellowship room of the temple and having to answer a bunch of questions about "your sickness." I have a friend at church who never could bring himself to talk about alcoholism. Instead, he would ask me in tones of great seriousness, "How's your trouble?" It was a long time before I could get him to understand that I didn't have any "trouble." What I had, and still have, is a disease. What is even more important, I have my church again.

Like me, thousands of other recovering alcoholics have turned to the fellowship of Alcoholics Anonymous and discovered the concept of turning the problem of drinking over to God, the God of their understanding. For many of them, this has replaced the formal experience of church attendance, even though AA is not a religious experience, but rather a spiritual one.

Why not both? There is a real joy in attending a church or temple service on a Sunday morning or Sabbath Day, and then going to an AA meeting. It sort of ties up the old week at the same time it helps begin the new week, with powerful tools of resolve and hope for the new, sober you.

I have discovered that the comfort level in returning to the church you walked away from can be so low that you actually think that they might not want you back. (This reminds me of the guy who wanted to attend a meeting of "Paranoids Anonymous," but no one would tell him where the meetings were.) You do get paranoid about so many things in recovery that it's easy to see how returning to a church or temple where you noticeably abused alcohol at times normally reserved for worship and praise could be difficult. So, once again, here are a few tools for your consideration to make the job easier.

BE AGGRESSIVE

This will not be an easy tool for you to handle, particularly if you were abusing alcohol to overcome your shyness and to be aggressive, sociable, and comfortable around people. However, it's important for you to be able to show others, as well as yourself, that you no longer need any kind of crutch to exchange greetings and accept well-wishes from fellow members of the congregation. The key is to remember that *they* are embarrassed to approach *you* for fear of offending you. It's as if they want to find a way to pretend that you never were gone from them in the first place. Yet they know that alcohol had taken over much of your life, so much that you had stopped even coming to church.

You have to make it easy for them. Be aggressive—walk up to people you have known in the past and greet them. You will instantly find they are pleased and no longer gun-shy about you. They will say how much better you look and how much weight you've lost. The reason they don't say anything else is because they don't know what to say. So you have to employ the next tool to increase your comfort level.

BE HONEST ABOUT YOURSELF

"Where have I been lately? I have been recovering from a disease," you reply. If you can say it for them, it will make it easier. You can overcome any paranoia by just assuming that rumors have been circulating about your drinking problem. What good would it do to let them continue to be rumors? Put them to rest with an honest approach. Tell your church friends how great it is to be back and how you've missed it all. Tell them about your bout with alcoholism. By helping them overcome their own embarrassment, you receive strength for yourself. You see, they don't talk about it because they don't know much about it. So I tell them openly I feel good about being there in church, and I'm glad they missed me.

When you invade these little groups of people who are standing around talking, you give a clear message that you are back and that you are approachable. "Approachable?" Yes. Have you ever stopped to think how many times your drinking problem was treated like some kind of leprosy? You know, the old "Careful! It might be contagious!" routine. Your willingness to be open and honest about your disease will accomplish two things: It will make others feel it's okay to talk about your past drinking. It will also make disclosure of the past much easier for you every time you do it. The church and the temple are ideal locations for this kind of disclosure.

One time I became aware that two ladies in the church parlor were looking at me, then talking to each other and looking at me again. I walked over, saying, "My ears are burning. What's up?"

"We were just saying to each other," one of them replied, "how good you look and how good it is to see you back in church." Well, you can't beat that kind of Warm Fuzzy. I never would have known about it if I hadn't been aggressive enough to take the risk and ask the question.

COME TO THE QUIET PLACES

In every church, temple, sanctuary, parlor, or fellowship hall is a quiet corner. It is your kind of place. It is the place for you to come before the rest of the congregation to have your quiet time with the process of making friends again with the God of your understanding. I like to go alone to the very front of the church, off to the side where I can sit in relative darkness, and just think how fortunate and grateful I am that freedom from alcoholism has helped me find the way back to my church.

This quiet communion is a rewarding process for your sobriety. It is here that you can find the kind of peace that proves it was you who did the walking out and not your God. Ten minutes is plenty of time to sit in meditation of all the joy associated with your being in this place. You don't dwell on the heartaches—all that is past. You concentrate on the present relationship that you are enjoying with your God.

This tool of a Quiet Place is even fun to search for. It's very much like the Laughing Place we spoke of in Chapter Five. It is a special place in your church or synagogue that you can call your very own for just a few minutes once a week. Does it take a little extra effort on your part? Sure. Sobriety takes a lot of effort, but this is one of those very personal rewards that I'm sorry cannot be enjoyed by people who have always been sober. It's not the same for them as it is for you. It is in your Quiet Place that you can be aware that the church itself never left, and the Divine Spirit you are talking with is to be found there as before. It's as if you had taken a short trip and have, over and over again, the thrill of realizing that you have come back.

When I see people alone in such a place, I assume they are in some sort of prayer. I don't do that in my Quiet Place. I have a little chat with my God, and I expect Him to listen. And as I leave my Quiet Place steady and upright, I am convinced all over again that He always did listen. He was just waiting for me to catch up.

HANDLING COMMUNION OR SACRAMENTAL WINES

I am indebted to many pastors, priests, and rabbis who have shared with me some ways that the recovering person can participate in the meaningful use of wine in the Eucharist of their faith. Alcoholics cannot, of course, handle even that little thimbleful used in many Protestant congregations as part of the communion service. You will want to, and should, participate in the service itself. Here are some ways to tackle the problem:

1. Your pastor, priest, or rabbi will know of your problem. They can insert a dose of straight grape juice or Kool-Aid in the tray with the other little cups. No one but the two of you will know the difference.

2. You can use the two fingers of the right hand and gently touch the chalice or common cup lightly on the rim. Then touch your own lips as you pass the common cup on. It's a very rewarding gesture.

3. You can take a private communion. Use Kool-Aid or grape juice.

4. You can substitute a dose of plain, clear water.

This last way requires further explanation. My pastor and I were searching for a new and meaningful method by which the celebration of the communion could be as symbolically powerful without wine as it is with wine. It was Pastor Del who hit on the idea of inserting a few words around the "Marriage Feast of Canaan," where the miraculous transformation of water to wine took place.

We simply used a small thimble of water, and Del retold the New Testament story about the water-to-wine episode. He added the words, "Receive this water, in the spirit of the wine which it was to become for all who are believers." It's a beautiful thought. I make use of this in private communion at least twice a year. Somehow it has taken on as much or more meaning than the old way. It is a simple tool, but I have shared it with a number of recovering people who have all reported back enthusiastically.

You can handle wine in the temple or synagogue in much the same manner. Your rabbi is anxious for you to participate in the worship service, and he will assist you in every way possible to do just that. The key, of course, is to talk it over with your spiritual advisor. You'll be in for a big surprise. You'll head into that person's study or office thinking you may be the only one in the whole congregation who is recovering. Wrong. He will put your mind quickly at ease by telling you that several others need to have communion or celebration wine handled the same way. They'll just make provision for one more. It's a good feeling. See, you are not alone.

GET INVOLVED

One of the quickest ways for you to say "hello" again is to insert yourself firmly into a church or temple activity, something you shunned when you were an active alcoholic. Choir, Sunday school and adult teaching, nursery, camping activities and the like are obvious and logical choices.

A word about the nursery job. I once had a female client who purposely set out to get the noisy task of running her church nursery when the position became vacant. "What in the world possessed you to tackle that job?" a therapy group member asked. The young woman replied, "I wanted those church people to see me being trusted with their most precious possessions, their babies. I wanted to show them I was a different person." It was an effective tool for this woman because she had the courage to take the risk and ask for the job. She gained the best reward of all from getting the job: a great big dose of self-confidence.

But don't bite off more than you can chew. Take it easy and look around a lot before you jump right in and find the pressures too much for you. If your church or temple has a library, you might want to help out there. Most of them I've seen could use more help than they ever get. The work is quiet, and you can go at your own pace.

Be sure that you don't confuse the task at hand. Bowling with the church bowling group is great, but it doesn't replace giving some of your time and talent back to your congregation. Hospital calling may have always been something you shunned as a very disagreeable task. It is in many ways, but as a recovering person you can reap new joy in your sobriety by paying a visit or two to those persons who are less fortunate than you.

Finally—and although this may sound like heresy at first—I would strongly recommend that you be open to visiting some new places of worship. You have the comfort and security of knowing that you are just expanding your horizons of sobriety. Take another AA friend, or ask to go to another sober person's church or synagogue. The point of all this is to reinforce the knowledge that your sobriety now allows you the richness of knowing that you have many ways and many places in which you can say "hello" again to your God. Before, alcohol was the limiting barrier to any kind of spiritual relationship you may have had. Now you are free to express your joy and your newfound gratitude in many ways and in many different places.

You'll feel a new comfort in places of worship that you never found before. When you walk out of a church or synagogue it will be with pride—not anger, blame, or mistrust. That was the *old* you.

MORE JOY (An Update)

I made a very major change in my life concerning religion since first writing this book. I left the church where I had been a member for many years to search for another one closer to our home, and perhaps closer to what I was seeking.

I recognize my recovery each day as my wife and I hold hands and say,

"Thank you, God, for another day of sobriety." I never forget, or at least try never to forget, my gratitude to my God for the strength of my own sobriety.

But I needed some other place where I could just be a part of the congregation. My previous church was a truly active experience for me; I was even honored by being in the pulpit many times, and by being asked to produce special plays, TV presentations and other pieces of highly visible work within the church. I was seeking the peace and quiet of just being a member and sort of fading into the crowd.

In our new church in the same Lutheran faith, I got caught up again in doing seminars, lectures, or workshops, and generally starting the old routine again. So I backed off, and I want you to know that wasn't easy.

The thing is, there truly is a joy in religion. There is also a joy in the search for new ways in which to worship the God of your understanding. By "new ways" I mean the exploration of different faiths and different settings. You truly expand your heart and soul by looking at a much broader spectrum of religion than what may have been in your life before.

It's comforting to know that no matter what physical setting surrounds your worship, the basic premise that a power greater than ourselves has had a great role in restoring us to sanity still rings true. I was the one who had to do the hard work of recovery, yet when the dark hours of those early days threatened to get even darker, I always knew somehow that my God would sustain me.

You hear people all over the country expound on what part God, a Higher Power, or a Universal Power played in their recovery. It doesn't matter what you choose to call the being or influence to which you turn in prayer and supplication. What's important is that you continue to acknowledge that you probably didn't do all the hard work alone.

In the darkest hell of my alcoholism I can distinctly remember asking God for help just to stand up straight, for hope that I was not permanently crippled by my drinking. What is it that happens in recovery that people forget the thanks due a Creator who heard their prayers and answered?

One time, doing research for an article I was writing, I discovered there are some seventy-five different names in the Bible by which God is called. Whether it's "Yahweh" or "Lord" doesn't really matter. What matters is that you become more and more reinforced with the importance of and the recognition of the joy of belief in your life.

I recall reading Albert Schweitzer's book on the historical Jesus, in which he gathered the foremost philosophers and scientists of the time and asked them to write on the miracles of Christ. As I pored, spellbound, through the book, one by one all the miracles as related in the New Testament were torn apart and explained in very scientific terms. Everything, from the changing of water into wine right down to the death and resurrection of the Galilean, was explained.

I was devastated that there could be explanations, both scientific and logical, that would destroy the entire premise of Jesus Christ as the Son of God. Schweitzer, however, put it all into great perspective when he asked in so many words, "if you don't have faith, then what is left for mankind to hope for?"

Keep the faith…whatever faith and wherever you choose to do it.

Fellowship is heaven, and lack of fellowship is hell; fellowship is life, and lack of fellowship is death...

William Morris

11

THE FELLOWSHIP EXPERIENCE:
AA REVISITED

"You'll never find *me* at one of those meetings."

"I walked in on one of those AA things and it scared the hell outta me."

"It's nothing but some dame talkin' about how drunk she used to get."

"I never spent any time in the slammer. What do I want to hear about his jail time for?"

And so it goes. All those reasons and at least a million others are why the fellowship of Alcoholics Anonymous is not for you, right? Almost every case history of persons coming into treatment for the disease of alcoholism reflects that they have either already formed an opinion about AA or have adopted someone else's opinion. What it eventually boils down to is that the person has had one or two bad experiences. By "bad" I mean visits to AA meetings that were not suited to that person's needs at the moment. Well, we are going to shop around a little and see if we can't find the kind of meeting that is just right for you.

Let's begin by understanding that active involvement in the AA fellowship as a part of the treatment for your disease is a dynamite tool. It is a lifelong process that will help to cement your resolve, sustain your courage, and forge strong links in the chain of support so necessary for living a life dominated by sobriety.

The friendships you form in the fellowship will be the strongest ones you will have throughout your life. These friendships continue to support the basic philosophy of AA. You can think, "If all the people in this AA room with me have stayed sober, if they have found ways to do it, then I must be able to do it, too."

What I want to do in this chapter is help you shop for the kind of meeting that best suits you.

You wouldn't dream of walking into a store and buying the first suit on the rack. Nor is it likely that the very first or even second model of car you see will be the one you buy. Humans like to make choices. You can remind yourself of this every time you try to find your favorite cereal on the store shelves, packed in with what seems like a thousand other choices.

So no matter what your previous AA experience has been, let's shop around and look at various kinds of AA meetings. Be aware that these groups are the ones I have used as a shopping list for myself and for others in the recovery process; there's nothing terribly official about the list. AA itself has taught from the beginning that all that is necessary to hold a meeting is two people and a copy of the "Big Book." I've known countless people who have done just that, many of them without even a book to aid them. They had only the desire to get sober and stay sober.

Here's my list, not ranked in any order of priority:

1. Closed Discussion
2. Closed Speaker
3. Open Discussion
4. Open Speaker
5. Closed Step
6. Open Step
7. Home Group
8. Special Interest Group
9. Women's Group
10. Gay Group
11. Specific Minority Group
12. Young People's Group

CLOSED DISCUSSION

This is my favorite group—the type that I have chosen for my own home group, the group I try to attend regularly. The closed discussion group is limited in attendance to only those people who are recovering. There are no spouses or significant other persons allowed. The exception to this rule is when a member may have, for example, an out-of-town visitor he or she specifically wants to attend. The alcoholic can request a group conscience vote for permission to have the visitor in attendance. However, the group may still elect, by vote, not to allow a guest.

The meeting is run by a selected chairperson who may or may not have a topic to discuss. If no topic is specified, the chairperson may ask if anyone in the room has a topic they want to bring up or a specific problem they wish to discuss. If you are new, the chances are you will be greeted with a round of applause. This recognition is not because you are an alcoholic, but because you have taken the courageous step to come to a meeting. If you don't wish to participate, you can politely decline with, "I think I'd rather just listen," or some such phrase.

Everyone who speaks at an AA meeting follows custom by identifying themselves and their problem. For example, "My name is Jack, and I'm an alcoholic." Now we know the problem. Still, so many people say, "I can't stand up and do that. What if I see somebody there I know?"

Boy, I love an opening like that. First, you don't have to stand up. You can remain seated if you want to. Second, if you see someone you know at an AA meeting, you assume they are there for the same reason you are.

The speaker then comments on the chosen topic. The speaker may pass to another person he or she knows, or may just call on someone at random and ask them to pass to someone after speaking. It's very casual, very informal. At any AA meeting you may get up and get coffee, even when others are speaking. You may leave the room and go to the restroom. You may leave early, although by tradition, AA meetings of any kind only last one hour.

The closed discussion meeting allows you and your fellow recoverers to let your hair down in a way that people who have not been afflicted with the disease may not appreciate. My home group, named Crossroads, has been so supportive of me. The years of my recovery have been joyous and bright because of the laughter, the tears, the meaningful discussions that have filled my life during the times I have been in that room. It can be that way for you, too.

There is very little formality in group, mostly traditions. There are three traditions that are standard no matter what kind of group you attend. You will be asked to join in repeating the "Serenity Prayer" at the start of every meeting, as you stand. It'll take you less than fifteen seconds to say (in unison, remember):

> God, grant me the serenity to accept the things I cannot change,
> Courage to change the things I can,
> And wisdom to know the difference.

Nothing to panic about there, right?

Next, the speaker will either read or will have chosen someone to read from Chapter Five, "How It Works," of the "Big Book." That's it for anything approaching a formality until the end of the meeting.

About five minutes before the meeting is to end you will notice a basket, plate, or empty coffee can being passed from person to person. Tradition suggests you put in a buck to defray costs of the meeting room, coffee, etc. (That tradition calls for groups to be self-supporting and to pay their own way.) My close friend David taught me years ago to "put something in if you have it. If you need it, then take something out." That's how it works. All for one, and one for all, to borrow from Dumas and *The Three Musketeers*.

When the meeting is over the speaker will ask, "Will those who care to join me in the Lord's Prayer?" This is another tradition, but notice that the choice is yours. More times than I can remember I have said this prayer standing side by side with a Jew, a Hindu, a Buddhist, or a Moslem. The choice is always yours.

The closed discussion group is a good one for you to investigate with another sober person who uses the fellowship of AA to gain strength in sobriety.

CLOSED SPEAKER

This kind of meeting may be the kind that turned you off about going back to AA. It may center around just one person, or at most three or four persons, relating what has become known as a "drunkalogue." It is essential that you understand the very great need for the speakers to be able to relate the horrors of their past active alcoholic life in order to share with you their profound gratitude for their sobriety. The closed speaker meeting may not be for you, but it serves a very important purpose. It certainly provides a platform for some absolutely outstanding people to talk with you, people who may be famous or totally unknown to you.

All the speakers tell their life stories or particular incidents that reflect in their harshest forms the ravages of the disease we all share. The main difference in this kind of meeting is that you do not participate. Instead, you listen to the speakers. Only recovering persons may attend a closed speaker meeting, but most clients with whom I have worked find this kind of meeting hard. They often can't relate. Again, if you shop around, even among the closed speaker meetings, you can find some that are real dandies.

Call Alcoholics Anonymous in any city in the country and in most cities abroad, and the people on duty can direct you to the kind of meeting you want, day or night, seven days a week. When you attend a meeting you like, pick up a free local directory from the table where literature is displayed. It will give you day-by-day listings, type by type, of all meetings in your area.

OPEN DISCUSSION

This is another spectacular way to revisit AA and become involved again with the fellowship. At this type of meeting your significant other, kids, roommate, or boss can attend with you. Most of what they will see or hear will be no different from traditions followed at regular closed meetings. The only difference is that the alcoholic shares with others in the room who may or may not be recovering.

I find these groups stimulating. I try to attend with my wife or one of my kids when I can. The open discussion meeting allows input from husbands, wives, and others who help show your own significant other that they have not been and are not alone. There is a lot of Al-Anon and Alateen feedback that can enhance a group such as this.

Often, a recovering person who attends with his or her spouse discovers the beginnings of what turns out to be a crackerjack couples group. For one evening a week, for example, you and your spouse can make attendance at an open discussion meeting a regular part of Quality Time experience. It's relaxing, beneficial, and fun. Yes, *fun*.

I use the word "fun" a lot in referring to the fellowship of AA. That's because it *is* fun. It is not the grim, lecturing, "cold fish" kind of experience you may have imagined or been falsely told it is. You'll never know, of course, unless you take the risk. I have rarely been to a meeting of any kind where some laughter was not part of the meeting. Many times I have witnessed outright gales of laughter, washing over the whole group like some miraculous spring rain that freshens the mind and the body.

The open discussion group is wonderful for the shy person who just can't bring himself to disclose he is an alcoholic, particularly in front of other people.

Many times I have confronted someone who has hidden out at an open discussion meeting. Invariably, after a few shots at this game playing, the person announced that he or she was recovering. That's great. It doesn't really matter how you get on the boat—just don't stand on the pier and let it leave without you.

OPEN SPEAKER

This is the vehicle most often used for the celebrity speaker and for local, state, or national conventions, when the benefits of what the speaker has to say should be heard by all, not just those in recovery themselves. It is also a meeting that is ideal for the person who needs and desires the support of friends who have aided in the recovery process. Bring them to an open speaker's meeting to hear more of what this disease is all about. You'll be much richer for it.

CLOSED STEP

In this type of meeting, the group discusses and comments upon one or more of the Twelve Steps of Alcoholics Anonymous. Again, the clue to what kind of meeting is in the word "closed." It means only you, the recovering person, may attend. This is a marvelous experience for the person new to the fellowship of AA. The people with more sober years, months, and weeks than you help you understand what the particular step means to your sobriety. Other group members share their opinions of what the step has meant to them and, most important of all, how they have used it as a tool in their complete recovery program.

Many times this is the type of meeting that your AA sponsor will want you to attend with him or her. AA is like any other tool to help you maintain lifelong sobriety. You have to use it for it to be of any value. The closed step meeting is a continuous study program that helps you understand the concepts behind the fellowship, and what has made them work for generations of alcoholics.

If you don't have an AA sponsor, get one. The sponsor is a person, usually of the same sex, who has more time in sobriety than you have. Your sponsor could be that special person who helped see you through your treatment, or a person you heard at a particular meeting. It's a great honor to be asked to be a sponsor. The person will not take it lightly when you ask.

I have seen a close friend, a member of my home group, proudly display a pearl necklace to which is added a pearl for each of the new women she sponsors in the fellowship. Ruby wears this necklace with more pride than the Queen of England wears her diamond tiara.

OPEN STEP

It's obvious that this kind of meeting is similar to the one just outlined, except, of course, it is open to alcoholics and nonalcoholics alike. The really great benefit of this kind of meeting is you can share a learning experience with someone you love or care about in a special way. Together, you can learn more about the Twelve Steps, and each of you can have your questions answered. Again, this is a very nonthreatening kind of meeting. It's the kind of meeting in which you can truly say, "We got sick together, so we can learn and recover together."

The open step meeting has ready-made subject material at hand. There is no pressure to come up with a topic. Your significant other can be as involved as he or she desires. Both of you can ask as many questions as you like. Hopefully, you'll be spurred to share experiences of your own around the use of the Twelve Steps.

HOME GROUP

This kind of meeting is not to be confused with the home group I mentioned earlier, which was the group you consider to be your home base for AA attendance. The home group kind of meeting is just what the name implies. Several of the fellowship, usually no more than twelve or so, alternate hosting meetings in their homes. The meetings are usually closed, although I have attended open home group meetings.

I have clients who have combined the best of two worlds: entertainment and group work. They meet weekly at one couple's home, and spend the first part of some allotted time in a group meeting, closed to the non-recovering persons. (The significant others meet in another part of the house.) Following these meetings, both groups get together and spend the rest of the night playing cards. It's a great meeting for them, and my clients have shared the benefits of their home group with me many times.

The same ever-present coffee pot is always on at home group meetings, just like it is at the others. Tradition still calls for throwing a buck into the pot to reimburse the host for expenses of having the meeting at his or her house. Needless to say, at most of these meetings brownies, fudge, or coffee cake and cookies magically appear along with the coffee.

The home group kind of meeting is often a favorite for professional men and women whose schedules make this meeting more attractive than the larger kinds. The home group meeting is also used when illness prevents a member from attending in a large or crowded place, but the desire to have a meeting is still strong and/or necessary to continued aftercare.

Home group meetings are very often the seedlings that grow into larger meetings, as the need to accommodate more persons in the fellowship of AA develops. A small farm community comes to mind as just such an example of where this happened. As word got around that there was a meeting, people from neighboring small towns began asking if they could attend. What started out as a home group of five or so eventually became a rather well-stocked group of twenty-plus, meeting in the town church one night a week instead of at a member's home.

SPECIAL INTEREST GROUP

Just as the name implies, this kind of group forms out of the need to share recovering experiences with others having similar interests. This is where the doctors, lawyers, pilots, or other groups may want to get together in fellowship because they feel they have some unique problems and that they will benefit each other more if they remain together. If you are such a professional person, you have only to inquire at any meeting you attend about the possible existence of a special interest group, and you will find it. The network of AA is so efficient that the word gets around in really expert fashion. This is due largely to the fellowship's desire to provide a meeting for everyone. If you express a need for a special interest group, chances are you'll have that need met.

Handicapped persons may, by choice, have a particular place where they have more mobility and access. This may start as a special interest group for them, but can and often does expand to include others outside the special interest. I know some teachers who formed such a special group, and it has been quite successful. It is growing in both the frequency of meetings and the number of people in attendance.

A particular special interest group common to many larger communities consists of men and women like myself who are both recovering and therapists. It is obvious that these men and women have unique needs as both alcohol professionals and professional alcoholics, as we like to refer to ourselves.

There is almost no limit to special interest groups that may be available. Again, if you take the risk and ask around, you'll turn up one or two.

WOMEN'S GROUP

I can't say enough about this kind of AA support group, even though it's obvious I can't attend. The comfort level of female alcoholics is considerably increased with participation in a women's group. Often it is the only kind of group the female will attend on any regular basis. If you are this kind of sober female, then I suggest you start with such a group. As your comfort level goes up, you can expand your horizons and attend other kinds of meetings.

The advantages of a women's group for those women with small, dependent children are numerous. Many such groups will have a nursery kind of setting so that the alcoholic mothers in recovery can get group support and still keep an eye on the little dears.

You may wonder why you can't just stay in such a women's group and never try anything else. Well, of course you can. Remember, though, that this is a book about the joy of being sober. Part of your joy comes from personal growth, from learning to meet new people, and from expanding your personal horizons. Thus, the more you get out of your too-comfortable modes and start growing a little, the more solid will be your joy. Use your women's group as your home group if you like, but make yourself venture out into the larger world of different kinds of AA meetings. It's well worth it.

Many women in recovery have found their first women's group through their sponsor, who takes them to such a group. Before you know it, as the months of your own sobriety build up, you will be asked by some frightened, unsure person who is a lot like you were to help steer her to a group. Then is when you will most value your women's group and the special fellowship it provides.

GAY GROUP

More and more, we are seeing gay men and lesbians identify themselves not only as members of the homosexual community, but also as recovering alcoholics who happen to have a sexual preference different from others. Thus, the gay group is the ideal setting for the AA fellowship. Once again, there are good and not-so-good gay group meetings, just like any other kind of meeting. It all depends on the makeup of the core group and on the willingness of the group members to put forth the effort for the group to function in as productive a fashion as possible.

Remember that the most important common ground of the gay group meeting is not that a person is gay, but that the person is an alcoholic. The fact that you may enjoy the gay lifestyle as a matter of personal preference does not submerge the fact that your sobriety is in as much jeopardy as that of straight people.

Again, a phone call to Alcoholics Anonymous, or to a treatment center or hospital, can help you find the gay groups in your community or the community you are visiting. You may find that gay groups will expand and have many different types of AA meetings such as step, speaker, and discussion meetings, open or closed.

The gay group is a most valuable tool for the recovery of the homosexual man or woman. You will find such groups to be highly supportive of your efforts to continue your life of sobriety.

SPECIFIC MINORITY GROUPS

There is no question that this kind of group work fills a very large need. We see it working constantly in the many fine Black, Hispanic, and Native American groups in our own community in Denver. Minority alcoholism is still alcoholism, and sobriety requires support. When members in recovery speak the same native language and/or share the same culture, the sometimes the understanding of the disease and its effects upon our lives becomes clearer. The resolve to maintain lifelong sobriety is strengthened.

Many minority AA groups will be identified by their names and will be easy to find. Some others may be a mixture of many ethnic backgrounds, and it will not be readily apparent that this is the minority group you might be seeking. The cardinal rule is, "If in doubt, go to the meeting." Go to the meeting no matter what. See if there is a person in that group who can direct you to more specific minority meetings.

We have a dynamite group in our area called "Black Rap." It is such a fine meeting that it is openly attended by many people, both Anglo and Black. See, it's the quality of the meeting that makes the difference. Once again, the common denominator is that everyone in the room is a brother in the fold of recovery from alcoholism.

YOUNG PEOPLE'S GROUP

You can find this kind of group almost anywhere. Often these groups are outcrops of another kind of meeting in which many young people find they want to narrow some fields of interest. It is in such groups that specific problems of nonalcoholic dating and peer pressure tactics can really be laid on the table and chewed over.

A young adult's group is often formed from a larger open discussion group. This new splinter group may grow and become a regular couples' group, still dealing with the problems of the young adult in recovery. It doesn't matter if the couples are married or not; the binding element is the age bracket. The problems of any young person in recovery are partially the same as those of others and partially unique. Often, the seriousness of the disease has not struck home as much for the younger alcoholic as it has for the middle-aged or older alcoholic. There is some sort of wishful thinking in the young that they have plenty of time; so what if they slip a time or two? A young people's group will help people like that understand that age doesn't matter. An alcoholic of any age is one drink away from the next drunk.

Again, a young people's group may be expanded to be an open group that will allow the influx of many Alateen people. Those are teenage significant others who have suffered from the effects of alcoholic behavior just as much as the active alcoholic. As a guest, I have witnessed some fine meetings of this kind. The lively discussions and honest approach to the problems of sobriety were refreshing and very stimulating.

Al-Anon and Alateen people are very special in their own right. Their participation in young people's groups—or any of the AA groups where they are appropriate—is a real plus for recovering persons.

So that's my shopping list for giving AA another shot. As a treatment professional, I realize the importance of Alcoholics Anonymous to the total recovery of the person afflicted with the disease. As a tool used in combination with treatment, I believe it is absolutely unbeatable. (AA does not take on the function of professional treatment for alcoholism as its objective. Treatment is the responsibility of the treatment centers and hospitals that are better equipped to perform those tasks. The power of AA as a tool of aftercare makes it the worldwide success it is.)

The fellowship of AA will go with you long after you have left formal treatment. It will remain with you as long as you live. It is a whole new and exciting world out there in AA-land. You may have had a bad taste of the AA experience, but just as with any other thing, you may have tried it and passed judgment too soon, without giving it a second chance.

What I hope you will do is pick up some of the tools available in AA meetings and try them out. You can be assured that wherever you are in the world, you can always find a meeting, and that in itself is one of the biggest joys of being sober.

AA means that the traveler doesn't have to sit alone in one hotel room after another with nothing to do. There's a meeting you can attend. You no longer have to think of yourself as a stranger in a strange town; you see, you have friends. Pick up the phone and find a meeting. Did your auto break down on the road, and you need a place to stay while the local garage rebuilds your car? You'll be amazed at how many offers you'll get for hospitality from members of the fellowship.

In short, make it high on your list of priorities to revisit an AA meeting. Remember, you already possess an addictive personality. So feel free to get hooked on AA.

MORE JOY (An Update)

The fellowship (or the program, or whatever you want to call it) is still going strong, although members' loyalty does waiver now and then. But the same rule works that I wrote about earlier—search out the meetings that provide you with what you need.

Like anything else, you get out of the program what you put into it. I am privileged to be asked to guest at several professional meetings that don't always follow the format of a standard AA meeting. Particularly with lawyers and doctors, these meetings accomplish what they set out to do—help reinforce sobriety—but often don't use the formal structure as we know it.

As I travel around the country and people introduce themselves to me, the conversations don't go on very long before someone will tell me they're a friend of Dr. Bob's or of Bill's. They are referring, of course, to the original founders of the Fellowship of Alcoholics Anonymous, Dr. Bob Smith and Bill Wilson.

Television programs such as *Hill Street Blues, The John Laroquette Show, N.Y.P.D. Blue,* and *Murphy Brown* have certainly done a lot to take the edge off any squeamish feelings about attending AA meetings. I think the motion picture that featured James Garner and James Woods as Dr. Bob and Bill was a good one. It helped explain the founding of the program and cast a pretty good historical perspective on the work of AA.

That work is definitely worldwide in scope. In fact, while one of my clients was on a combined business and pleasure trip to Moscow before the breakup of the Soviet Union, he was directed to an AA meeting by an In-tourist person.

I'm most comfortable attending a meeting when I travel. Often meetings in Denver will have either current or former clients in attendance, which can make it difficult for me. Frankly, I won't stay—it's not my place to share my personal life with people with whom I work or have worked on a professional basis.

Usually when I spot such a person, I leave so I don't take away the chance for him or her to utilize the strength of the meeting. I don't feel disappointed, however; when you have been in practice in the same place for more than twelve years, a good many people have crossed your threshold, and it's always a great feeling to see them still attending meetings and strengthening their program.

People often ask me the reason I don't incorporate Twelve Step work in my treatment program. It's simple; I refuse to charge people for something they can get for free. It never made sense to me, and still doesn't, that some programs charge the amount of money they do in view of that fact. More than half the time a person is in treatment in one of those programs, they are working the steps of AA, and paying to do it.

To me, treatment is not what AA was ever designed to do. Its mission is lifelong support in conjunction with treatment. Together, the two make a dynamite package for lifelong sobriety. I certainly encourage my clients to continue their meetings while seeing me for individual therapy. You can't get enough of the support and strength that you need to win your battles.

So munch on, crunch on, take your nuncheon, breakfast,
supper, dinner, luncheon!

Robert Browning, Pied Piper of Hamelin

THE JOY OF MARTINI-LESS LUNCHES

Have you seen that television commercial in which people are asked at random, "What did you have to eat today?" No one can remember, except of course the people who are eating the particular brand of cereal being pushed.

Drinking your lunch was a lot like that, wasn't it? Didn't matter a whole lot where you ate, or *if* you ate, as long as the martinis kept coming around. (If martinis weren't your bag, then please substitute whatever your favorite noontime libation was.) Well, there is a real joy to having lunch sober. Not only do you care what you're ordering, but you can become very choosy about where you eat and with whom. Seems fair enough, doesn't it? Consider that the main idea is to take a midday break and put some sustenance into your body. You remember—vitamins, minerals, all the good things you need to carry out a full afternoon of work or pleasure.

During your drinking days you forgot the real reasons for having lunch and got right to the real joy of your noontime—drinking. A friend of mine, when ordering a vodka martini, used to tell the waitress, "I want you to think of the driest vodka martini this place has ever made. I want mine drier." We laughed then. Now, in sobriety, it's kind of sad, isn't it?

What can happen to you in sobriety is that you begin to make a festive occasion of going out to lunch. You can actually look forward to it for a whole new set of reasons. You can make lunchtime an event that can brighten your whole day or salvage a dismal week.

As a newly sober person, you need some new ground rules about lunch:

1. Pick places you didn't go during your drinking days.
2. Try to lunch with people who don't drink much, if at all.
3. Be good and hungry (this is no time to diet).
4. Set limits on the time spent at lunch.
5. Set a regular weekly time and place to meet.
6. Have your own transportation, if possible.

NEW PLACES

You are a creature of habit—your past drinking habit. You need to break that habit. Don't return to the scene of the crime. You will have a tendency to spend too much time reminiscing about how the old days were and remembering how drunk you got at your old favorite places. All that belongs in the past. Let it stay there, while you move on to the present and the future. Do this by looking around for the places where you have wanted to go with your friends or by yourself but never did.

There is no point in trying to find a place that doesn't serve alcohol, because they are so rare that they are almost nonexistent. (I am, of course, excluding the fast food operations. I am talking about nice sit-down establishments that make your lunch an occasion.)

A good rule to follow is to make sure there is a separate dining room. Don't try to grab lunch in the dark confines of a cocktail lounge. If the restaurant you choose serves lunch in the lounge, don't sit there, even if it means waiting awhile to get a table in the main room.

A really nice bonus from sobriety right off the bat is that you can afford to eat more. Wow! I mean, do you realize what you used to spend on just the booze tab? You'll be absolutely amazed at how two people can have an elegant lunch in a nice place for well under fifteen bucks. There was a time in your life when the bar tab for lunch ran over twenty dollars. Right away you will see that you can afford this luxury of eating out more.

That's what makes picking new places so exciting. There's practically no restaurant beyond your financial reach once the bar bill is out of the picture.

NEW PEOPLE

This sounds a lot harder than it really is. Remember those times when you wanted to have lunch with someone and didn't make the effort because they *didn't* drink? Of course, the way you were drinking then would have made them uncomfortable. Now you can make up a list of people you always wanted to have lunch with but were embarrassed to ask before. Just think of that. You avoided taking people to lunch who couldn't or wouldn't keep up with your drinking, so you never had the pleasure of their company. Now all that can be changed. Just be honest with yourself and bite off only what you can chew, if you'll forgive the pun.

Don't start off by meeting six people for lunch. You can't handle it emotionally, and probably not financially, either. Which brings up an important point to remember: It is not essential for you to pick up every lunch check. You did that when you were drinking because it was a way you could order more drinks and no one could complain.

What happens if your luncheon companions want to order a drink for themselves? Will you help them with their quandary? Of course. You have the alcohol problem, not them. But your friends won't know how you'll react if they want a glass of wine or a martini. Help them out by saying, "Please feel free to order something from the bar if you like." They're going to say something back to you like, "Doesn't that bother you?" You say, honestly, "Sure. Sometimes, but drinking for me means sure and premature death." Or answer with whatever you feel comfortable saying.

The point for you to stress is that alcohol and your life are inextricably intertwined. You are not about to monkey around with the odds. What I've suggested for you to say is what I say. You choose your own words, as long as you get the idea across to your friends that you are allergic to the chemical alcohol. *You,* not them.

Your newfound friends at AA are ideal lunch companions, but you don't have to limit yourself to people who don't drink at all. You will be able to handle, say, your spouse taking a drink before or with lunch. You help yourself out by ordering something to sip along with your companion. Iced tea, regular or decaf coffee, or a soft drink are all great choices. (We'll discuss more specific drinks for the alcoholic in another chapter.) But don't allow yourself to dawdle over a pre-lunch drink. Get on with it, which brings us to:

BE GOOD AND HUNGRY

Since you are no longer drinking, food tastes better to you. Yes, you've probably put on a few pounds, though not as many as you did when you were abusing alcohol. What you want to do is really enjoy lunch for what it is—good food, and good friends. If you are not properly hungry, the temptation to dwell over the pre-lunch drink your friend is having might be too strong. Now is the time to break old habits. It is not necessary to wait for a second round for your friend before ordering your lunch. When the cocktail person comes to the table to see if we need more drinks, I'll say, "I'm ready to order, but maybe my friend wants another." Most times (most, not all) my companion will shut off his drinking and order lunch.

With a new friend I have invited for lunch whose drinking habits I may not know, I say, "Are you ready to order?" This puts the ball squarely in his court. If he does order another drink and the cocktail person wants to know if I'll have another of whatever I am drinking, I'll say, "No, thanks. I'm ready for you to take my order." This sets a limit, and my companion can pick up on the hint that this is an eating lunch. It also helps you:

SET LIMITS ON THE TIME SPENT AT LUNCH

In the beginning you are going to be a little nervous just sitting without a drink in front of you. So be prepared to set limits. My friends and I act crazy together at lunch every Wednesday at 11:30. At 11:30 we get a table without waiting too long, and we can be back at work by 1:00. The secret here is that the longer you delay getting started, the longer you will want to spend at the lunch table. This is too reminiscent of old habits.

If you have a set lunch hour and can't go as early as I have suggested, try your best to set one-and-one-half hours as the maximum time to be at lunch. If you are a brown bagger, it's even easier. Use lunch as an opportunity to assert yourself and meet new people. You have a ready-built safety valve when you see another person with his or her sack lunch. You know they are not into drinking for lunch, so you can feel secure right from the start.

Taking your lunch to work is a good way to help yourself through a rough time or two. If you worry about going to a restaurant, you can set a limit by telling a friend, "I only have an hour for lunch." Then suggest that maybe you can brown bag it together. This will be a novel idea for you, even if you don't usually take a lunch to work. You can make a picnic out of it—an open space and imagination are all that you need. Try it a time or two, until you feel comfortable enough to handle a restaurant situation with liquor all around you.

Again, whatever you do, make your social contacts in the new world of your sobriety more frequent and less lengthy. More one-hour lunches with new people will do you more good than one big two-hour blowout once a month.

SET A REGULAR WEEKLY TIME AND PLACE

In sobriety you need something fun to look forward to, something you can count on to bring brightness into your new world. Setting a regular weekly luncheon with one or two friends is a great way to meet this need.

I mentioned earlier about getting crazy with some sober friends at lunch. We are all recovering people, and we meet every week at a favorite restaurant of ours. No one has to call and confirm; we all know where we are going to be on that special day, and we mark our calendars accordingly. We have been known to get up and sing "Happy Birthday" to friends or acquaintances we see in the place. It doesn't matter whether it's their birthday or not (it never is). We do it just for the sheer joy of it.

This weekly lunch is a miniature AA meeting of sorts. Often a person in the group will bring a new member of the fellowship along, to show them that sobriety is not all doom and gloom.

This regular luncheon is a very bright spot in our week. It is a tool you can use, too. Midweek is the best time. Choose a place flexible enough to handle two to six people for lunch. Other than that, you only need to take the risk and start a weekly gathering of your own.

This is positive reinforcement that the joy of being sober is a constant celebration of just being alive and free from the bondage of alcoholism. If a member of the group has a problem or is downcast, you can depend on the rest of the group to help cheer him or her up. You'll find more exhilaration in a sober lunch than you ever experienced drinking, and find yourself not wanting to miss this date with other people who constantly reaffirm that the sober life is the only life for them.

Recently I overheard another restaurant customer ask a waitress if "those people are drinking or what? They're so happy—they must be." Our waitress stepped in and said, "Those folks are in here every week, and not one of them has ever ordered a drink." We stopped to think about it, and realized that in more than two years of lunching at this particular spot we had never mentioned that we were recovering alcoholics. We never had to. No one has more genuine fun and celebrates the joy of life more than a recovering person. You'll see!

HAVE YOUR OWN TRANSPORTATION IF POSSIBLE

This is important for your comfort level while trying this new drinkless lunch plan, because the very nature of your disease has made you restless. You may feel boxed in and slightly claustrophobic. When that kind of anxiety attack occurs, you usually want some form of reassurance that you can get up and leave the place. If you have your own form of transportation—car, bike, or supply of bus tokens—you can leave if the pressure becomes too much. What you want to avoid at all costs is the idea that you need a little drink to calm your nerves. That's a disaster in the making.

So be sure you have your own way to and from the meeting. Be independent if possible, and then there will be no excuse for you to remain at the restaurant in an uncomfortable situation just because you are beholden to someone for a ride.

This uncomfortable feeling of anxiety will pass as you become more secure with your sobriety. You'll realize that you can handle all, or nearly all, social situations without feeling the pressure to drink. Being open with a friend who says, "It's silly to take two cars" is the best and only way to be. Inform your friend that you need your own car in case you feel too pressed by the situation. It's no different from getting out of the hospital after an operation and not wanting to tax your strength too much.

You are coming off a disease that has altered your life and will require time, patience, and honesty to help you heal. Be honest and tell your friend that you're not yet sure how strong you are for this social situation without alcohol. Your friend will help you if he or she understands what you are trying to accomplish. You need whatever security you can muster, such as your own car, to help you through the trying new times. This tool may seem like using a crutch, but use it anyway until you build your "CQ," or Confidence Quotient.

Having lunch out in the company of someone you really care about, having a business lunch to really talk business, and savoring the taste of your food are some of the rewards of the martini-less lunches.

You've heard about the woman who, dreading her husband's pending retirement, said matter-of-factly, "Honey, I married you for better or for worse, but not for lunch." Well, you can make lunch more than just a break between breakfast and dinner. In sobriety you can make lunch a refreshing experience, not something during which you spend time, trouble, and money making yourself numb with alcohol.

Bon appetit!

MORE JOY (An Update)

Well, I think the Internal Revenue Service has done a whole lot for martini-less lunches since I wrote this chapter. In fact, the whole idea of the business lunch has changed, and I think for the better. We are a very health and fitness-conscious nation these days. There isn't nearly as much lunchtime drinking in evidence compared to ten years ago.

These days, tons of people grab some yogurt and a piece of fruit after walking, working out with weights, biking, or running and jogging during their allotted lunch time. I think this is the best use of the lunch hour. Before I was hurt and had to give up running, this was my routine. I used to see people all over the country following the same kind of plan.

When I am at professional conferences in other cities, I try to stay at hotels with fitness rooms or some similar exercise facility. There are those of us who like to spend the time normally devoted to putting away tons of calorie-laden food taking weight off instead.

The trendy bottled waters made the scene long ago. And have you noticed all the so-called nonalcoholic beers and wines? I say "so called" because those products still contain one-half of one percent alcohol by volume, so they are not really alcohol-free. I think you should stay away from those drinks anyhow, because of the psychological mind games they trigger. Why would you want to have something that even *looks* like beer on your table anyhow?

These days, the best joy for me at lunchtime is that my wife Cyn and I have begun using it for real quality time. We both work long hours and well into the night, so dinners at our house really are sort of passé. Instead, we decided that we would try to have lunch together at least three days a week. Sometimes she comes to my office with a packed lunch for us both. Other times I travel ten minutes away to her office. We eat on a small patio set on the balcony outside her office, or meet and have lunch at a restaurant.

Either way, we've discovered a new way for us to enjoy both our lunch and each other at a time of the day when we can really communicate with one another. It is far different from when I was drinking my lunch.

You can do the same thing. I have most of my couples in therapy meeting one another once a week for either a picnic lunch or grab-a-bite fast food. Either way, they spend more time together, finding new ways to celebrate their personal joy in being sober.

Another thing that has turned out to be fun at lunch (but does require more than the traditional hour) is a picnic bike lunch ride. In this case, one of you takes care of packing and bringing a lunch on your bike. Your partner bikes to the designated trysting place such as a park, bike path, or greenbelt. If you both work in the downtown area, check whether your city has downtown bikeways. The two of you can make it work if you put a little effort into it.

We have found that an extra half hour is enough if we picnic. If we want to bike to a restaurant, I haul our bikes via car carrier to Cyn's office. Then we bike together to someplace two or three miles away, have lunch, and bike back, usually in forty-five minutes to an hour. Try this new way to spend a martini-less lunch. If you're really bold, substitute rollerblades for the bike idea. However, I take no responsibility for the potential hazard to your body from that idea.

Reach out . . . reach out and touch someone.

The Bell System

13

THE JOY OF CARRYING THE MESSAGE

"Sometimes I think I could shout it from the rooftops!"

"I look at those people standing around boozing and think, 'That used to be me. Don't they know what they're doing?'"

"Every time I tell someone else about how super it is to be sober, they look at me kinda funny. Sooner or later, though, they get what I'm talking about."

"My God! Everyone tells me how great I look since I've been sober."

Carrying the message—that's what it's all about. This business of finding the joy of being sober is too good to keep secret.

The remarks quoted above have come from people just like you, both the newly sober and those with a longer amount of time in recovery. They have all learned what is essential to continued happiness and joy in recovery: if you feel that good about yourself, then carry the message to someone else.

This is the main work of Alcoholics Anonymous. It is also the main theme of the New Testament, which urges Christians to take the Gospel, the "Good News," to the whole world.

Now let's consider the how and where of your journeys—how to carry the message and where to do it. And don't forget the issue of how to do it without preaching or sounding "holier than thou" when carrying the message.

What *is* the message? It is what this whole book is about. There is a joy in being sober. Your life can be fuller, more enriching and rewarding than you ever thought possible when you have separated yourself from the bonds of alcohol.

So many people, including yourself at one time, didn't want to break the mold, didn't want to "test the waters" of sobriety. You were convinced that life after booze was no life at all. Now you know that just the opposite is true. What you thought was "life" before was really a nightmare of drunkenness, hangovers, debt, and disasters of the worst kind in all your interpersonal relationships.

Alcohol for you meant a poison in your life. For you, to drink was to die, not live. So you have an obligation of sorts to carry on the message of what sobriety can mean to someone else. Yes, I said "obligation." The reason for making it so strong is well-known among all who carry the message: by telling someone else about alcoholism, you keep yourself strong in sobriety. Simple, isn't it? Why complicate things when the truth of the statement stands out and slaps you squarely in the face? If sobriety can bring joy to my life, it can certainly do the same for you.

HOW TO DO IT

Carrying the message begins with a complete understanding that honesty will always be your best tool. The collection of statements heard at various gatherings from recovering alcoholics who can't deal honestly with their sobriety is endless. Some of my favorites, collected from patients and clients, include these:

"My doctor thought I ought to take off a few pounds, so I'm not drinking."

"My blood pressure was getting up there; thought I'd lay off the booze awhile."

"I thought I'd better cut down on my drinking a bit."

"Well, I've been having a bout with the flu—the stuff doesn't taste as good."

(From a pregnant woman): "I thought I'd lay off until after the baby comes."

"I'm on some kinda antihistamine thing that gives me a reaction when I drink."

(From a Jew): "I never drink during the High Holy Days."

(From a Catholic): "Gave it up for Lent."

And then my all-time favorite, one that has been used forever by people who are uncomfortable with their sobriety: "I'm on the wagon."

What wagon? The water wagon, of course. If you're on the wagon, you're abstaining from alcoholic beverages. But can you see how these statements skirt the real issue? You, as the newly sober person anxious to reinforce your sobriety, should continually say, "I'm a recovering alcoholic." Or, if that's still too tough right at this stage, "I've discovered that I'm allergic to the chemical alcohol." And that's the truth. No hedging there. There is something in your genetic makeup, both psychologically and pathologically, that makes you unable to assimilate alcohol in your system like "normal" drinkers.

I prefer that you plunge right in. These days, "I'm recovering" is generally all you need to say. Most everyone will understand, and the beautiful part of it is the reaction you will get—it's worth the price of admission. Once you have honestly disclosed your disease, you will begin to hear most of the statements I just quoted. Now, however, you'll hear them from people you talk to as projected plans of action for themselves.

For example, you'll hear "Gee, that's great. I'm really proud of you. You know, (here it comes) my doctor thinks maybe I should cut down a little."

Or, "Really? I never thought you had a drinking problem. Well, I'm giving it up for Lent this year, myself."

How to help carry the message, then, is to begin, continue, and end with honesty. You can respond to any of the people you know who have a drinking problem of their own by telling them to be honest with themselves. "I have the disease of alcoholism," you say, "and I'm doing something about it. How about you?"

Well, no one is going to jump up and down with joy to hear they might have a disease of any kind, much less alcoholism. But you can point out to them that if alcohol is becoming a problem in their lives, then maybe they need to think about it. That's carrying the message.

There is a vast distinction between carrying the message and "carrying the drunk." You can't "carry" the drunk by trying to *make* him get help. You can only share with others what your sobriety has done for you. They must take the step themselves of asking for help, but you are a constant example to the most hardcore drinking friend you know. "It can be done" is the banner you carry everywhere you go.

The longer you delay calling your sobriety a direct result of your battle in the alcoholic war, the longer you delay building your own strength and the ability to share that strength—that joy—with others. Go ahead and choke over the words "recovering" and "alcoholic" for awhile if you have to, but spit them out every time you have the chance. Use them every time you are confronted with "Why aren't you drinking?"

You'll be amazed at how many positive responses you will receive. Your honesty and your successful attempt to do something about your alcoholism will garner you many pats on the back. What about the business of using "recovering" as opposed to "recovered?" You can do as you like, but my strong recommendation is to keep using the term "recovering"—the present tense. This states two facts about your disease:

1. Recovering is a lifelong process that never ends.
2. You are just one drink away from the next drunk, no matter how long you have been sober.

In more concrete terms, the disease of alcoholism is treatable, as we have mentioned many times. It is not curable. Using the expression "recovering" indicates to yourself as well as others that you are engaged in a process that will require your attention every hour of your life. But the accompany message is, "How worthwhile that process is."

At various AA meetings you may attend, you will hear the message being passed every time someone introduces himself or herself. The message may be, "I'm Peggy and I'm a grateful alcoholic," or, "My name is Jim, and I'm a sober alcoholic." You will always hear the word "alcoholic" in the greeting, even though the speaker may have a hard time saying it. Every time you acknowledge your disease, you own up to the fact that you are dealing with a deadly chemical in your life—for the rest of your life.

Is there joy in knowing that you are learning how to get on with the business of living without that chemical? You bet! So why not be up front with people when they present openings for you to disclose your disease and how you're conquering it on a day-to-day basis?

If you walked into a room with a mangled arm dangling at your side, sat down at a table, and painfully hauled the obviously broken limb up on the table, people would be aghast. "What on earth is the matter with you?" they would cry. "What haven't you gotten that treated?" Can you see yourself replying, "Oh, *that.* It's nothing but a broken arm."? The protests from your friends would be overpowering: "Why isn't it in a cast? Aren't you going to do something about it?"

The next time you walk into that same room, your arm would be in a cast, as is proper and necessary to the healing process of the broken bone. Everyone would rush over to you to sign the cast, an expression of their desire for you to get well.

Well, your disease is not outwardly visible, except when you were manifesting it through the alcoholic behavior patterns of your life. It's still there, and you are simply treating it as if it were in a cast. Why not, then, allow your friends to "sign" the cast of your recovery by telling them about it and showing them how they too can become healthier?

Every time you carry the message of your recovery process, called sobriety, you help not only those who hear the message, but also you as the carrier. You are applying a little more gauze, tape, and plaster of paris to the break. By doing so, you make the healing process stronger.

WHERE TO DO IT

It has been a policy of mine since my own recovery began to spend Christmas Day and New Year's Day at a hospital. I visit either a detox ward or the inpatients who have not been able to go home to their families. These people are suffering from the same disease that is in my body and yours.

This holiday idea was passed on to me by a recovering doctor friend of mine, Blair Carlson, director of the Alcoholism Recovery Unit of St. Luke's Hospital in Denver. Blair follows the practice himself, even though he, like any of us in the field, works with alcoholics twenty-four hours a day.

Spending an hour with people in detox or on the ward reminds you that you have much to be grateful for. You are sober this day, and you can offer that same message of encouragement to the poor, sick person who lies there in that hospital bed. That's where you go to carry the message.

A client of ours recently found herself doing something that she never thought possible. She spent part of Mother's Day with some strangers in a nursing home, some mothers who wouldn't have any visitors from their families on this special day. For our recovering friend, it was an act of carrying the message of her newfound sobriety by sharing her wellness with others who needed contact with wellness.

You can do it, too. Your church or synagogue has a heavy load of hospitalized or homebound people who would welcome a visit from you. Who are you doing this for? Yourself *and* them—it's okay to be a little bit selfish in deciding to visit with another person.

The theory here is sound. By giving your message of sobriety and the joy of being sober to another, you add to your own joy. It's simple, and it does work.

You don't have to wait for holidays to do this, either. Many times I have recommended to people new in recovery that they pay a visit to a hospital when they feel a Dry Drunk coming on. It's great therapy for you and the person you visit in the hospital. It will remind you of how far you have come in your sobriety, and at the same time it will remind you of how quickly you could be back in that detox ward, in that hospital bed.

Combine a visit with an AA meeting and you won't have to worry too long about your blues or depression. Carrying the message and hearing the message are dynamite one-two knockout punches for Dry Drunk Syndrome and Pity-Pot sitting.

Schools can also use your message-bearing efforts, either through organized citywide programs or directly through a local PTA or concerned teacher group. One of the most rewarding experiences you can ever have is to sit in a classroom of junior high, high school, or even elementary school kids and answer their very bright questions about the disease of alcoholism. You don't have to be an expert. You can simply share your story of what it's like to be free from alcohol.

This takes guts on your part, because it's making a public commitment to your lifelong sobriety. But that's what you want, isn't it? You can garner all the invitations to speak to service clubs, women's groups, or other organizations in your hometown and not be afraid to take the wraps off your "trouble." Steel yourself and be proud to share your story of recovery with others. Somewhere in every audience you speak with is someone who is in trouble with alcohol. You might just be the flicker of hope for that housewife, lawyer, or teenager who hears you talk about your recovery.

You will be amazed at the interest from, say, a church group of yours, or the teachers themselves at your local school. But what if it's a school where your own kids attend? Do you still make yourself available for a program dealing with alcohol and other drug abuse? I just asked myself, "Did I ever show up at this school in a state of alcohol abuse that embarrassed me or my kids? How do my kids feel about me disclosing my disease to their peer group?" The answers gave me the reassurance I needed.

Each person has to make these decisions for himself, but I think the benefits of speaking to these groups far outweigh the disadvantages. Your alcoholism didn't fool anyone, even though you were convinced that you were fooling everyone. Your kids probably took a whole lot of abuse when you showed up half-smashed at the school fair, play, or bake sale. What a marvelous opportunity for you to reappear, carrying the message that you have found joy in being sober and that your life is so different now that alcohol is no longer a part of it.

When a few people in group therapy discussed this means of carrying the message, most found it unthinkable. A few weeks later, however, two members of the group disclosed they had taken the risk and volunteered to be part of a panel discussion on alcohol abuse at their children's schools. The panel groups were part of a citywide awareness week on alcoholism, so the two group members were at different schools in different parts of the city.

Their reports back to the therapy group were very stimulating. The recovering persons found some new friends in recovery (one of them her son's homeroom teacher). Even better, all the friends of their children had taken special pains to thank the speakers and express their pride in knowing them.

One father told me in an individual therapy session how his son had been so proud of him for coming to school and talking to his class. The son even found some new friends as a result—children with alcohol-abusing parents who were still actively drinking. The kids were glad to hear and to meet another kid who offered visible hope that things could be better.

So carry the message, not the drunk. Carry it everywhere you go and to as many lives as you can touch. It will bring you unbridled joy.

MORE JOY (An Update)

Many things have changed in the way I carry the message these days, but I still try in my own way. There is no longer an opportunity for me to visit inpatient facilities on Christmas and New Year's. The entire face of treatment has changed in the past ten years. The new trend is to get people in and out of detox or "special care" and into intensive outpatient as soon as possible.Dr. Blair Carlson now heads the Medical Department of the Kaiser Permanente Chemical Dependency Program, whose administrator is my former partner, Paul F. Staley. Many, many changes.

Instead of doing what I had done for so many years, I decided to celebrate my joy in a different way, particularly on Christmas morning. I started volunteering to usher at our church for a Christmas Day church service, even though we attend services on Christmas Eve. It may not seem like this is a way of carrying the message, but for me it is a personal testament to my ongoing recovery.

Of course, as a working therapist I am very fortunate to always be carrying the message to others. In a sense, every prospective client to my practice is someone who is receiving the message, "If I can get sober and find joy in it, then so can you."

There continue to be ample resources for you to share the good news of your own recovery. As I discussed previously, the "friends of Bill W. or Dr. Bob" continue to make themselves known to you, sometimes in very strange ways. Nevertheless, they let you know they are carrying the message and passing it on for you to pass it on to someone else, and so on.

It's very common for people to come up to me at a book signing or lecture and without any prompting, disclose that they are also recovering. I always congratulate them, and they invariably want to know how long I have been sober. But I never disclose that, and I'm not going to here, either. The reason is that I don't want anyone to base their sobriety or their dedication to recovery on what I have done, but rather on their own personal dedication to a newer, better life.

You carry the message in simple ways: when you are able to accomplish some physical task that you would not have tackled before; when you balance your checkbook the first time; when you remember your sister-in-law's birthday without being told. You get the picture. When you begin to reinvest yourself into life better than ever before, you are carrying the message.

I can't emphasize too much that your job is not to reform the world of drinking. Your job is to set an example of how much better life can be. Earnestly live that life in a manner that sets an example for others who have an alcohol problem, but don't try to force them into doing something about it. Send the message—don't preach it.

Party is the madness of many for the gain of a few.

Jonathan Swift

The sooner every party breaks up, the better.

Jane Austen

HANDLING THE COCKTAIL PARTY

Perhaps the question most often asked by a recovering person is, "Why can't I drink like everybody else?" We've already discussed the reasons you must stop asking why. Move on to more positive questions like "what" (can I do about it?) and "where" (do I begin?).

The second most popular lament is, "How am I ever going to be able to go to a cocktail party again?"

The answer is simple. You just go. Here are some new rules and tools designed to help you have fun at a cocktail party instead of spending every moment in sheer agony.

The first thing to understand is that cocktail parties are designed for one purpose: to consume great quantities of alcoholic beverages. That's the name of the game, and you've been playing it for years. So let's decide what you're going to do instead of putting away your share of booze. These are new rules, so we'll call them that.

NEW RULE #1

The recovering alcoholic will make it a point to decide on the exact nature of the purpose for going to this party in the first place. Ask yourself, "Is this really an important event for the advancement of my or my partner's career?" Armed with the appropriate answer, you follow with: "What happens if we decline the invitation?" Or, if you are operating solo, "What are the consequences to me if I decline?"

Knowing the purpose for attending can often give you the kind of support you need to set limits on what you can handle at the event. Which leads us to:

NEW RULE #2

The recovering person will stay at a cocktail party for no more than forty-five minutes, give or take ten minutes. Just about everything that's going to happen at a party will happen in the first forty-five minutes anyway. You will have made all the bright remarks you're going to make. Your friends will have made all the extracurricular passes that will be made. And you will have had most of the numbers worked on you that would have been tried for the whole night had you stayed.

All that action will happen in the first forty-five minutes or so of just about any cocktail party. From that time on, the same old tapes play over and over, with different people moving in and out of the picture, getting progressively more inebriated. So why stay and play old tapes? You can make a very acceptable appearance and accomplish the purpose of having been there in the first place without staying any longer.

To follow this new rule, you have to do some groundwork with whomever is going with you to the affair. If you are the recovering person and you are escorting someone who is a social drinker, then attendance requires planning and agreement before you ever leave your place for the party. You present that groundwork and agreement as follows: "It's necessary that I not stay longer than forty-five minutes at this party. Is that going to be okay with you? If it isn't, then I probably shouldn't go."

You then outline the reasoning just the way I have given it to you. You might emphasize that it is perfectly acceptable and socially proper to not overstay at a cocktail party. If you are talking about a cocktail hour before a banquet, you can propose, "Could we agree to split the difference? We can go for the cocktail hour thirty minutes ahead of dinner instead of the full hour called for on the invitation." Thirty minutes is more than enough time for you to give your companion the option of having one or two cocktails, and you don't have to manage your stress points quite as long before you go in for dinner. (I have discovered that I can use up thirty minutes just standing in line to buy my wife a cocktail at one of these events.)

If you are double-dating for the affair and you feel you are imposing on the other couple by following this new rule, then you have these options:

1. You can explain the pressure points of cocktail parties to them, which, of course, helps your honesty program.

2. You can agree to meet them during the cocktail hour and go into dinner together (although this may not be a very satisfactory arrangement for a double date).

3. You can suggest meeting at your place at the time the cocktail hour or party was supposed to start. You can offer your guests the first drink at your house, leave after that one drink, and still arrive very fashionably for them to have a second round, if it is desired. All of these options help keep you in control instead of being the controlled person.

By following New Rule #2, you won't make anyone angry at you for being a spoilsport, nor will you offend the people who invited you. You will make sure of the latter by bringing New Rule #3 into play.

NEW RULE #3

The recovering person will make sure he or she greets the host and hostess or chief "muckamuck" as soon as possible after arrival. That way they will know you have been to their party, and therefore won't be all bent out of shape when you leave. Even if you are staying for forty-five minutes only, other folks can get pretty snockered by then. You want to make sure that your appearance is known before everyone gets such a glow on.

A friend who has honed most of these rules to a fine edge explains New Rule #3 this way: "I make damn sure everyone knows I've shown up," he says, "'cause most of them won't remember in the morning."

I try never to leave my wife's side during these events. Sometimes I hurry her along to greet the host right off the bat, even though it made her uncomfortable the first few times we pulled it off.

You may be wondering, "What's a few minutes more or less going to matter? I'll get around to the host or hostess eventually." That's the very point. By the time you have stopped and chitchatted with everyone else, most of your allotted time is up. Instead you hit the hosts first, a task made considerably easier if they greet you at the door. (This becomes more difficult, however, as cocktail parties get larger, making it harder for the host and hostess to stand by the entrance. All the more reason to make a beeline for your benefactors, boss, or whoever is in charge.) Thank them for the lovely invitation, make quick small talk if you can, and beat it around to exchange more greetings. You want folks to be able to say, "Ol' Charlie was too there. I saw him." And you can also score a lot of points for your self-esteem if you send a thank-you note as a verification that you did attend.

The reason for all this emphasis on being noticed is that many people will not want to include a recovering person on the invitation list for a cocktail party. They will think it will be too difficult for you, that you might start drinking again. Well, they just don't know you, do they? They don't know that you have found joy in being sober and that you don't want to be left out of the fun. And it can be fun.

I developed a game for myself which I now pass along to you. I imagine what people would look like if I had the power to remove the glasses or beer bottles or cans from their hands. Try it. It's a scream to imagine the little knots of two or three people making party talk, standing in that peculiar bent-over stance, but without the glass in their hands. The ridiculous poses make them look like so many comic strip characters.

Another trick I recommend to help cement your fun at a party is to tell your host or hostess how nice it is to really enjoy a party for a change. You might find yourself being among the minority of guests who can say that honestly to them, especially on Hangover Sunday.

The host and hostess appreciate hearing that people are enjoying the efforts they have put forth. Otherwise, an hour or so later they may wonder why they didn't just throw all the booze up for grabs and forget about having any kind of social mixer.

NEW RULE #4

The recovering alcoholic will absolutely never pretend that the drink he or she is carrying around is "real." Boy, this is one of my pet peeves. I have angered some folks, I'm sure, by calling this dishonesty to their attention as game-playing. You are not carrying around an alcoholic drink, so why pretend you are? The whole idea of your sobriety is to break old habits. Walking around with a Virgin Mary, or a drink that looks like vodka and tonic but is really just tonic and lime in the same kind of glass, is not being fair to yourself—or anyone else, for that matter. (More on this in a few pages.)

Honesty! That's your battle cry from now on. It's too easy for some well-meaning friend to refill your drink glass with the real thing, and before you know it you'll be a goner.

Avoid punch bowls like they are filled with bubonic plague. There is always some clown at every party who believes that the punch needs a little pick-up. The best-intentioned plans to offer nonalcoholic punch as an option will go down the tubes when a bottle of gin is slipped into the "safe" punch.

So what *do* you drink?

ALTERNATIVE DRINKS

You will find that the very habit of carrying something around in your hand is a hard one to break. You may feel somewhat naked without a glass in your hand. Conquer this habit by switching to coffee at a cocktail party. Now, I know that may drive you up a tree; here are all these folks doing their best to consume as much liquor as they want, and I'm telling you to walk around with a cup of coffee in your hand.

You don't have to do it every time—just at the beginning if you are a newly sober person. Trust me, please. It may feel a little awkward to try to balance a coffee cup and saucer, but I'll let you in on what every recovering person already knows: if you'll ask the bartender or cocktail waitress who is circulating the party for coffee in a mug, you'll probably get more than you bargained for. Lots of folks like drinking coffee/liqueur combinations, such as coffee and kahlua or coffee and brandy, so the party will probably have some of those coffee mugs for just that purpose. So even though you can't have a mug, make the effort to take a cup of coffee or decaf as your drink. There are two reasons for this: The first is it helps identify that there is a new you at this cocktail party, one who no longer has to have alcohol to be part of the scene. Second, it will help you explain your sobriety by simply telling inquiring people, "I choose coffee as part of my recovery." "Recovery?" they ask. "Yep," you say, and the door is open. They may say things at the beginning like, "What? You're drinking coffee? What in God's name for?" You can reply, "I'm allergic to alcohol and so coffee is my drink now, okay?" The "okay" is to help establish that you mean business, and to enlist their support in not pushing alcohol on you.

On a summer day, you can't beat iced tea and fresh mint with a lemon wedge. If the weather is cold, I prefer to stick with black coffee, though hot tea may be your beverage of choice. If you like orange juice, try this for a terrific drink: ask for one-half orange juice topped with sparkling soda. It's refreshing, and the sparkling soda gives a delightful "bounce" to the drink. Hang onto your glass, though, as it could be mistaken for an orange blossom or screwdriver, and you don't want that. One way to help make sure that folks know there is a difference in your drink is to ask the barman to put a fresh orange slice on the rim of your glass. Orange blossoms and screwdrivers are rarely served this way, so you are flying a different flag on your nonalcoholic drink.

Perrier mineral water or any of the other waters are, of course, acceptable and taste good. I like Perrier because I can ask for the bottle with the drink (no chance for it to be mistaken for something else). If there are small tables at the party, I can set the Perrier bottle in plain sight, which labels me a nondrinker. The same goes for tonic and lime or plain club soda with a lemon or lime wedge—if you can set the small bottle on the table with your glass, then it's okay. There's not much danger of it being confused with an alcoholic beverage.

This is a good place to mention a very serious no-no for you at any function where liquor is served and you are standing at the bar to get your order. Never accept tonic, soda, or plain water that is dispensed from a multiple head shot-gun. These heads will often be switched to dispense gin or vodka along with the other beverages I mentioned. Don't hesitate to ask for your tonic, 7-Up, or club soda from a bottle.

Cola drinks often don't require any explanation. The old word of caution is to use the can rule. Either carry the soft drink can and plunk a straw into it or have the can sitting on the table with you. All of these drink suggestions lead to:

NEW RULE #5

Always inform your barperson and/or cocktail waitperson that you are recovering. These people are the best friends you will have at a cocktail party. Even at private home parties, if there is a circulating server, take him or her aside and ask, "Will you please help me out tonight? I'm recovering." That's all you have to say. There isn't a bartender, waiter, or waitress who won't watch out for you. They approve of your courage and are anxious to help.

Some people I've given this rule to say they feel silly asking "to be taken care of"—that is, until they try it once. Then, they report back, "I've never had a more relaxed evening. I didn't have to worry the entire time."

I have observed many bartenders who, when asked to watch out for a recovering person at a party, will tell a waitress, "You come directly to me for this person's drinks." This same New Rule works with servers at those banquets where the dessert may be "wine sundae" masked under a fancy name such as "Virginia Dare Delight."

Get your waitress' attention, and when she comes over by your place, simply tell her, "I'm recovering. Is there some other dessert I can have, like plain ice cream?"

You may think this is going to cause a big stir. Well, it isn't. See, other folks have been drinking, probably a lot. They are wrapped up in their own conversations and won't even notice the little bit of talk you have with a waiter or waitress. The same goes for any embarrassment you may feel about standing at the bar and telling the bartender not to give you your soft drink from the shot-gun. He or she will know instantly that you are a recovering person if you simply say, "May I please have a Coke, and not from the gun dispenser?"

Many bartenders will automatically respond with, "You don't have to worry. This is strictly for soft drinks," or something like that.

If there are people around you when it's your turn to order, again you must remember that they have been—or are—consuming alcohol, and they don't much care what anyone else orders except themselves. Plus, you'll be surprised at how softly you can give instructions to a bartender and be heard. The very change of voice level alerts them to listen, and you can give your order in a perfectly normal tone of voice. It's the people who are drinking alcohol who continue to raise their decibels, usually in direct proportion to the amount of drinking they are doing.

I once gave this as an assignment to a therapy group: go to a crowded function and elbow your way to the bar. Try the New Rule #5 of informing the bartender of your recovery. Tell him in a normal voice.

 Four people reported great success with the experiment using New Rule #5. Two or three others said they had to shout to be heard, but guess what? Nobody else paid them the slightest bit of attention. Try New Rule #5, and the more you use it, the more comfortable it will become for you.

NEW RULE #6

The recovering person will be attentive to his or her companion. This should be a new twist for you, since most cocktail party behavior is bad to say the least. By "bad," I mean the first order of business for so many couples is to play "ditch 'em" the minute they hit the door. That may have been your lifestyle before, but now you will invoke New Rule #6 and pay a lot of attention to the person who has accompanied you to the party.

Again, you are trying to break old habits and to reinforce the sober life. In your drinking days, you may have thought the thing to do was circulate. As a result, both you and your companion may have had some terrible times. If you were the outgoing "life of the party" type, then your companion probably felt left out, ignored, and totally useless. If your spouse was the "party animal" and you were the drinker, you may have drank even more to combat the hostility you were feeling at having been dumped.

You probably didn't remember most of what you said and did, and yet had to make numerous apologies the next morning for what you *were told* you did. So New Rule #6 does a bit of intervening for you. By using it, you're saying, "I am proud to be seen here with you, and will make you the object of my attention as much as I can." Before, alcohol ruled the way you behaved (and misbehaved). Now you can further cement your sobriety by changing the way in which you act at cocktail parties. What you are doing is setting up a perfectly logical formula that says: "Before, when drinking, I needed drink to be the relaxed, charming person I thought I was. Now I no longer need drink. I am recovering, and I choose to spend time with you. It is you who can help me be relaxed." The "charming" part is up to you, depending on the manner in which you conduct yourself.

The feedback from invoking New Rule #6 will be good. You'll hear things like, "This is the way I always wanted things to be," and "It was such a pleasure to be with you at the party—not just be dragged there by you." Use this New Rule and going to cocktail parties will not be the drudge that you may have decided they were destined to be. You will also find that you are the envy of many other people who wish that their companions could find them stimulating just for themselves.

THE HOSTILITY METER

The more people drink, the edgier they get. The more they drink, the more quarrelsome they can become. As a sober person, you need to be aware of these changes in personality which you will see, and about which you will be utterly amazed.

I call it the Hostility Meter. As you are engaged in cocktail party conversation you will notice that many things you say are being picked up on. Points of view you thought you could express freely suddenly seem to be starting arguments. This is the escalation of the needle on the Hostility Meter—you need to watch out for it and extricate yourself from the situation as soon as you can. Why?

Because people who are drinking can reach your soft spots pretty quickly, and your new sobriety is still making you tender in the emotional area.

As you see the Hostility Meter needle rise, you know there can be trouble brewing on the horizon. The conversation can be about most anything—sex, religion, politics, company policies. It doesn't matter. The more alcohol consumed by your companions, the more the needle goes up.

That's because alcohol is loosening up emotions and, remember, inhibitions. Name-calling and bitter remarks can be exchanged in a big hurry as the Hostility Meter begins to reach the red line. For you, this is a direct threat to your sobriety. You begin to hear that small, always sleeping snake stir in your brain, ready to strike. That snake is saying, "If this sonofabitch keeps going at me, I'm gonna take just one little drink so I can handle him." We already know that one little drink can lead to the next drunk.

Ignoring the Hostility Meter can mean disaster for your recovery. If you visualize that every person you are talking to at a cocktail party has this meter painted on their forehead, you can be safer. As they begin to look bent out of shape, visualize the needle rising toward the red zone. When you hear positive clues that the person you are talking with is getting just a little hostile at either something you are saying or doing (such as not drinking), then bail out as quickly and politely as possible. Leave the conversation or group of people where the action is starting. You sobriety depends on you taking evasive action before nerve endings get too exposed.

The Hostility Meter is another good reason to have your companion close by your side. He or she can learn to read the warnings on the Hostility Meter with you, and together, you can keep out of trouble.

By being able to read and interpret cocktail party Hostility Meters, you can count on not having to answer a series of apologetic phone calls the day after. Better yet, you won't have to make those calls yourself because you let some red-line situation get out of hand. The real joy of being sober at a cocktail party is that you get to observe people and their actions and reactions to the world around them. You get to see them as one who is thinking and acting clearly.

All that's been said certainly doesn't mean that every cocktail party is one big lost weekend. It does mean that for you it can be a trying time unless you are willing to apply these new rules. Turn them into working tools that will help make you feel comfortable around other people in drinking situations.

The cocktail party is still a great American pastime. You can enjoy the people, the action, the companionship, all for the very low price of knowing and using these few methods to help you keep your recovery intact. And you can do this without appearing to be either a reformer/crusader or a "holier than thou" person.

Just remember how great it's going to be for you to wake up the morning after and know what you said and did, who you were with, and—probably the greatest joy of all—how you got home.

MORE JOY (An Update)

The cocktail party still seems to be a unique American institution, but it certainly has changed in nature over the years. It is not the same totally alcohol-oriented affair that it used to be. Something new has been added: There is usually a plethora of soft drinks being offered—nonalcoholic drinks, bottled waters, and fruit juices.

All this ties in with America's health-conscious kick, and I for one applaud. However, the same pitfalls I originally wrote about are still there, and you have to be aware of them and steer clear of the rocky shoals of cocktail parties. My wife and I still practice the rule of each of us taking our own car if she has to stay at the party.

To this day I will not drink from any punchbowl, even if it is labeled nonalcoholic, any more than I will take the word of anyone else that such a punch exists. I've met too many people who have been burned by that one to trust it. The later you arrive at a party, the greater the risk that the punch has been altered by some well-meaning (at least they think so) guest who wants to liven things up.

I think that today's hosts and hostesses are much more in tune with how many of their guests may not drink, and so they provide an easier atmosphere for the recovering person to handle these parties. It's still a very good idea, however, to plan your arrival time closer to the stated dinner hour. That way you won't be subjected to interminable minutes of others imbibing while you wait for the chow.

I still try to carry around a soft drink in the can so there is no question about what I'm drinking. I certainly do like the hot and spicy tomato juice and tabasco mixes used in a Bloody Mary, but I try to put that mixture in a glass different from those real Bloody Marys are served in. That's as much for me as for anyone else.

Clients are always asking me when I think they are ready to attend a cocktail party, or go to Las Vegas or Atlantic City, where there is so much access to free alcohol. My answer is that they're ready when they do not dwell on being at a cocktail party and can just enjoy the company, and when they are interested in the shows and entertainment rather than the drinking at the tables.

Still, Las Vegas is a great place to help you with New Rule #5. Every time I have asked a "harem princess" or a toga-clad server to please make sure I don't get served an alcoholic beverage, they have been right on my side. Many of them will tell me, "Don't worry, I'm recovering too," or, "I'm in the program...don't worry." Cocktail parties are probably always going to be in existence, and you can't always avoid them, but you can take them for the crowd-mingler that they were designed to be instead of for the getting-sloshed affairs that they may have been in your past. There's a real joy in being able to spend your allotted forty-five minutes at such a party and feeling absolutely no pressure whatsoever around the cocktail part. The only pressure, I find, is keeping the jokes new.

...And it was always said of him, that he knew how to keep Christmas well, if any man alive possessed the knowledge...

Charles Dickens, A Christmas Carol

15

HOLIDAYS AND HOW TO COPE WITH THEM

It is one of the rare events of my life. Every time we trim the Christmas tree, I think of a note hung on the tree the first year of my own recovery. It was written by one of my daughters—I don't remember which one. The note said, "Dear Daddy, it's so nice the only things under the tree this year are the presents!"

It had a touch of class. Too many recovering people have spent too many holidays as blurs on the landscapes of their lives. Holidays were an excuse to increase the drinking time and to find more reasons to drink earlier, heavier, and faster than at other times.

Well, we're going to help you change that. From now on, your sobriety is going to allow you the opportunity to find the joy of the major (and, yes, even minor) holidays, all without having to have one alcoholic drink.

It doesn't matter if you're a Christian or Jew. Most of our national holiday celebrations overlap during the same periods of the year anyhow, so you can use the same tools for coping with either religious persuasion.

Notice the word "cope" in both the title of this chapter and in the emphasis on the use of tools. Coping can be very hard during festive occasions. Almost everyone around you is really into the spirit of the holiday, and you are inclined to share company with your Grey Ghost. Your Pity Pot groweth larger as the holly and the mistletoe abound.

It isn't just at Christmas or Hanukkah, either. Easter, Passover, your own birthday, even—people all make a big thing out of making alcohol an absolute must. Some people think there must be drinks not only before and after an event, but also during the celebration. No wonder you get your hackles up. No wonder your jaws turn to steel mandibles when someone sloshes a glass of claret all over your gift of Irish linen napkins for sister Susie's birthday. It sure doesn't help your coping abilities.

So what we're going to do here is list a few of the biggie and some of the not-so-biggie holidays. We'll look at the pressure areas that can wreak havoc with your recovery plan unless you face them squarely and make alternate plans. First the holidays and their gremlins:

1. Christmas or Hanukkah—Overbuying and overspending.
2. New Year's—Parties; staying up until midnight; "pressure kissing."
3. Thanksgiving—Family dinners and reunions.
4. Halloween—Kids in general.
5. Memorial Day—Sadness; the "must" visit to the grave site.
6. Fourth of July—Beer busts; company picnics.
7. Labor Day—Last-big-holiday-of-summer bash.
8. Easter—Overbuying; wardrobe pressure.
9. Your Birthday—Turning thirty, forty, fifty, whatever.
10. Your Kid's Birthdays—They're "growing up and away" (Empty Nest Syndrome).

To begin with, remember that all of the tools you learned in Chapter 14 about the cocktail party also apply to coping with holidays. Now you can strive to understand these additional pressure areas, and by understanding them, change certain things so there is joy in the holiday instead of heartaches, hangovers, and harsh words.

You can rearrange the list above in order of importance to fit your own needs, religious beliefs, and traditions. I list them in the order that they caused the most pressure for me, which is also the order in which I give them to clients in recovery who are having the same problems.

CHRISTMAS OR HANUKKAH

There is no question that we all get caught up in buying and overspending during these greatest commercial holidays of the year. No matter how many vows you have taken to stay within your budget this year, no matter how you have sworn that you will use only the money that is in your Christmas Club account, you will overspend. Why? Because you're an alcoholic. You will do everything to excess in keeping with your addictive nature and your grandiose ideas of what is important in life.

You will have completed your shopping list, and then the perfect gift for him or her or Uncle Harry or Aunt Meg will show up on the shelves. You'll buy it. Your alcoholic behavior patterns will whip that old Visa or American Express or Floogle Department Store card right out of your pocketbook or wallet, and you'll buy, buy, buy.

Then, if you play the old tapes in high fidelity, you can find yourself engaging in an almost endless round of drinking, partying, drinking, and partying. The bills and the upcoming financial obligations get pushed back farther and farther, to the farthest recesses of your mind. They stay there until later on Christmas Eve or Christmas morning, when the last package has been torn into. Then reality hits, and hits hard. "There is nothing more over than Christmas," a friend of mine once said. How true. Suddenly you may need to reach for a Bloody Mary, Screwdriver, Brandy Alexander, or six-pack. You realize that all this stuff that was so important a few weeks and days ago now has to be paid for.

Well, try something new. If you'll go back and consult your past bills, you'll find that most of your splurge spending or spur-of-the-moment gifting happened in the days just before the final day or evening of celebration.

I started a little game for some folks in recovery called The Twelve Days of Christmas. The rules are easy. If you are a family, each member puts his or her name in a bowl. Everyone draws a name, but does not disclose whose name. Then the fun begins. You are limited to two dollars for spending for each of the Twelve Days of Christmas. It's pretty obvious you won't be able to trot out and buy twelve lords a' leaping or even a partridge in a pear tree, unless you are really clever. Each evening (or whatever predetermined time you choose), you and your exchangees gather and open these very simple, inexpensive gifts, still not divulging who is the benefactor.

You will be absolutely amazed at what you can still get, either buying or creating, for two dollars. People have reported finding cookie cutters in the shape of partridges. They make the cookies, put the cookie bird on a branch of a tree in the yard, sprinkle some glitter or Ivory Flakes on the thing, and have a really clever gift.

When I first tried this, I had a lot of small kids to buy for. Colored pencils, packs of new colored chalk, rubber bands, file cards, hair bows, and balsa wood gliders were high on my list. The reason this little game works for you in your sobriety is it satisfies this craving you have for buying without breaking you.

You are not allowed to buy for more than one day of the twelve days at a time. Twelve separate little excursions will let you savor the excitement, hustle and bustle of the holiday and still not face an undue amount of debt. Does this replace the major gift or two on your list? Of course not. But it does enable you to share more of what the spirit of giving is all about.

If you are a sober single with no particular member of the opposite sex to buy for, then pick a relative or friend and send twelve different Christmas or Hanukkah cards. When one client tried this with a few friends, she reported back that she had simply signed her cards as "Your Angel." She drew a little angel on each card and included no return address (something I'm sure didn't please the post office, but it certainly gave her some joy). She told me that she heard from a bunch of old friends as a result of this. Some had deciphered the postmark of where the card was mailed and deduced it must be her. It wasn't until after the holiday that she divulged her true identity to each of the folks she had selected for her Twelve Days of Christmas. Now, two years later, four of them choose each other's names and play this simple game.

She has told me many times of the thrill and joy she gets from getting out of her apartment in the evenings and going to the various little card shops and art stores to select her inexpensive gifts for the twelve days. One of her friends got so intrigued that he started making his own cards. They are a delight to everyone who is lucky enough to receive them.

Another way to curb the pressure to overspend is to wait until the last minute to shop. I didn't believe this when it was first suggested by another recovering friend. "Heck," he said, "if I wait until a day before Christmas, most of the really expensive things I would have bought are gone. I have to settle for something that turns out to be cheaper and just as much appreciated." You would think that the opposite would be true, but it really can work that way. Try it yourself and see if you don't spend less than in your drinking days.

Another new tool for Christmas pressure-spending is to make a gift of yourself. The money you would spend on a lot of gifts might be better used to go home for the holidays. What nicer gift than to take yourself back home or better yet, bring someone to you. It's one cost that can be fairly large, but one that will mean a great deal to you. If you are the present, no one need expect anything else. And if you decide on such a gift of travel, your airline or travel agent will help you work out a way to prepay your fare in installments, like Christmas Club payments. A prepaid trip eases your money pressure and allows you the freedom to enjoy your holiday without going overboard as you did in your drinking days.

Finally, make it a point never to give liquor of any kind as a gift. You don't need even one trip into a liquor store, no matter how strong your sobriety is. Alcohol has no place in your list of priorities, and if you keep giving liquor you are not being honest with yourself about the importance of alcohol in your sober life. Better a box of premium chocolates than that bottle of scotch in its tempting Christmas wrap.

There is so much that is free around Christmas that you simply won't believe it until you look around. There are concerts of sacred and traditional music, ballets, and plays. And of course, the real joy of attending children's Christmas pageants in a sober state can't be fully described until you try it yourself.

I have tried each year to investigate some new form of celebration of the meaning of the holiday. Last time it was the discovery of a new brass group playing in a local church. A freewill offering was the only charge, but the evening was a memorable return to what sobriety during celebration of a holiday can really mean.

Be sure to include as many AA meetings as possible as you get nearer to Christmas itself. There is nothing like it for your ongoing support; no pressure to drink, no pressure to overspend. For many clients and for myself, I like to recommend attendance at a meeting before or after a Christmas church service, or at least within one day of it. It is a wonderful "bow" to put on anyone's Christmas package.

NEW YEAR'S EVE

You may think that you can handle all the New Year's Eve late hours, but you're wrong. Your energy level is still not what it might have been when you were pumping all that alcohol into your system, and you can get tired more easily than you think. So pick your party carefully. Use all the other party tools you have learned, but remember this one particularly: make sure you have your own way to get home from that New Year's Eve party.

As people drink, remember, their Hostility Meters run higher and higher. You need to protect your means of retreat from whatever pressure situation may be building up. Your New Year's Eve companion, for instance, might overdrink on this occasion when he or she might not at other affairs. The pressure to overdrink is there for everyone, you see.

An additional element you need to be aware of is the seemingly written-in-concrete concept that you must stay at a New Year's Eve party until the stroke of midnight. Well, that's okay for people who have put a lot of alcohol away for several hours, but it's damn tough on you. If the whole thrust of the party is to make sure you are there to ring in the New Year, then I suggest you arrive at the party at around 10:30. That takes a lot of heat off of you to stay for hours and watch other folks hit the booze. (You can get a lot more visits to a lot of different gatherings in if you invoke the forty-five minute rule and make the last party the favorite one where you want to be when it is time to salute the New Year.)

When the stroke of midnight arrives you will meet another enemy of your sobriety, and that's the pressure to kiss everyone and their brother. When you were drinking, your inhibitions were well-blocked. You may very well have been the leader in this form of merrymaking. Now that you're sober, it may be difficult or even embarrassing and awkward for you to exchange kisses with close friends, not to mention strangers. Your discomfort may be overwhelming.

If you've come to the party with someone special, explain this little pressure to him or her and ask that you not be pushed into it. If you have come alone, you can give a quick smooch on the cheek to your host or hostess and split the scene. Or you can always just extend your hand before you are forced into this pressure kiss. (Don't laugh—I've seen a couple of people break into tears over just thinking about this terror that was very real for them. Fortunately, they worked through it with the aid of friends.)

Again, if you are with sober people to start with, your own comfort level is going to be so much higher. Warm Fuzzies in the form of New Year's kisses will be okay, because you know that everyone—including yourself—is in total control.

Visit an AA meeting. Visit a hospital ward. Both will remind you that you are ending a year that may have been spent partially in recovery and partially in the sickness of alcoholism. In any case, you will know for certain that this New Year will be one of joy, hope, and well-being as you continue your program of sobriety. (If you have had your sobriety for the whole year, then you already know the real meaning of "Happy New Year.")

THANKSGIVING

Here's the one holiday in the year that is so family-oriented that it's almost considered a crime against Norman Rockwell's view of American life not to have at least fourteen people gathered for dinner. If this has been one of the great chores in your past (preparing for and hosting all those folks at your house), then you know what a temptation it was to have a little nip or two while you were preparing the dinner. Well, you can't do that now. Maybe you ought to look at some alternatives to that kind of pressure.

What's wrong with asking for a little help from other family members, if possible? How about a more buffet-style repast instead of a big sit-down-at-one-table bash? These two points are well taken for sobriety. Asking for help, even if it hasn't been done before, spreads out the pressure among a few, instead of leaving it all to you. Remember that almost all of your dear ones are inclined to give you more credit for your strength in recovery than you actually have. Big tasks take a lot out of you, tasks that often led you to drink just to get through them. I'll never forget hearing Phyllis Diller convulse her Palmer House audience by saying the only way she ever got her ironing done was to "put gin in the steam iron and invite all the neighbors!" Share the pressure.

Call up your honesty forces and share with your sister, brother, or other relative that you need help to feed the whole gang. Remind them that there have to be new ground rules for celebrating such things as big family get-togethers. Don't shirk the task if your turn has come up in the rotation cycle among your family, but don't be shy about asking for help. No one is going to think you are just passing the buck. Your honesty about how doing these things increases your anxiety level will help them understand.

Admitting to yourself that putting on a big family dinner or reunion is an emotional pressure cooker will help you keep a firmer grip on your sobriety. There isn't anyone who would expect such an effort from you if your arm was broken and in a cast. There is no shame in reminding them that you are still recovering from a disease (even if it's been several months), and you need understanding and help.

Why try a buffet-style dinner? Because you need the freedom not to be confined to one spot at the table answering questions and getting more and more anxious. This is particularly important if your sobriety is fairly new. If you are at a buffet dinner, everyone kind of picks who they want to sit by or with. As the host or hostess you can be free to move around a little more and discharge what I call "anxiety adrenalin." When the initial panic strikes you and you think that having a drink is the only way you might get through a big sit-down dinner, then you change the game plan. Don't have the big sit-down—go buffet. So what if it's Thanksgiving? The purpose of the holiday in the first place is to take time for expressions of gratitude for life's blessings. Chief among these is your sobriety and continued recovery.

The whole family can gather, holding hands in a circle if you like, and offer a word of thanks. Then you can have the buffet-style dinner. You are much freer to spread yourself among all your family and friends. Plus, you can relieve the pressure and anxiety about not drinking as it comes upon you instead of letting it build up. That's important. Many times I have urged newly recovering people not to let anxiety build up, but to deal with it right then. The buffet dinner is a way you can deal with it effectively. How do I know? Because I did it, and it worked like a charm.

HALLOWEEN

A client told his therapy group that he had always loved Halloween because he could go trick-or-treating with his kids. He took them around the various blocks in their neighborhood, carrying a scotch glass. Every few doors or so, he would holler "Trick or treat" with his kids. They got the candy, and he got his scotch glass refilled. No wonder he loved that holiday.

But now, in sobriety, you must deal with the pressures of this harmless little holiday, and those pressures are the kids themselves. You no longer have alcohol to insulate you from the doorbell-ringing, or their hounding you to get started on their rounds the minute you get home from work. You may not have realized how irritable you become when you can't have some booze to get you over these little annoyances.

When a group therapy session kicked this around, a really positive idea or two developed that I now gladly pass on to you. You are going to exhaust your energy level much more quickly in the early days of your sobriety, making it harder for you to cope with little irritations, not to mention big ones. Use the family car to take the kids, and if both you and your spouse can go together, then you can trade off every block or so. She stays curbside for a few houses and you walk your kids on their trick-or-treating adventures. Then change places—you stay in the car and let your spouse handle the supervisory chores. This trade-off procedure keeps you from getting absolutely crazy trying to cope with this kid's adventure. I know it's a lot of work getting in and out of the car, and it may seem like you're creating a lot of extra bother, but you'll find the whole experience will be more rewarding for both parents and children.

Here's another idea. Get a camera—a Polaroid or Kodak Instant is ideal. As kids come to your door, take a minute and invite them in. That's the fun of Halloween—to see how creative they've been with their costuming. Take their pictures and begin to enjoy this event instead of considering it something you have to do to keep your windows from getting soaped. When you take the time to let the kids show off their costumes, you also encourage them not to treat the night as just a grab the candy-and-run game.

What adds strength to your sobriety around this little holiday is that you are able to enjoy it. Taking a few pictures also helps remind you that you are in control of yourself again. It's a positive reminder of sobriety that you're able to do a simple thing like take a few pictures—I've had many people say this was something they always messed up when they were drinking. They wanted to take pictures of their own kids in their costumes, but were rarely able to do so because their drinking interfered with even the simple operation of a camera. Now that you're sober you can reward yourself by doing this Halloween bit with the camera and being able to say, "Hey, look at this one. Pretty good, eh?"

If you're alone and have no children of your own, you may dread this night as a real bother. Don't avoid the night, however, by shutting off the lights and pretending you're not at home. Let the little buggers in and let their pure joy rub off on you. It will help keep you off the Pity Pot, even if the nerve ends get a little frayed. Getting them to stay just long enough for you to snap a picture will help remind you that you are not alone, though you may have thought you were. If there is one underlying joy to being sober, it is the one that builds on your need to share your own happiness with others. Taking an extra minute or two with the neighbor kids before giving them their treats will make you feel better about rejoining the human race.

MEMORIAL DAY

It used to be called Decoration Day for a reason. I can recall this as being the day when a visit to the cemetery was a dreaded must to decorate some loved one's grave. You probably went through the same thing. In recovery, however, death has been temporarily put on hold in your own life. Your decision to get alcohol out of your life means that you are not going to drink yourself to death.

Visiting the grave site of another person is still traumatic. You may think that you can't handle it. If you can't, say so. Don't let the unspoken pressures turn into real pressures that might jeopardize your sobriety.

One of the ways you can handle Memorial Day obligations is to do the grave-tending on the very first day of the holiday weekend instead of on the last. Since it is now a three-day affair, this means you go to the cemetery the first thing on Saturday, or even better, on Friday evening, before the start of the weekend.

This promises to put any trauma around the occasion at the front end of the holiday, so you can make the days following ones of joy instead of sadness. You want to return to work in a good frame of mind, not one that shows stress and strain from having waited until the last minute to visit the grave, or whatever place you pay homage to the departed.

When I had to bury my mother in a far-away state, my wife and I planted a new tree in her honor in our front yard. We did the same in memory of a favorite aunt. Now, for us, Memorial Day does not have to be a pressure-building scene. We can enjoy the memories of our loved ones every time we go out our front door. We named the two trees in honor of our dead relatives, and we can and do tend them much more frequently than one day of the year.

I started giving small trees away to other friends who lost loved ones in lieu of funeral flowers. The response from them is always so positive, but another joy in it is what it does for my sobriety. It keeps a healthy picture before me, and a reminder that to drink is to die. To be always sober is to enjoy the living and the growing things of life.

Coping with Memorial Day grief and sadness in the ways I've suggested may seem a little selfish to you until you give it a try. You'll find your own comfort level rising with every year's practice of these methods of dealing with Memorial Day memories.

FOURTH OF JULY

Beer busts and company picnics are the big gremlins on this holiday. Once again, the rule for you is to make all things meaningful. You should volunteer to be a part of the company picnic. Be one of the barbecue cooks or tend the watermelon table. If you love sports, make sure you participate. Play softball or volleyball, even if you're lousy (like I am). It's the joy of being able to do things you couldn't do before that helps make the coping easier on this holiday. You can laugh and play just as hard without the beer.

If you are worried there will be no soft drinks, then bring your own cooler and plenty of pop. You'll be a big hit just for making an alternative drink besides beer available; others will welcome the chance not to have to bow to the social pressure at a kegger. Advertising your sobriety by bringing your cooler of pop or jug of sun tea is a great way to meet other nondrinkers at big company parties and

Fourth of July barbecues. Just stand around your own cooler and see who flocks over with a "thank goodness you brought something to drink besides beer" attitude.

When you participate in sports and games, you prove to yourself and others that this is a new you—one who may not be the greatest athlete, but who has turned his life around. That makes you a winner.

Again, it will serve you well to plan your appearance well within the time limits of your energy. Three hours for one of these picnics is probably the top end of that energy scale. If you are getting tired, that means you may also be starting to build some anxieties. Pack up and leave. It's okay.

LABOR DAY

Since this is the last big holiday of the summer, there is always pressure to make the weekend a long and enduring one. That's not okay for the newly sober. You will have a tendency to burn out very quickly if you have to cope with over-crowded beaches, mountain highways, or seaside resorts full of people trying to cram the best of all the summer into one three-day affair.

I find that Labor Day is a good time to adjust to the fact that summer is winding down. But here's where you can be one up—why accept that all the pretty weekends and all the bright times are suddenly to be put in mothballs just because the calendar says so? For the newly recovering person, you are probably better off foregoing a long weekend that will put you in heavy return-home traffic, or a trip to a place where some services have already begun to close because the tourist dollars are also heading home. This is pretty depressing stuff. Avoid being depressed.

Instead, don't think of Labor Day as the end of anything. Stay home that particular weekend. Pick the weekends right after to begin to wind down summer activities. This is the best time to go to some of the places off the beaten path, places that are open to serve you all year instead of only during the tourist season. By extending the time when you change over from a more lazy mode to a more frantic pace, you give yourself time to adjust.

It has been my experience that changing anything rapidly is a mistake for your overall recovery. Think of how nice and joyful it will be for you to take a series of little summer "closer trips" instead of one gigantic (and sometimes depressing) three-day goodbye-to-summer foray.

When you were drinking, you did everything to excess. You don't have to do that now. There is no need to abruptly force yourself to wind down from the sunny days of summer. Don't try to wage a battle against the swimming pools

Holidays and How to Cope with Them 167

closing on the Labor Day weekend. After all, what happens? Does the water suddenly become less appealing the day after? Of course not. It's a matter of not having the personnel available to keep the places open. So, I suggest taking your last day or weekend at the pool before the Labor Day weekend. Choose any wonderful time to just lie there, get good and hot, and soak up all the sun you can handle. Then you won't have any end-of-season blues.

You see, you need to feel free to change the ways that you've been doing things, things that have put emotional pressures on you. Again, don't worry about what other people think. You're the one in recovery, and it's your comfort and coping levels that have to be kept high, no matter what anyone else's opinion might be.

EASTER

Overbuying and "New Wardrobe Wantitis" are the pressures that seem to come into play for this holiday, much like the splurges of Christmas. For the recovering person, traditions sometimes have to give way to better judgement. That's a hard pill to swallow, but swallow it you must. In the past, you drank to abandon and spent money the same way. You've changed one, and now it's time to change the other.

One way you can cope with new clothes pressure is to start to buy whatever it is you need for your Easter finery well in advance of Easter. Pick up several small, inexpensive Easter cards or candy bunnies as soon as they appear on the grocery shelves. With each item you buy, attach a card or small bunny to the box to support the fact that you have bought it for Easter. This practice will be less painful on your pocketbook, and will give you some instant reward-identification. Or, keep a picture of the suit of clothes you want in a prominent place. Each ten-dollar payment you put away for the suit earns an Easter card pinned beneath the picture of the clothes. By the time the holiday arrives, you will have paid for the suit and have secured a variety of Easter cards to send to relatives and friends.

There is a joy to Easter you may have forgotten. Get back to dyeing a dozen eggs. If you don't have any children to give them to, children in your local hospital will love having a basket of Easter eggs to help them enjoy a holiday they are spending confined to bed.

With each little gift like that you can pass on the message of what it means to you to be getting healthier each day of your sobriety. My only problem with egg dyeing is that for me, one dozen is never enough.

YOUR BIRTHDAY

The "birthday" celebration that should mean the most to you from here on out is the celebration of the years that you have remained free from alcohol. Your natal birthday pales in comparison to those your family and your AA friends will share as being the most important.

When you put this amount of significance on your sobriety, it doesn't really matter what the chronological years say. Your real joy is to know that your first, fifth, fifteenth, or thirtieth birthday of sobriety has brought you more of a gift than could ever have been dreamed up by the most fabulous store.

So it becomes easy for you to gather family and friends for a celebration of your twenty-first, twenty-ninth, thirty-ninth, or (God forbid) forty-ninth birthday. Your real birthday (you proudly claim) is the number of years, or even weeks or months that you have had your sobriety.

How many times I have sat in a meeting and listened to a person proudly announce, "I'm celebrating my birthday today. I've been sober thirty days." I last heard that message from a woman who was fifty-eight years old. Her age didn't matter to her, not one bit. Her real birthday had been just one month ago when she began her sobriety. That's the joy of being able to celebrate your birthday, but in a different and more meaningful way than you ever have before. If you share this feeling of joy with your loved ones, with your friends, coworkers, or whomever your life touches, then those old-fashioned regular birthdays will be a bore.

Plan your party around this important fact of your new life and the celebration marking the day you were born will be a breeze. You will be able to cope with being whatever age you are, because you are always going to be younger in the years of your sobriety and recovery.

YOUR KIDS' BIRTHDAYS

This is the last of the so-called troublesome holidays that I think you need to be concerned about. As your children celebrate each new birthday, you may be inclined to feel very much alone. This is particularly true if you have not resolved much of the guilt about all the times you spent drinking instead of sharing time with your children.

You may be afraid they will grow up and leave you, turning their backs on the protection of your house and your arms. What will you do when they are gone? This "Empty Nest Syndrome" is a very real cause of depression. Left unattended, it can cause you serious problems. What you don't want to happen is to have this syndrome rock your boat of sobriety.

Everyone has his special way to deal with kids growing up and moving out. A way for you to help yourself through the feeling that "they're getting older, and soon they'll be gone" is to reverse the feeling from dejection to gladness that they will soon be out of the nest.

The gladness comes from knowing that in your sobriety you will be free to do and to be what you could never be in a state of alcoholic confusion. You can and will be a better parent, in-law, grandparent, traveling companion. You can mark your children's birthday celebrations as days of happiness that your freedom from alcohol will enable your children to live their own lives free from the worry that you are going to drink yourself to death. That's one hell of a present for you to give, and it's a great cause for celebrating your kids' birthdays with sheer pleasure instead of sinking into depression. Your sadness at their growing older becomes gladness that you are witnessing another year of their lives while you have your sobriety.

Let the guilt die. Bury it and commit it to the soil. It will not take back one minute of any shouting, harassment, or general bad parenting that you did when you were actively alcoholic. Go on to the future with your children and   celebrate their birthdays confident that you will see better years ahead for both them and you.

GATHERING RELIGIOUS STRENGTH FROM THE HOLIDAYS

What I have been talking about in this chapter has had to do with learning to deal with the social pressures of various holidays. But the recovering person must also press hard to appreciate the religious experience of a Christmas, a Passover, or a Thanksgiving. The search for the God of your understanding will be even more fruitful as you let the spiritual meanings of each of your holidays take priority over the commercial aspects.

For many, there was never any significance to Easter or to Passover. Maybe now, in the freshness of your sobriety, in the dawn of an era of understanding about yourself and the disease that has controlled your life, you will be free to explore the further joys of being sober on a special holiday. Those joys are in knowing that you have the ability to put spiritual meaning into your life. Pick up the tools as you come across them in your daily life of sobriety. You just may surprise yourself by finding they have been there all along.

MORE JOY (An Update)

As I was rereading this chapter I couldn't help but think how much things—

little things—have changed over the years since I first wrote this book. When I suggested getting a Polaroid or some Kodak Instant camera for those Halloween pictures, those were pretty much all that were available.

But now it's "grab the camcorder" and "where's the disposable?" that you might hear echoing in your home. Who would have thought you could just go to your supermarket, pick up a disposable 35mm camera at the last minute, do your thing with it, and then have the pictures developed while you wait? Well, these changes in technology only make the real fun of holidays even better for you to enjoy in a state of sobriety.

Cyn goes to her birthplace of Lubbock, Texas for part of the Christmas holiday every year, so we prepare a videotape for her to take as we decorate our home for Christmas and prepare for our annual Christmas party. The folks in Texas get a kick out of our little tape tour each year. We enjoy doing it, as it adds to our own appreciation of a sane and sober holiday.

As a society, we have added some holidays to our national calendar in the last few years. Martin Luther King's birthday is now celebrated in most of the country. It is not uncommon for larger companies to grant an employee's birthday as a paid holiday, so that person can have the day off even though the rest of us may have to work. I don't believe either of these events is cause to worry about a threat to sobriety. Nevertheless, you still have to be concerned when you may find yourself with too much free time, especially if you are new in recovery. Make sure that you have something planned for your celebrations, no matter what they are. (It doesn't make a lot of sense for you to work yourself into a mental snit about not having big plans for some holiday, either. Just take a look at every holiday situation for what it is, with special regard to being with people for the biggie holidays like Christmas and Thanksgiving.)

Some friends of ours make it a point to hold an "orphan's" Thanksgiving dinner. That's a dinner for adult friends who for one reason or another can't make it to their homes for the holiday. This is a really nice idea, one my daughter Tracey has carried out with great success for many years. If you are a recovering person, it would be really great for you to look around for other recovering people with whom you could get together for these major holidays. Your favorite AA meetings will always be a good source for folks like that.

One year in my early recovery, I invited three people with whom I had been hospitalized home for dinner. It was relaxing. It was supportive. It was what Thanksgiving was all about.

All nature is but art, unknown to thee; all chance, direction which thou cannot see.

Alexander Pope

THE JOY OF RISK-TAKING

Take a chance! When we were children, how often were we taunted by friends to do just that? As we grew up, the chances we were willing to take grew less risky, as priorities for how we wanted to live grew in importance. Dreams of the extra-fast sports car when you were in your twenties gave way to the desire for more sedate models as you took on family responsibilities.

A friend of mine always talked about how badly he wanted a motorcycle. When he finally could afford the one he wanted, he discovered that the desire to have a high-powered machine had been replaced by more "mature judgment," as he put it. "Why," he told me, "should I take a chance on breaking my fool neck at this age?"

However, when it comes to sobriety and the disclosure that you are recovering from a disease, risk-taking is quite another matter. For you, it is a matter of wanting to get that all-important comfort level operating at peak efficiency. It isn't easy to stand up and say, "I'm an alcoholic." On the other hand, as we have discussed in earlier chapters, it is essential to the solid base of your recovery that you are able to say just those words. It is an admission that you are, as AA teaches, "powerless over alcohol," and isn't that okay? Sure it is—you should also feel powerless over the effects of an atomic bomb, or over when the sun will shine. It's okay to admit being an alcoholic, to say to those you care to inform that your system is not capable of handling this drinking business. There is a joy in taking the risk of calling your disease what it is, instead of trying to hide or deny it, which is what you did while you were drinking.

That's what being in recovery does for you—it enables you to look at past behaviors and freely choose to do something different.

"But if recovery and sobriety aren't automatically going to make significant changes in my life," you might ask, "what good are they?" The answer is that they are absolutely necessary if you want to make things different for yourself. Get all you can out of them.

If you keep the joys of your life a big secret, what fun is there in having them? Would you be really happy to have saved and saved and finally found a way to purchase a diamond necklace you had always wanted, and then never wear it? You might be terrified of it getting ripped off your neck by a mugger, but you sure wouldn't want to just have it locked up somewhere with no opportunity to show it off.

I've never met anyone who drove a new car home from the dealership and then put it on wheel blocks in the garage. Collectors don't even do that for very long. Your sobriety is the same way. It needs to be shared, and by sharing you are nurturing the seedling that has taken hold in your brain, the very hard realization that you can't and won't drink alcohol again and live.

With whom are you going to take the risk? What are the benefits and the pitfalls? Here are the basic groups of people who form the core of support in recovery, as I see it. Your particular situation may be different, but it's pretty certain that your supporters will fit at least two of these categories:

1. The Significant Other in your life
2. Your employer
3. Members of your family
4. Your banker
5. Your spiritual advisor

I have purposely not included AA members because it is understood that in the fellowship you will be among friends whose priority in their lives of recovery is to admit, freely and with joy, "I am an alcoholic." So let's look at the other categories of people with whom you can find joy in risk-taking.

THE SIGNIFICANT OTHER

This is probably someone other than a spouse who, we assume, is very much aware of your recovery. The person I'm primarily concerned with here is the special girlfriend or boyfriend, the roommate, the person with whom you have been keeping company, and your relationship looks like it could be the start of something big.

The Significant Other is that person who is most in contact with you on a social, personal basis. That person is someone in your life whose own wellness can depend on your wellness.

Your Significant Other's life will be greatly affected by disclosure of your disease of alcoholism. So you are in a dilemma, or at least you think you are. There really is no choice, for your relationship with this person hinges on honesty. There is no more honest disclosure you can make than that of your recovery process.

A young man who was a client of mine had wrestled for some time with the problem of whether to tell his lady friend about his alcoholism. He was feeling pressure to take her to various places where liquor was a mainstay: bars, dances, and private parties. As he began to feel more and more anxiety about his disclosure, he felt like he was "between a rock and a hard place." His lady friend was a social drinker. They had been dating more and more frequently, and the newly sober client was in a quandary. Then he took the risk of telling her about his alcoholism and about his recovery process. Suddenly the romance was over. The woman dropped him because "she didn't want to change her lifestyle."

Where was the joy for him in taking this risk? At first there just plain wasn't any. He was disheartened and a little angry that I had urged his risk-taking when he thought he might have gone on with the charade a while longer. It was only a few days later, though, that this young man shared with me that his disclosure was the best thing that could have happened to him. He was feeling very free of guilt for the first time in a long time, and was actually glad that he had taken the risk. "What makes you glad about this?" I asked him in a session. "I know now that I can be honest with myself, and that's the whole ball game for me," he replied.

His risk-taking cost him a very special girlfriend who was unable or unwilling to be involved with someone who could not and would not continue to make drinking the important event that it was to her. Your own Significant Other may only be aware that you *have had* a drinking problem. That's not good enough, because it intimates that it is possible to clear up such a problem permanently. The problem drinker and the alcoholic are not very far apart as it is; if you have made the realization that you were and are powerless over alcohol and that you are an alcoholic, you know that your problem will be with you for the rest of your life.

In the words of Sir Walter Scott, "Oh what a tangled web we weave,/When first we practice to deceive!" And it's true. The more you try to fool or put off your Significant Other, the deeper you will get into a morass of anxiety and guilt. It will be very hard to extricate either yourself or the relationship from that morass. So 'fess up. You will probably do no more than confirm suspicions that the Significant Other has already had but was unable to approach you about.

Once you have taken the risk and determined that your Significant Other is sticking with you, your next shared joy is to involve that person in your recovery. Take him or her to group therapy if you are in a treatment program and such a group is available. Take him or her to an open AA meeting and let them see for themselves that AA is more than whatever stories they may have heard. By taking the risk of disclosure with your Significant Other, you are able to share the real joy of that risk-taking. You can plan activities together that you might not have in the past. You can breathe a lot easier after learning the true feelings of your special person and how he or she is willing to be a part of your recovery team.

You may indeed suffer some temporary setback by risk-taking with a Significant Other. On the one hand, you may lose the relationship. On the other, you may learn that the relationship will grow even stronger through your trust, your sharing, your risk-taking. Again, I urge you to go for the gold on this one.

YOUR EMPLOYER

Federal law prohibits any employer from discharging you because you have the disease of alcoholism. They can fire you for being drunk on the job; they can fire you for other reasons, like not showing up for work, being constantly tardy, embezzlement, etc. But just being an alcoholic is a no-no in the firing department. What's to keep you, then, from sitting down with your employer, supervisor, or department head and telling him or her about your disease?

Fear, that's what. The fear that if anyone at work knows about me, I'll lose my job. Well, we hear that a lot from people who have made the choice to enter treatment.

What you need to understand and be comfortable with is that your employer, nine out of ten times, will be one of the most supportive people on your team.

Why? Because if you are a good employee you are valuable, that's why. It has been estimated that it can cost as much as five thousand dollars to replace just an average production line employee. Companies may threaten to fire the employee who refuses to get help for his or her alcoholism, but that's a different matter. Your employer would far rather share the cost of your recovery in treatment than incur the cost of firing and replacing you. That's why so many corporations are using the employee assistance program concept to help their people identify and do something about their drinking problem.

Your employer wants less tardiness, less absenteeism, fewer sick days, and improved productivity out of you. If his knowledge of your alcoholism and your treatment and recovery can help him have all those things, why wouldn't he want to know? Firestone Tire and Rubber reports saving about two million bucks a year through its employee assistance program, where about half the caseload is alcohol-related.

No one at work is going to know about you unless you tell them. Insurance companies and other third party payers are not going to disclose that they have been helping pay for your treatment. Your counselor or therapist isn't going to tell anyone, because federal law protects your confidentiality. Unless you sign a specific release of information form, nobody can learn of your treatment for your disease. You will have an ally in your corner in this battle if you confide in your immediate boss. If your company is one with clearly established lines of authority, then you will know the person in whom you should confide.

I know of many instances (I see them daily) where the company EAP person is the only one that knows or has to know. He or she reports to the big boss that So-and-so has a problem and has been referred for treatment. And as long as So-and-so is doing his or her job and keeping the recovery program strong, that's the end of it.

So there you are, applying for an important new position with a new company, and the application form asks, "Have you ever been treated for alcoholism?" Do you lie? No. An unqualified no! If you want to live the rest of your life as one big lie then go ahead, but you will be the loser. Answer the question honestly, and then attach an explanatory letter of the details of your treatment program and the success of your sobriety. Ask for a personal, additional interview to elaborate on this point. You'll get your chance to be open and honest with this company right from the start. You may be surprised at the number of administrators who will disclose to you their own battles with the bottle; they will take the same risk with you as part of their program of recovery.

Employers want good people working for them. Your risk-taking in sharing the exact nature of your disease can only work for you in job security, advancement, and performance rewards. If you fail to get a job and you think that you have been discriminated against because of your disclosure of alcoholism, then report that company. If you had another, more "acceptable" disease, you wouldn't be turned down unless it was clear that having the job might prove risky to you and the company. Don't be bamboozled about the issue of your alcoholism. The American Medical Association recognized it as a disease in 1956, and you're entitled to the benefits of that recognition.

MEMBERS OF YOUR FAMILY

I don't know why this usually seems to be such a big problem. So many recovering people will say, "My wife knows, but my folks mustn't ever find out." That's downright ridiculous. You need the support and strength of those who have loved and cared about you no matter what, and to deprive them of the joy of your being sober is just not right. If you counted on members of your family to bail you out of difficulties caused by your drinking—and you probably did—then why in God's name wouldn't you want them to know of your recovery?

If you have been afraid to take this particular risk because of the fear that family members will disown you, or because there hasn't been any such alcoholism in your family before, you may safely dismiss that fear. Logic should tell you that any family member who stood up for you in your alcohol-imbibing times will be only too glad to stand up with you in your sober, joyful days. They won't have to worry about you anymore.

As for the other point about family alcoholism, you may be doing a great disservice to those you love by *failing* to disclose your disease. There might be a brother or sister who is going through what you went through, who lives in another state or town and would welcome getting their own support around the problem. If you take the risk, maybe they will come forward and seek the help they so badly need. Trying not to rattle any family skeletons is absurd. I subscribe to the genetic theory of alcoholism, which tells us there is a genetic tendency for the disease to be passed from generation to generation.

In the majority of cases the alcoholic in treatment will have at least one family member who also has the problem. Some are just stubborn to admit it, that's all.

Once, during a question and answer session after one of my lectures to hospital inpatients, I made the same point I've just told you. A lady patient blurted, " No, sir, you're wrong." I pressed her, "What do you mean, I'm wrong?"

"I'm from a strong farm family, and we didn't have any alcoholics in our family." She was pretty righteous now, and I could tell she was fast winning some converts from the other patients. So we began talking about what life was like for her on her family farm. She told of hard work and little recreation, except for big family dinners on Sundays, when other relatives from neighboring farms would join her family. Suddenly, she turned almost white, and let out a cry of amazement. "What is it?" I asked. "My God," she wailed, "I almost forgot. Every now and then we had to take Uncle Ed's head out of the mashed potatoes." Well, the whole room broke up with laughter. This poor woman had forgotten about someone in her family tree who obviously had an alcohol problem. As it turned out, she had filed the incident away for a very good reason.

When I asked her why she never considered Uncle Ed to be an alcoholic if his behavior at the dinner table was as she described, she replied (with some dignity I thought), "Because my mother didn't allow any alcoholics in the family." In long-term therapy, this woman, now well on the road to recovery, discovered several other family members who weren't "allowed" to be alcoholics, but have been clearly identified as such.

Share with those who make up your family, close or not. The risk you are taking will be minimal compared to the joy you will bring to an aunt, a sister, or a cousin who has, perhaps for longer than you know, been praying for a miracle to come into your life. Sharing the joy of your being sober today can help answer those prayers.

YOUR BANKER

This is repeat business from Chapter Six, but we need to bring it up again until it is a decision that you make in comfort. After all, what is the worst that can happen if your banker knows of your alcoholism? He can turn you down for a loan. Well, that's not all that bad. You may simply have to shop around until you find someone else, perhaps an AA member who doesn't have a prejudice against you because of alcoholism. Or, you might find a way to do without the loan.

But no matter what, your strength in financial recovery will be tenfold if you take the risk of disclosure. This doesn't mean that every teller in the place needs to know. It means you ask for an appointment with your own banker, the loan officer or personal banker who handles most of your special needs. You are confiding a trust to him or her that is very important to you, and he or she will not betray that trust. That person will respect your risk-taking. Your particular request may still be refused, but you will at least know that it had nothing to do with your alcoholism. How will you know? Because you'll ask, that's how. You come right out and make certain that you are being treated solely on the basis of whether you meet the qualifications of the bank, not whether your past affliction has colored the bank's judgement. By taking this risk you will add another strong block to your sobriety foundation, a block that says, "I can be judged on how I am now, and not on how my behavior was."

Your banker doesn't just control your money. With him or her on your side you will have a staunch ally in many things that affect you and your standing in the community. In fact, your banker may be beside you in many situations that you never even know of at the time they happen, but will come to light in later years.

If you take the risk of disclosure with your banker, you will have increased your own personal worth far more than you may think. A banker looks at many elements of a balance sheet, not just the figures. The particular thing you may be denied by your bank today may be possible tomorrow, and your honesty in disclosing your disease and in sharing the joy of your present sobriety will pay handsome dividends.

YOUR SPIRITUAL ADVISOR

If your priest, pastor, rabbi, or other spiritual advisor has been with you through the tough times of your drinking, then he or she already knows of your alcoholism. But supposing this is a new church or a new congregation? Suppose you are anxious to involve yourself as part of your recovery (Chapter Ten) but are unwilling to take the risk of sharing the fact of your disease? Are you uncomfortable as to how to do it?

Rest easy, and invite the person to lunch. I love having lunch with my pastors whenever their schedules and mine permit. It's very open, low key, and full of joy, laughter, and warmth. It's at lunch that such a disclosure can be made quite easily. When the cocktail person approaches your table for your order, you can ask your companion to make a choice. When it's your turn, and you decline or choose something nonalcoholic, you have a natural opening to disclose in the most comfortable way you can.

When my pastor and I had lunch at a favorite restaurant of mine at Christmas time, we were presented with a bottle of champagne with the compliments of the management for my "good customer" status with the place. Pastor Del and I had a warm laugh over that for many months. Our Christmas lunches are a tradition for just the two of us. It was at such a lunch that I made my own disclosure, not knowing that my alcoholism had been common knowledge to everyone but me.

Your spiritual advisor shares a very special place in your life, for he represents a tie to your life from the past, to the present, and into the future. Even if he is a new person in your life and you are new in his congregation, the quiet luncheon with the opportunity to lay your cards squarely on the table will bring you an element of rare peace and joy.

Many ministers and priests suffer the same affliction. Many more deal with it on a daily basis, and their ease with the subject can very well be the turning point in your life for becoming comfortable with the risk of disclosure. Remember that any time you make a disclosure, it should be to strengthen your sobriety, and your spiritual advisor is part of your total recovery plan. This makes him considerably different from just being your confessor; your spiritual advisor lends help in the ways you ask to keep your recovery strong. When he cannot help, he reverts to being your friend, and as such, a person who is willing to listen.

The joy of risk-taking is as much a joy as any of the others that we've talked about. It is a way that the boogeyman can be brought out of your closet, and you can unload the years or months of guilt you experienced around your past alcoholic life. When you take a risk you also cast a long line out into the world in which you live, love, work, play. The mere opportunity for you to help someone else who has been hiding in darkness about their problem makes the risk-taking worthwhile.

As a member of the fellowship of Alcoholics Anonymous you can do just that, remain totally anonymous; that's the protection it affords twenty-four hours a day, and no one will quarrel with your decision.

But if the spirit of adventure is in your soul, if your heart likes the feeling of lightness and guilt-free tranquility that your sobriety can bring, then you may want to do a little more risk-taking, and you have the freedom to do that, too. The joy will be in how you handle it, in how you learn that the ways of taking risks in sobriety are endless. You may lose a few rolls of the dice, but the odds are that you will come up a winner more often than you ever thought possible.

MORE JOY (An Update)

I don't know that there is much to update here. The longer I have my sobriety, the easier it is for me to disclose it to others, and of course, the more I am known, the less need there is to disclose. Therefore, not much risk-taking is involved for me anymore. However, I still believe that the wider and stronger you can make your base of support, the better your chances are of avoiding relapse.

Each time you take the risk of telling someone new that you are recovering, the bigger your army of supporters will grow. I still have clients who do so much back-pedaling around the issue of their alcoholism that I wonder where they get the energy. For all the time they spend trying out different angles to avoid the issue of being in recovery or avoid admitting their problem, they could add days of joyful sobriety to their lives.

There is an incident engraved on my mind, and I hope it will add to your sense of how much trouble it is just to avoid the good news of recovery. Many years ago, a client of mine entered group one night and began to hand out copies of a *Newsweek* magazine article by a person who wanted America to give up the nomenclature of "alcoholism" and "alcoholics" for "Jellinek's Disease." This thoughtful piece suggested that it would be so much easier for someone, anyone, to share that they had Jellinek's Disease instead of alcoholism. Not only would this honor a man who had done much for the treatment of alcoholism, but it would be (the writer proposed) a better way to help people live with their "problem." Well, my client finally was told in no uncertain terms by other members of the group that eventually someone would ask "What's Jellinek's Disease, anyway?" and the person would be stuck right where she was before—disclosing she's a recovering alcoholic.

All the effort to gloss over a subject and to make things appear to be what they are not belongs in the field of stage magic as far as I'm concerned. It is a privilege to share with others who mean something to you the new direction your life is taking and the high esteem that you have for them. Let them be a part of your recovery.

As I said in the original work, you certainly never had any problem letting the entire world see that you were drinking, so what's the big deal about letting a few important people in your life know about your sobriety? I use the disclosure of being in recovery as a constant protector against my eating or drinking foods that might contain alcohol. For instance, as much as I like hot mustard, I don't use a certain brand that is made with white wine. It's not because I believe the mixture will make me break my sobriety, but rather that alcohol in any form is not a part of my life anymore, and hasn't been for a long time. Therefore, I advertise my sobriety when it will continue to protect me, and I acknowledge recovery to strengthen my resolve.

However, there is not a day that goes by when I am not keenly aware that, like all other alcoholics the planet over, I am just one drink away from the next drunk as long as I live. And you know what? It is that thought—perhaps more than any other—that really contributes to the secure knowledge that my sobriety is my number one priority in this glorious life.

(So maybe there *were* a few things to update, after all.)

Man therefore can, with a rigid surface and a properly designed apparatus, repeat the maneuvers of ascension and direction performed by the soaring birds...

Louis Mouillard, L'Empire de l'Air

17

FLYING WITHOUT DRINKING
(HOW TO LET THE BOOZE CART PASS YOU BY)

"No way! I gotta be six sheets to the wind just to get near the airport."

"It's just pure goddam agony for me to go anywhere on a plane. I'd never make a trip without drinking."

"If I have to fly, I drink. If I can't drink, I'm not flying."

Well, well. Is this you I am quoting? Are you the newly sober person who just dreads the idea of your first flight, knowing the booze cart will have to pass you by so you remain in recovery? Probably. It's more common than you may think, particularly when you may have been skittish about flying in the first place. That little miniature bottle or two set on the fold-down tray in front of you certainly helped the flight go smoother, didn't it? I mean, there is no question in your mind that the turbulence was easier because you were politely getting sloshed, is there? It's amazing how all that electronic gear and massive machinery works in direct proportion to the amount of vodka you run through your own engines.

What we'll attempt to do in this chapter is show you some ways you can actually feel okay about flying and let that booze cart sail right on down the aisle. I have collected some of the basic fears that seem to come up about flying, anxieties that spring from a lack of understanding about what's happening to you and the machine you're in. Together we'll create a checklist for flying without the need to drink before, during, or after the flight.

There is a basic premise here that needs to be your personal motto from now on: "There is absolutely no mechanical, electrical, or hydraulic linkup between my alcohol consumption and the operation of the aircraft." There won't be any scientific prize for developing this axiom in your own mind, but if you say it out loud enough you'll understand the value of realizing that whatever happens— including the majority of really smooth, wonderful flights you take—happens because of sources or circumstances beyond your control. Drinking in order to fly simply means that you have not come to grips with your life, not to mention the joy of getting on a jet, going somewhere, and really enjoying it.

So, let's look at the Basic Checklist for Flying. The entire flight crew goes through a checklist for every stage of your flight in preparation for all contingencies. They go through it step by step for every flight, no matter how many hours of experience they have logged. You can and should do the same thing. The checklist consists of:

1. Preflight preparation
2. Boarding procedures
3. Start-up and taxiing
4. Takeoff and "climb"
5. In flight
6. Descending
7. Landing
8. Leaving the aircraft

Obviously, this Basic Checklist is not nearly as complex as the manual the captain and crew have. (By the way, I spent a number of hours refamiliarizing myself with this manual, as used on a Boeing 727 aircraft in preparation for flight training. I would like to report that my cockpit simulation flights were as successful as those I have made as a passenger; I'd like to, but they were not. I have been able to pilot an airplane since I was a boy, spending all my lunch hours and job pay on flight lessons, but mastering some of the fine points of being a pilot has eluded me. My jet flight instructor, my helicopter instructor, and many other pilot friends of mine keep hoping for better performance from me than I can return.) While I may have had trouble working the pilot's checklist, however, the Basic Checklist for Flying is very workable. You just need occasions to practice it. Use it every time, and never vary from its basic principles except to add to it for your own enjoyment. Ready? Here we go.

PREFLIGHT PREPARATION

Virtually every airline wants you to arrive at the airport at least one hour before departure. Forget it. You don't need to sit around on some concourse watching a lot of other "happy" travelers make their steady (and sometimes unsteady) way into the many little cocktail bars that the airport provides. So you need some planning to prevent you from being tempted to break your sobriety, either because you're hanging around the airport too long or because you cut it so close that you almost miss your flight. I suggest that you try to arrive as close as possible to one half-hour before the aircraft is ready for boarding. If there is a delay and you are in the seat selection line when the row numbers are being called, rest assured they are not going to leave without you. (Seat selections can be made ahead of time with many airlines. The more you can do this, the better.) What is ideal is for you to arrive at the departure gate, spend no more than ten minutes there, and get on the aircraft.

But suppose it is impossible for you to use this technique. You may have to spend an hour or more at the airport before boarding an international flight. You certainly will have to if you are waiting for a connecting flight, although the popular hub-and-spoke system of air connections used by most major airlines seems to cut that between-plane waiting time considerably. If you do have to wait, you can incorporate any of the techniques for meeting people from other chapters, or you can read and listen to music. Now wait a minute—don't get panicky. You *can* meet people without going into the bar. There are hundreds of folks at airports who are flying and waiting to fly, and like you, are spending some hours in a concourse lounge.

You have part of your problem already whipped, because those you see waiting in someplace other than a bar are obviously going to do what you're going to do—fly without being tanked. If you are a newly sober single female, you can just sit there, and more people than you would like may try to start a conversation. You handle that any way that makes you comfortable. But let's say, for instance, that you really just want to read and/or listen to music.

About the music—airlines won't let you play those AM/FM personal portables while in the plane because they might interfere with the aircraft's own communications system. However, you can use them in the concourse lounge. Better are the personal cassette players that are so popular and are coming down in price every month. You can put in your favorite music for reducing anxiety about flying. Put those miniature earphones on and you're set. You can even take that kind of device into the plane with you and play it all during your flight if you wish.

Most of the larger airlines supply stereo headsets and programming right at your seat, but we'll talk about that later. For now, here you are in the concourse waiting area, listening to your music. You decide you want to read. Now, you've probably made a basic mistake. You've probably brought along at least two new books or articles that you have been meaning to get to. Your flight seems like the ideal time, but it isn't. Your anxiety level about flying without drinking may be pretty high at this point, and your level of concentration is practically nil. You won't do anything with a new book but start over and over and over about three hundred times between checking your watch, going to the bathroom, reshuffling your briefcase papers, or rummaging through your backpack, handbag, or carry-on luggage.

Nope. You want to read something that you're already into, something that you are so engrossed in that you can get right back into the story or narrative quickly. Save the new book or magazine to read in your hotel room, or while lounging around the pool. Your brain needs to be instantly occupied with something other than worry, nervousness, anxiety, or outright panic. Familiar characters, plots, and dialogue will help get you into a less frantic "head space" than trying to catalogue, sort, and digest new stuff. (The one exception is for work materials. If there is a new report to read before you attend the meeting you're flying to, then read it. Bear down on the concentration. You probably already carry a notepad or, like I do, a legal-size binder and pad. Use it. Make notes, even if they are lousy notes. The idea is to occupy your mind with the report, not what is about to happen when you have to get on that damn plane.)

The brain, you know, is a marvelous organ. It has trouble concentrating on more than one thing at a time. If you are engrossed, if you force yourself to concentrate on what you are reading or writing, you simply can't have space to worry about your flight. And in recovery, more so than at other times in your life, you can't do two things at once, at least not well.

So concentrate on the work or reading material before you. Don't pay attention to the activity of others around you in the lounge. Your personal music will help that, but if you don't have one of these gadgets, just concentrate harder on your reading. Read at least one full page before allowing yourself to glance around at lounge activity. Reassure yourself that everything seems to be okay, then go back to your reading (and/or making notes). This time, read at least five pages before looking up and around. Another five to ten minutes will have slipped by, depending on your reading speed.

As part of your preflight preparation, ease off on coffee and other high-caffeine drinks. Your state of agitation will be increased when you start pumping a lot of coffee into your bladder. Try to remember that caffeine fuels anxiety, especially when coupled with too much liquid that is making you have to leave your seat and go to the restroom every ten minutes.

Call anxiety what it is. Tell yourself, or your traveling companion, "I'm nervous about flying. I'm nervous about flying without drinking." The sharing of that information will help you in your preflight portion of the checklist. The mere verbalizing of your anxiety takes the major sting out of it. You can't be too scared of something you can talk about; remember that. You deal with your anxiety by letting it happen.

About ten minutes before you think boarding is to begin, close up your work or your reading. Shut off or put away your music. Get up and walk over to the nearest window where you can observe your aircraft in its final preparation stages. If this isn't possible, look at some other plane that is being readied. Look first into the cockpit. Most aircraft are parked "nose-in" to the jetway, and you can see the flight crew. They are going through their preflight checklist. Observe them being at ease. They may be laughing with one another or may, having finished part of their preflight list, just be looking back at you. Go ahead—wave. You've always wanted to do that, now haven't you? They'll wave right back if they're not busy and if they know you're waving at them. It's a good feeling for you to know those folks are just like you. They love life, too, and they're going to have a safe trip right along with you. How about that?

I'll bet that you, now sober, never thought about that; these folks in your flight crew are going with you on your trip. They want to get there and back every bit as much or more than you do, in safety, comfort, and with ease. So why would they want to do something to make you uncomfortable when the same thing would make *them* uncomfortable?

Look at the other activities that are taking place around your plane. Your food is being loaded, they're topping off the jet fuel, and the last carts of luggage are being brought to the aircraft. Can you spot any of your luggage from where you are? Concentrate on the numbers of people who are all working to make sure that your aircraft is ready for you. You might see a member of the flight crew walking around the outside of the plane, looking up into the wheel wells. "My God! What's wrong?" is the message that your nondrinking body receives. A moment of panic. If you were still in your active alcoholic days you could have cared less if anyone was even jumping on the wings, much less looking in a wheel well.

Well, there's nothing wrong. That's the flight engineer or second officer, possibly the first officer or the captain, making a routine check of the aircraft. It's as normal a part of his job as when you take a quick walk around your family car. He's looking in the wheel wells to make certain there is nothing to interfere with gear retraction. He is checking, visually, things that his cockpit instruments also will confirm, such as that hatch doors are shutting and locking, wing-tip lights and underbelly strobe lights are operating, etc.

By now you will have more than used up any of those ten minutes you were trying to pass before boarding.

Here's an important final point about your preflight preparation: Don't try to make a last-minute dash for either the bathroom or the telephone. You will have already said your temporary goodbyes, so no one needs to hear from you again. Terminate this link. You are going to get on board. You will call loved ones or business associates upon your arrival. What you are saying to yourself is, "I'm ready. Let's do it."

BOARDING PROCEDURES

Item two on your Basic Checklist for Flying: you are now walking down the jetway or across the "apron" to arrive at your aircraft. Don't push or shove. Not only is it dangerous, but you will just keep your anxiety level high by rushing. When you arrive at the boarding door of the aircraft, take just a second to look to your left, into the cockpit, if the door is still open. I make it a point to say hello even if I don't know the flight crew. These folks are just like family, and I appreciate the job they are doing for me. You'll like seeing them going through their procedures. It won't block things up for the folks behind you, either. Just a quick look in, see all the instrument lights on, the flight crew adjusting seat belts and harnesses. It's okay, do it.

Next, thank your flight attendants who greet you at the door. They are welcoming you into their second home for the next couple of hours, and you are glad to be there (even if you are quaking with anxiety and wondering how you'll ever get through it without a drink or two or three).

Use little mind tricks like "Thanks for having me," or "I'm looking forward to this trip." She or he may not have time to respond right away, but these professionals will usually remember someone who took a moment to say something pleasant, and they'll remember you. It may be later in the flight, but many times I've had some flight attendant recall my boarding comment and take a moment or two to respond.

Get to your seat and buckle up right away. This helps you say to yourself, "I'm secure. I'm not going to fall, either out or down." I hope that you will select a window seat when you get your boarding pass. It will be a greater help to your learning to fly without drinking than any other seat.

If you have selected something other than a window seat, or could not get one, then the order of seat preference is:

1. Any seat over the wing
2. Any aisle seat
3. Any seat directly behind the first-class bulkhead

If possible, avoid the seats in the very tail of the plane, where turbulence may be felt more severely than elsewhere. Middle seats that are somewhat cramped may cause you to feel a little claustrophobic, so avoid those as well.

Next item in your boarding procedure is to look up and around after you are seated. Notice how roomy this plane is. It's probably bigger than your bedroom, and sure has a lot more headroom than your recreation room. If you are in a window seat, see that your window shades will go up and down. Just like home—maybe better.

START UP AND TAXI

The door is shut, and you say to yourself, "I've done it. I actually am seated here on this plane and I'm going to make this trip without booze." Now pay attention to the flight attendant giving you and everyone else the basic safety instructions. This time really listen and pay attention. By riveting your attention on what he or she is saying and demonstrating, you (once again) can't concentrate on anything else, like being anxious. So, in addition to paying attention to potentially life-saving instructions, you help yourself overcome an even more primary fear—the drinking and relapsing fear. This fear says, "I'll have just one when it's offered, to overcome my anxiety." The fear part is even thinking that you might do it, and hence undo all the time of your recovery and sobriety that you have worked so hard to build.

You will hear noises now, and they are all accounted for. It's okay. The engines are being started and "spooled up" to taxi speed. In the cockpit, your flight crew is checking them for proper temperatures, performance, etc. Look out the window at the wing. You will see, at the same time you hear them, the flaps coming down on the wing. This is in preparation for your takeoff. You'll want to observe these flaps later, so watch them being lowered. When they are down in position, the whirring noise you have been hearing stops. What you heard is the drive gear that raises and lowers the flaps. Get used to hearing, maybe for the first time in your sobriety, the chime that summons the flight attendant to the cockpit. There's a moment's panic: is something wrong up there already? Nope. The Captain or another crew member may want something from the galley, or may need to relay some flight delay information to the senior flight attendant. No big deal. If it's important for you to hear it, you will, firsthand.

Now, look at and reset your watch. This is the first time that you should, in my opinion, reset your watch to reflect the time zone into which you are flying. The trick here is that if you are heading east, you can see that quite a lot of your trip time has already elapsed. Tell yourself, "Hey! This is going to be shorter than I thought." If you are flying west, you move your watch back, and you can say, "This is great. I'll have more daylight to spend at my destination than I thought." Substitute whatever you like, but make yourself aware of the time. You'll use it later on during the flight to see what good progress you are making. If you are going east, the time has already marched along by more minutes than you thought. That's good. Use all these tricks and more to keep your anxiety level down. You are not going to have to drink.

As you are in your taxiing check, notice that many folks have already closed their eyes and appear to be asleep, even with their seatbacks still in an upright position. "Well," you say to yourself, "they must feel okay about flying, and they're on the same plane I am." See, what used to happen to you was that you let your anxiety start making you believe that only you were involved in this activity. You've got company, and no one else on that plane is holding a drink in their hands, either, although many of them may have been drinking before they boarded. Doesn't matter. At this point, as you are taxiing, you are all equal without alcohol in your hands. Therefore, doesn't it stand to reason that the plane is moving without your help?

TAKEOFF AND CLIMB-OUT

Usually you will have an announcement by some member of the flight crew telling you that your aircraft has been cleared for takeoff. You may not have this announcement, but simply feel the acceleration and the pull of gravity on you as the plane reaches its lift-off speed. Look out the window and notice that those flaps are still down. Feel the aircraft tilt or "rotate" its nose to the upward climb level. The jet engines are not increasing in noise level, but are producing a steady, powerful whine.

As you become airborne, it's time to unclutch your hands from the seat and observe two quick things that will help you to calm down. First, if you're on an international flight, the "No-Smoking" sign is turned off. Second, those flaps you saw go down are beginning to wind themselves back into the wing. You now know for a fact that everything is okay and that your crew has "trimmed" your aircraft for flight. Nothing's wrong. You now hear and feel the landing gear come bumping into its nest underneath the plane. Another good sign. You are okay and, just imagine, still no need to drink.

Just when you are feeling okay, you suddenly feel the plane go into a fairly sharp turn or "bank." "Oh, oh," says newly sober and alert you. "What's happening?" Simple. No need for panic. Your captain has been told by Departure Control to clear the airspace above the runway so that planes behind yours can take off. Your aircraft has already been cleared to an assigned altitude, and the sharp veering away from the runway enables you to get where you're going and allows other airplanes to use the runway. You may also hear, shortly thereafter, all of the engine noise decrease. You believe that they are slowing down, and you're right. Again, the traffic controllers handling your flight have asked your captain to maintain a certain altitude while they clear traffic at the assigned level for your flight. Cutting back on the engine power reduces speed and maintains that altitude, usually for a brief period. Then you'll hear the engines "spooling up" again as your crew begins climbing to the assigned flight altitude.

So far you are convinced that everything is okay, but the real test is starting. While you are asked to remain seated, your flight attendants have begun to ready that formidable monster the "booze cart," lurking there in the shadow of the galley. You know it's there. You sense it, and your anxiety still may be high enough that you wonder how you're going to handle it. You *will* handle it.

Don't look in the direction of the galley. When you are told you can move about the cabin, don't get up and go to the restroom if you can help it. If you have to go, walk toward the rear of the plane where any booze carts being prepared are not likely to be out in the aisle yet. Most airlines prepare their first class, up-front service first, so going to the rear is a safer bet.

If you don't have to go, stay in your seat, use the convenient stereo provided by the airline, and crank that little puppy up as loud as you can handle. If it's your own cassette, do the same thing. The idea is to get you to a state of irritation because of the loud volume as quickly as possible. When the music is so loud that it almost hurts, slowly reduce the volume until it's at a comfortable listening level and the noises of the aircraft cabin seem welcome. What you have done is show yourself that you are capable of reducing anxiety (symbolized by the manual reduction of the volume control). You are in control, therefore it will not be necessary to turn to a substitute (alcohol) to help you gain control of anxiety.

IN FLIGHT

So now there you are, level, sober, and feeling like you're going to make it after all, when down the aisle comes that cocktail cart. You stare at it, wondering if the new, recovering alcoholic person that you've become can let that thing get by you. Are you still frightened? Are you still digging your fingers into the arms of your seat? Have you hit a little clear air turbulence, or has it been a little rough ever since you took off? Maybe the answers to all those questions are "yes." Once again, you need to remind yourself that no matter how much alcohol anyone on that plane consumes, it will not affect the flight or the machine itself. So, go ahead and look at the booze cart. What do you see?

When you were drinking, you automatically saw that little cart just loaded with drinks on its top shelf, and it couldn't get to you quickly enough. Now, look again. There are no little miniatures of liquor in view. You may very well see champagne or wine bottles, but the hard stuff is kept in a drawer underneath the cart. What you have conditioned yourself to see are all of the "set-ups," the plastic cups with ice in them, surrounded by the lemon and lime wedges, olives, cherries, etc. that go into mixing a cocktail. You think they're filled with alcohol.

But you are not looking at endless glasses of cocktails. Now, pay close attention to how few people on board the flight actually order alcoholic beverages. It's amazing. When several flight attendants who are in their own recovery were confronted about this observation, they reported back to group that they had never noticed it much before, but it was true. Most of the folks on the plane with you will have a soft drink, coffee, or tea. A few people will drink a lot. They are the ones you notice. Sure, a number of your fellow passengers will take wine or champagne, but remember, those are not quick-fix beverages, so they must not need them to reduce anxiety. Neither do you. Make sense?

My own personal choice for taking something off the drink cart is orange juice and a diet 7-Up or Sprite or Fresca, something bubbly that puts a little effervescence on top of the orange juice. You try it yourself and see if you don't like it. You get a sugar boost and a little bubble fallout. It's quite refreshing.

When the booze cart is past your row of seats, think of it as totally gone. You will not need it anymore, even if you want another juice or soft drink. You may find that your meal is coming right on top of the drink cart or perhaps just before it. Eat something. Even if you can't tolerate airline food, you need something in your stomach to counteract possible anxiety build-up. The blood that will have to be used to digest the food you eat is blood that will help drain your brain of being quite so "hyper."

Now you can check your watch again. See how much flying time has elapsed and how well you've done. It's the same principle you have been practicing throughout your entire recovery period: you will live your life one day at a time, and if necessary, one hour at a time. You can say, "Good for me. I've made it for (insert number of minutes or hours) flying without a drink." You are now beginning to understand the basic premise we spoke of in the beginning of this chapter: alcohol intake by human beings on board an aircraft does not affect the flying capabilities of the machine.

One or more of the flight crew may do some walking and visiting in the cabin after meal service is completed. They expect to be asked some questions, and if you are still feeling anxious about something, stop the crew member and ask. It's what you don't know that is likely to cause you to create the "scaries." It's your own conjecture about what is happening as opposed to what actually is going on that can be your undoing.

If you are in some rough weather and you see the wing tips flapping, it's because they're supposed to. They're built to handle many more times the amount of stress than that the average flight is subjected to. If you hear noise underneath the plane on take offs and landings, it is because you *should* hear it; ninety-nine times out of a hundred, everything that you hear or see is perfectly normal for your flight. It is safer to fly today than it is for you to drive on your own state's highways.

Go back to your book, the one you already have been reading. Or keep your stereo on, and you might even (saints forbid!) take a little snooze. Kick off your shoes. There's nothing quite as nice as flying in your stocking feet. It makes you feel right at home, in addition to being downright comfortable.

DESCENDING

As your plane starts its descent you may have some more anxiety due to the old tapes you are playing about needing a drink to cover certain nervous situations. If there are clouds below you, you may be making your descent "blind," on instruments, as your flight crew skillfully threads their way down into the assigned landing pattern. Here are some things to remember: Many times, even though you can't see outside your window, your flight crew sees the various breaks in the clouds as they make the way down. Another thing—a good many people are all concentrating their efforts to bring your flight in safely.

Cutbacks in engine power do not automatically mean trouble. They mean just what they did when you felt the plane climbing. The captain has been asked to "reduce speed." Then he may pick up the speed a little, then cut back again. All these things are quite normal in landing. Rest assured that if something comes along that is not normal and requires your attention, you'll be told. You can have fun watching the flaps descend again. Even if you are in weather you will see them, and then perhaps you'll see the set of "slats" pull away from their in-line position on the wing and form a wind barrier in front of the wing. You'll hear the landing gear go down, and you can say to yourself, "The captain has just been told that the gear is down and we have green lights." (The instrument panel in the cockpit has confirmed that the gear is down, locked, and ready by lighting a green light for each gear.)

Look at your watch for the last time during your trip in the air. You can take pride in knowing that you spent "X" number of hours and minutes conquering a fear you've had without using alcohol, without breaking your sobriety and your recovery process. That's great, isn't it? One more notch to add to your belt as you whip this disease of alcoholism. If you're still feeling nervous during the descent, use this trick. Crane your neck up and down the aisle. There is no booze cart in sight. There is no alcohol to interfere as you deal with your anxieties or emotions. You can rely on your own pride in your recovery and your own inner strengths, the help you receive from the God of your understanding, the calm assurances of your fellow passengers, and finally, the tool of communicating your nervousness to your companion or seatmate.

Verbalizing such anxiety with, "Landings and coming down through weather always makes me nervous," has an amazing effect. The minute you give voice to it, the less nervous you are. Try it sometime and see for yourself.

LANDINGS

An obvious continuation on your Basic Checklist for Flying is the landing. As the wheels touch the runway, and just before the craft settles to the nose wheel, look out the window again and observe the wings and the engines (if you can see them). As the plane settles on its nose wheel, the pilot reverses the thrust of the engines to help brake the plane's speed. You will see vents and cowlings open up and appear to fly away from the engines. This is so the engine thrust can use those vents to push air against the plane, slowing it down.

Watch the flaps come up again as the plane slows, and listen for the cabin music to come on. Look around you at the happy faces of your traveling friends. Feel good about yourself and say to yourself, "I've done it." Make it a point on your checklist to say, "That was a good trip," even if there were some rough spots.

Look at the wing again. A new set of "spoilers" is up. This set is on the back surface of the wing and acts as a brake that is used for landings. (You didn't see them employed on the takeoff since you wanted to go then, not stop.) Make everything as memorable in the way of an audio and visual effect as you can. Remember the sights and sounds of landings, and the next time you will expect them and will be more comfortable with them.

LEAVING THE AIRCRAFT

This is the last item on your Basic Checklist for Flying. You use this item to reinforce the fact that you will be flying again. To do this, make it a point to thank your flight attendants. Tell them, "I'll see you next trip." If the cockpit door is open when you leave, say goodbye and thanks to your flight crew. They may still be busy going over their afterflight checklist, but mostly they will be completed with enough immediate detail to acknowledge your word of thanks.

You will be back in the air again. You have taken a great step in overcoming the basic thoughts and actions you harbored for all the time of your active drinking. That basic premise was, again, that the plane's performance and safety was all dependent upon the amount of alcohol you consumed. Now you'll arrive at your place of destination without a booze headache caused from drinking too much, too fast, or at high altitude. You will be able to function, and that's always one of the best joys of being sober. You will have mastered the siren call of the drink cart and its dangers. Best of all, you will have learned that it didn't affect the flight of the plane, either. You just thought it did all those other times.

MORE JOY (An Update)

You know, I am constantly amazed whenever I fly when I notice how few people order cocktails. It's a far cry from when I used to choose the seat closest to the galley, where I thought the booze cart was stored. Didn't want to miss a chance to be served first, you know.

Now, again largely as a result of Americans' conscious choice to have more fitness in their lives, we seem to be drinking much less on airplanes. It's like the no smoking regulation that finally made flying comfortable again, even on a flight from Denver to New York or Washington, D.C.

Once again, the recovering person should examine the reasons that he or she needed to drink in order to fly. As I have discussed, fear of flying is really fear of not being in control, of not being in charge of your own destiny. It's interesting to note, however, that we never give that a thought when we climb in and out of our automobiles several times a day. It's curious how we think we are any more in charge of our destiny than when we are flying, yet statistically, flying is considerably safer than driving. We certainly don't have highway controllers (other than traffic signals) available to guide us and keep us safely apart the way our sophisticated air traffic control system does.

When you think of flying, think of the fact that the crew is just as anxious to have a safe flight as you are. How does that compare to the fact that any nut can pour booze into him or herself, climb into a car, and wreak havoc with anyone who happens to be in the way. Give me flying anytime.

I have had the extreme pleasure of being involved with many airline pilots in my therapy practice. I continue to be pleased with their dedication, their skills, and their willingness to adapt to the changes necessary to affect whatever the therapeutic problem is.

Someone once asked if it bothered me to work with airline pilots who were abusing alcohol. I still answer that I would be much more concerned about any flight crew personnel who were still in denial about a possible problem and avoiding getting help. And again, think of statistics—how many accidents caused by drunken airline pilots have you ever heard of, and how does that compare with the number of auto accidents caused by drunk drivers? The airlines are especially vigilant, and a pilot who is an alcoholic must go through treatment before he or she is ever allowed to get back in a cockpit.

The thing I want to emphasize is that you are free now to really enjoy flying. You can fly for business or pleasure and know that you don't have to be half in the bag. You won't make a damn fool of yourself when an important client meets you after your flight, or humiliate your spouse with the way you act on board. And did I mention the money you save by not flying first class, something you always did to be sure to get all the free drinks you could hold?

Enjoy your flight. Enjoy going and arriving with a firm handle on the fact that you don't have to be in control. Very highly skilled and keenly trained personnel who have wives, sweethearts, husbands, kids, significant others and family members, all of whom are important to them, are in command. Relax! Put on your headset, recline your seat and enjoy. Or if you absolutely have to be like me as I am writing this, type away on the laptop computer sitting on the fold-down tray in front of you. Ah, progress!

Which of us...is to do the hard and dirty work for the rest, and for what pay? Who is to do the pleasant and clean work, and for what pay?

John Ruskin

TRYING DIFFERENT WORK

It seems almost sinful to talk about the possibility of changing jobs when our economy is such that just having a job is a real blessing. So let's begin by saying that the newly recovered person certainly shouldn't run right to the boss or personnel manager and turn in a resignation. That will only complicate your recovery and make it more difficult for you to realize the joy of being sober.

What I am interested in having you do is to consider the possibility of adding to your work with activities you may have always thought about doing, but never had the right impetus for doing. Your sobriety and your new outlook on life may be just the ticket you have been looking for to urge you on. There is a little Walter Mitty in each of us, a little bit of the dreamer who imagines the sky's the limit. That's part of what contributed to our drinking behavior, but it can be put to good use in sobriety.

A recovering friend said only recently, "When I was drinking I felt ten feet tall." Another recovering person said, "Now that I'm sober, I'm just trying to get back to being five feet eleven inches (his real height)." When you were drinking there wasn't anything that you couldn't do, or so you thought. Now, in sobriety, there are many times when you wonder if there is anything you can do and do right.

It's okay to let our Walter Mitty imagination lead us to the brink of discovery, to examine whether what we are doing for our life work is really what we want to continue to do. There is no question that stress and tension are a part of any job, but the alcoholic is inclined to justify his past drinking by laying all the blame on job pressures. You realize, I'm sure, that was just an excuse you may have used. The reason you drank was that you have a disease and were unable to stop drinking without help. The job you have gone back to is probably exactly the same one you had when alcoholism finally caught up with you. It still has pressures and tensions, but there is one basic difference. You are now able to handle those pressures. You're sober. What seemed like monumental problems at work before may still be problems. However, there are solutions in sight, and your sobriety allows you to deal with those solutions.

Often, people are inclined to worry about climbing the highest ladder in the company, reaching the top echelon. What I suggest is that you don't worry about climbing to the top until you've learned how not to stumble on the stones in your path.

Changing jobs will not alleviate pressures. It might *add* to them, and you might just find yourself under more stress and strain than you ever bargained for. Worse, it could lead you down the path to a drinking episode, eventually breaking your sobriety.

Instead, let's think about adding a new job dimension to your life. Trying different work means letting out the reins of your imagination and experiencing some different types of work as part of your recovery. For example, you could get a paper route. (I took a sampling of jobs that turned out to be fun for people who wanted to add a new dimension to their lives while they worked their program of recovery, and having an adult paper route headed the list.)

I'm not talking about beating some needy kid out of a job. There are generally loads of car routes for adults available in almost any size community. One couple I know started out with a small route to help her in recovery; it helped her get needed exercise and earn a little extra money. Her husband agreed to help, and what started out as just a few-hundred-delivery route ended up six months later as a district route of several thousand papers. It helped this recovering lady get a new outlook on her life. She needed to know that she could tackle something new and make it work. You can do the same, if you're willing to make the extra effort.

One of the best options is to try retail selling in local department stores, particularly for seasonal employment. You won't make a lot of money, but you might be offered a courtesy discount which will help with your holiday shopping. You will also gain a sense of confidence that you can meet people, and the knowledge that you can actually use an intelligent sales routine without an alcohol booster to make you pleasant. Alcohol has done funny things to you that way; it had a tendency to make you very unpleasant and quarrelsome. Working in the public sector and learning to cope with the pressures of the day without the bottle is good for your recovery. You can do amazing things if you are willing to take the risk.

Finding additional work, something out of the ordinary from what you normally do, allows your fantasies to run the full gamut. A most refined lady in recovery had always wanted to try her hand at being a waitress. She really had not had to do much menial work of any kind before, having been born into a moneyed family. She actually wanted to experience the hard hours, complaining customer encounters, and aching feet that go with food service jobs. However, she didn't need the money as much as some other people in her community, and she received some rather severe criticism for "taking food out of others' mouths." This lady told me that she got tired of making up reasons to explain why she needed her waitress job. Finally she took the risk of disclosing to a few people that she was a recovering alcoholic. "I've never had to work hard in my life. I just sat around and drank," she confided to them. "It's important for me to know that I'm worth something as a person."

She didn't keep the job long—maybe three or four months. But it gave her much-needed confidence in herself as a sober person. She tried another position, this time as a receptionist in an automobile dealership, a greeter who welcomed people into the showroom and put them together with whatever salesperson was due to work with the prospect. This lady was quite good in this area of public relations. She moved up and asked for the opportunity to try auto sales herself. The dealership gave her the job, and she is doing extremely well in it. Her sobriety is intact. Her feelings about herself are in top-drawer condition, and she attributes this to "getting off my duff" and trying different work.

A man in recovery told me he took a job delivering telephone directories. It was menial work, and it was not what he was accustomed to doing. But his doctor had suggested that it would be good for him and would help clear the cobwebs of grandiose alcoholic behavior out of his mind. When he completed treatment, he took the directory job before going back to his profession in broadcasting. It did him a world of good.

I remember a client from another state who was so good at sewing that she was encouraged to try it as a business. Her recovery was secure—that is, she was in a "good space" with her sobriety and was continuing an outpatient program of support. She started her sewing business in her home, in the basement. She got some orders, starting with just simple alterations. She finally began to get requests for custom tailoring. This lady, who had never done this kind of work as a profession, finally opened up a store in the community where she lived. Two of the shirts in my closet are from her skilled hands. Her sobriety gave her the confidence to begin life anew with different work.

Changing job positions in the company where you currently work is another rewarding experience for the recovering person. You may have been considered before for promotion, only to either shoot yourself down with your own behavior or to have your employer not feel right about you. No one confronted you about the many absences or late arrivals to work as a result of hangovers and general "stinkin' thinkin'" attitudes caused mostly by your drinking.

Now, newly sober, why not try again? Approach the supervisor or the head honcho himself and take a stab at a promotion to a position that might be a step up for you. Be careful, though. You will not be able to handle giant strides all at once. Take it easy and feel your way slowly into areas that call for more responsibility.

The best thing to do is employ your tools of honest disclosure with your supervisor or boss. Ask him how he feels about you taking on the new position. Try to get open discussion and honest evaluation of what will be expected of you, what the high anxiety and pressure areas could be, and what kinds of help you can get if you feel overwhelmed.

A young man in recovery was confused about his chosen profession. He had been an elementary school teacher, but was feeling that his recovery might allow him to expand his horizons. He did so, trying a number of rather menial positions until he discovered that he liked retail sales. He worked first as Christmas help when he was off from his school position. He applied for management training with the retail firm, took a leave of absence from teaching at the proper time, and went on to work through a series of training and management seminars in the retail sales field.

This was something the young man had never mustered the courage to do until his sobriety. In recovery, he discovered that there was a new joy in doing something different. The Walter Mitty in him burst forth, and he is still hard at work in management of retail sales today. He is happy and feels he is reaping the rewards of being sober in quite a different way than he had ever imagined.

Before you can determine whether you are interested in trying different work, it's a good idea to look, in sober fashion, at the work you are doing now. Ask yourself:

"Do I like what I'm doing, or is it just a way to earn a paycheck?"

"Do I look forward to going to work, or is every day 'Monday' for me?"

"Is there a chance to move up?"

"Do I find myself getting bored easily?"

"Are all of my potential talents really being used with this job?"

These are all questions that may not have even mattered when you were an active drinker. As long as the money arrived when it was supposed to, and as long as you were getting by, it may have been good enough. In sobriety, however, you begin to question a good many things about what your life is all about, where you are now, and where you want to be in the near future. So, take a little time and be honest about your present job. If it is not meeting some personal needs as well as the basics of life that any employment provides, then you are going to find the winds of dissatisfaction blowing more steadily around you.

You can help yourself establish some criteria for job satisfaction by making a list of what you think are your best qualities—those things that make an employer interested in you. It's equally important to your joy in being sober to make a list of the qualities that you think are lacking. Come on, now. Be open and honest with yourself.

Many times in therapy sessions I will ask a client to bring in such a list. It is to be marked, "Ten things I dislike about myself." Easy enough. But when I say, "I also want you to bring in a list of ten things you like about yourself," there is hesitation. Many people won't have any trouble in lambasting themselves. I've had lists come back to me that numbered fifteen, twenty, and even twenty-five items. When I ask for the list of ten likeable traits, I've been handed as few as three or four. That's fairly typical of the low self-esteem a recovering person can have. There is so much guilt, anger, and shame around the alcohol issues that it comes through as a portrait of "poor, pitiful me."

In sobriety, you have the ability to reexamine those lists. You can begin with job qualifications that are perhaps basic to your line of work. Typing speed, short-hand, drafting, accounting, and writing abilities are some of the examples. Then go to other, more personal skills you possess.

"I maintain a professional appearance in dress and manners."

"I am punctual."

"I get along well with most people."

These are all items that could well be on your list. And don't forget to add to the list, "I don't drink." That's something to be proud of, and something that is a pleasure to see on anyone's list of job qualifications.

Examine the technical skills you have, but perhaps have not used just because your present job doesn't call for them. How many times have you seen a particular piece of work come across your desk or pass through your hands and found your-self muttering, "I could do a better job of that." We tend to bury our talents to fit the needs of what we are doing at present. This is particularly true when we are given a job that was not quite suited to the particular skills we possess.

Often we apply for a job, find that it is not available at the moment, but dis-cover there is an opening in another department. We take the second-best posi-tion in order to meet the needs of having work, a salary, and a way in the door. However, as alcohol became a more dominant part of your life, you may never have moved out of the temporary niche you accepted. The particular job pressures and anxieties of a job that you were not really interested in from the beginning became excuses for your drinking.

Now, in sobriety you can take a new look at what happened to the job or position you wanted in the first place. You still have those skills to offer—your sickness with the disease of alcoholism didn't take your talents away from you. It simply put them on hold, or more accurately, on ice (with several ounces of alco-hol poured over them). You can begin the big thaw of these talents now that you have your sobriety. Listing all the extra skills you possess, even if they do not apply to a specific position in your company, still gives you a personal and fresh inven-tory of what you have to offer.

The use of a skilled vocational counselor is very important to the recovering person. These special counselors help you find the untapped reservoirs of your job and career potentials. You can remove many of the job pressures that you find are making you a nervous wreck when a vocational counselor helps you analyze your skills and potentials.

In the process of making your personal list, you can examine the skills you have and compare them with the skills that are demanded by the job you are performing. Many times you will uncover a pressure area or two in comparing those lists. A client of mine uncovered just such an area when she found, in making her lists, that more mathematical work was being required than she was capable of handling with comfort. "I could always get by in math," she told me, "but the more responsibility they gave me, the more complicated the damn time sheets, expense reports, and budget records became." The simple math that she knew wasn't good enough anymore for the position she was filling. It was causing an enormous pressure on her to just be able to keep up with the job's demands, and she attacked the problem with alcohol abuse instead of by dealing honestly with the job.

In treatment she realized she was using those job tensions as excuses for feeding her alcohol habit. Sober, she was able to confront her weakness in math, and exchange that weakness for her company's new use of her talents in writing, editing, and overseeing the publication of the company newsletter.

This was a fine example, by the way, of an understanding employer who was very supportive of treatment for his employee, and who was instrumental in finding better use of her talents in sobriety. He, the employer, knew he had a valuable employee, and he was unaware of her alcohol abuse until it became painfully obvious. Instead of firing her, however, he gave her the opportunity to gain her recovery through treatment, and he was able to preserve the investment of years the company had made in her as an employee.

The real joy of trying different work is that you are able to let your imagination soar. You may not be able to pilot a jet plane, but by golly you might be able to go to flight school and get the private pilot's license you always wanted. Your sobriety will allow you the use of your faculties again. You can be freer to look for more challenging areas of work than may have been possible during your active drinking months or years. Volunteer work, while not adding one bit to the old coffer, is still an area where much of your newfound sobriety can be put to its better uses. The hospitals, fire departments, and many civic organizations of your community that are always short-handed can use all the talents you have been keeping in mothballs for so long. If you are in a job position that is okay with you but is just a little dull or unexciting, volunteer work is a great stimulant to put a little sparkle back into your life.

Most community theaters, dance troupes, and local music and arts groups are composed of people with a little or sometimes a lot of time to channel. They usually participate in addition to their everyday work jobs, to better enrich their own lives. When you were drinking you scorned this kind of thing. Now that you have your sobriety, these kinds of different work can be a big booster for you.

I have recommended adult tutoring to many recovering alcoholics as a very rewarding method of enjoying and strengthening their own sobriety. There are so many people in your own community who do not possess the basic skills of reading, writing, or arithmetic necessary to get a high school diploma or GED. You can use your own skills in these areas to do a little adult tutoring. It helps the people who are being held back because they lack these basics, and it helps you rediscover the joys of leading a sober life, where care for others has overcome the selfish behavior patterns of the active alcoholic.

Many times, the newly sober will want to channel the burst of energy that comes with sobriety into starting a business for himself or herself. There are basic rules for anyone who wants to go into business that certainly must be remembered. The principles of sound business practices aren't any different for you, but as a newly sober person, you need to take some special precautions. First, it is important that you don't bite off more than you can chew. Your newfound sobriety can be deceiving; you may not possess as much energy as you think you have, and the particular bounce you feel from your recovery can plummet to fatigue and burnout. Starting a new business requires enormous drains upon your personal energy—you must be able to budget your strength as well as your money.

Another important factor for the recovering person to keep in mind is that your tension level can become dangerously high over fluctuations in personal money. The rule of thumb that says you shouldn't start a business unless you can afford not to have a salary for at least six months (and probably even a year) applies even more strongly to you. Money is always a problem in recovery, due either to the aftereffects of your alcoholic behavior and wild spending, or to mismanagement of your resources both during your drinking days and during your recovery.

Starting your own business will take not only the usual start-up monies, but will also bring many hidden extras you may not have considered. These drains on your money will lead to pressure, tension, and a lot of anxiety. Your recovery will not be immune to these pressures, and your sobriety can be threatened if you let the situation get out of hand. A good rule of thumb for the newly sober is to try not to make any major changes in career or other personal matters for at least the first six months of your sobriety. That's not going to work all the time, obviously. You may have lost a job, a marriage, or a place to live. If any of these are the case, you will have to make changes. But if you can avoid jumping "from the frying pan into the fire," you will give yourself better insurance for your long-term recovery.

Starting a new business may appeal to your vanity. It may be the lure of the siren, and could be a disaster just waiting for you. Ask for counsel from all your resources before you jump into those pressures that naturally accompany starting and operating a new business. Remember that in this area, as in all others we have talked about, your Number One Priority Every day (NOPE for short) is your sobriety. All else must be relegated to secondary positions after that first and foremost endeavor. A new business can be the realization of all your many hopes and dreams for the future, dreams that were blocked for so long by alcohol abuse. But starting that new business can also dash you against the rocks of financial and personal ruin, and possibly back into the sea of despair. That's when alcohol use and abuse can become the desperate driftwood you reach out to cling to, hoping against hope not to sink to the bottom once again.

Take it easy. Approach the ideas of new work, a new businesses, or a new career with full awareness of the challenges they afford; but also approach them with the knowledge that your strengths and weaknesses will no longer be masked by alcohol, nor will alcohol enhance and build up what's not really there. So move with caution. Finding different work and meeting the challenges of relocating your career and redefining your life's work are exciting. They can be the elixir of the new life that you are choosing to lead, one day at a time.

For the newly sober, the joys are all around you—at the desk where you spend your working days, at the drawing board, the production line, in the field, or in the barracks. It doesn't matter what you decide to do to shape your future, if you are courageous, strong and honest in your risk-taking. Doing something different can be the topping on your ice cream, or it can be the new main course of your sober life. In recovery, all things are possible for you. In the grips of your disease of alcoholism, very little was possible except mere existence, and that is not good enough for you anymore. Look around you and explore the ways that your talents, abilities, and ambitions can be channeled into the new energy of your sober life. Don't overdo it, and your joy of sobriety will increase.

MORE JOY (An Update)

One thing for you to definitely consider now that you are sober is your further education. I'll bet that you have thought many, many times that you sure would like to have gone to college or finished your degree. Or what about that graduate degree you always dreamed about?

Where is the specialized training you talked about getting, and what about those watercolor classes you were going to take when you got around to it? Well, now's the time; you have a clearing brain in your head and the alcohol is not soaking up (pardon the expression) all your potential tuition money.

I can't even count the number of people I have goaded into going back to school and finishing or getting a degree or two. My wife, Cyn, didn't need the goading, but she got my enthusiastic and full support to go back to college and complete her undergraduate degree and her Master of Science.

It wasn't easy, holding down a full-time job, trying to keep a relationship alive and vital, and handling the financial stress. But she did it—summa cum laude in her undergraduate work, and with honors in her graduate program at Regis University.

My son Jackson did the same thing. Married with two children, he completed his undergraduate degree summa cum laude, and then his law degree with honors from Georgetown University. As of this writing, he is working on a Ph.D.

The money can often be found in student loans that are available. We used every resource, and so can you. There are federal, state, and sometimes city funds available to anyone who wants to try for them. You would be amazed at the loans and grants available at the institution you elect to attend. Don't be afraid to explore absolutely every source to allow you to return to school or to go for the first time.

One or two of my clients are taking arts and crafts classes that are available for less than thirty dollars, including materials, offered by local parks and recreation districts. Is it making a difference in their recovery? You bet. It's something they were always going to do before their recovery—they just poured another drink instead. At Christmas I generally receive some example of their work, and I am always pleased, honored and proud of the ways they have used their sobriety in such productive ways in their new lives.

Don't limit yourself in either the thinking or the planning stages; be prepared to get "yes" answers from the sources of higher education in your city and state. That "yes" means they have faith and confidence in you. Taking up the challenge of getting or completing your education is a definite reward of your sobriety.

For Satan finds some mischief still/For Idle hands to do

Isaac Watts

19

THE NEW IMPORTANCE OF HOBBIES

You've got some idle time on your hands now that you're sober. Now, wait—don't protest too much. If nothing else, you have time available that you used to spend sitting on a bar stool, or parked in front of the tube "pigging out" on chips 'n' suds (or whatever your particular drink happened to be.)

You have idle time. The purpose of this chapter is to get you started with a creative hobby of some kind that will do some important things for your recovery. What things? Well, for one, starting and completing a hobby project will be positive reinforcement that you have begun the sobering process. When you were drinking, you may have started a half-dozen or more projects. Oh, you started them all right, but how many of them ever got finished? In sobriety, you will realize how good it feels to finish what you start. Another strong point for hobby-in-recovery therapy is that you will regain skills or find hidden talents that have lain dormant while alcohol dominated your leisure time.

Before, you probably were among those who scorned people who did things like collect stamps or coins, cultivate rose gardens, tinker in workshops, or paint with brushes and oils. You need those things now—they're stepping stones back to the world of joyful recovery. So, here are a few tools designed to help you take another look at the new importance of hobbies in your life.

FRUSTRATION LEVELS

Perhaps one of the biggest barriers for the new hobbyist is frustration. It may have been just downright discouraging for you to try a particular hobby because your frustration level got too high for you to cope. So you tossed the work aside and popped the tab on another can of beer.

Your sobriety isn't going to increase your tolerance for frustration. As a matter of fact, you might be a little more short-fused because you no longer have alcohol to temporarily ease your anxiety and stress. So the kind of hobby you choose is going to be important.

Considering you might get easily discouraged, which leads to frustration, I suggest you pick a hobby that does not have a seasonal time deadline. For example, if you have decided to try hooking or weaving a rug, don't begin by saying, "This will be just perfect for Amy for Christmas." Buying the materials and starting work on the project is okay, but forget about pushing yourself into a corner around a deadline. It will become an unspoken frustration builder. As the days get closer to the holiday, the more you will feel that every little mistake is setting you back from completing the project in time for gifting. So, avoid the time deadline, at least until you have completed enough projects that you feel okay about increasing the pressure on yourself a little.

Another frustration-builder is tackling something much too complex for your new sober self. I'm thinking, for instance, of the many electronic projects that are on the market—enticing kits to make stereos, television sets, and home computers. These, even with their most simplified, easy-to-follow directions, can be real frustration projects. You will invest a pretty sizeable amount of money and then find yourself getting uptight about the project instead of enjoying the positives you are supposed to derive from the hobby.

Make your first project a simple one, maybe something that doesn't require constant attention. Choose something you can put down for several days and then pick up where you left off without getting bent out of shape about where you're "supposed" to be in the project. To help you do this "put-down-and-pick-up" stroke, get in the habit of keeping a small notepad and pencil with your project.

When you are ready to quit for the day, take a few minutes to write a simple note to yourself that says, "Begin with section two (or whatever), on page seven (or whichever)." Attach the note to the top of your work. It will help you get back in the mood of the project quickly, and will enable you to see that you have already made a good start.

This note-writing will work with any hobby, even collecting. If it's gardening you're doing, put the note on your potting stand or tuck it in the cuff of your gloves. If you will keep the notes you write from day to day, you will have visible proof that you are making progress on your project. Your notes become a good road map for your recovery.

Another idea to help you control frustration is to share your work with a special person in your life. Hearing commendations of the steps you have already accomplished will reinforce your future progress.

My own work with oil painting comes to mind. The work seemed to go so slowly that my own frustration levels built very high. Then I showed a work in progress to a friend, and was helped considerably when he suggested switching from oil to acrylics. That would allow me to finish a section of a painting, go back over it and make corrections if necessary, and still see some real progress in the painting. Struggling with the long-drying oils and not being able to hurry the work was only frustrating my need to get something done that I could not have done while drinking. My friend's comments and praise, and his suggestion to switch mediums, helped reduce my frustration level.

I'm not dealing here with the possible merits of hurrying through a project. For the person who is new in recovery, it's probably more important to start and complete something than it is to make a lasting contribution to the art world. Before you select a hobby to start, though, you should carefully consider how much frustration the project may impose on your still-fragile temperament. With that in mind, here's the second tool:

PICK SOMETHING FAMILIAR

There is a very solid foundation for your sobriety that can be built by picking up a hobby you have tried before. In your active drinking days, you may have completed many projects of a particular hobby and thought they were pretty good, or as good as you could make them. Now, in sobriety, you've a chance to go back and do something really well. You can show yourself that what you did before was not really your best effort at all. Many times I have looked through the "mistake box" in my workshop and wondered if many of the items I completed when I was drinking wouldn't have been better off staying in that box. In sobriety, my work is cleaner, more finished, more polished, and thus shows more loving care and attention to detail than work done before. Your returning to a familiar hobby will give you the same or better satisfaction. Remember, though—there is no need for you to apologize for work you did before; it still was a good effort. What you will see in the new work, however, will be the result of an alcohol-free mind and body working in harmony to utilize your talents to their fullest.

A client of mine once shared an experience about going back to paint-by-number kits again. He discovered that during his drinking days, about half of the time he had ignored the numbers called for in the painting. He only discovered this because he decided to repeat a picture he had done before. He was convinced the kit manufacturer must have made a mistake—the wrong numbers seemed to be called for—until he dug out the old painting. This revelation of how his drinking had confused his brain was a graphic example of what his recovery was doing for him. It has continued to play an important role in this client's unwillingness to ever return to those befuddled days.

Another person, new in recovery, went back to her stamp collection to find that in the last few weeks of her active alcoholic days, she had nearly ruined an entire book of stamps by placing her new acquisitions on the wrong pages. "They looked like the right spots when I did them," she told me. "But when I hauled the books out again after starting my recovery, I found all the places I had screwed up." For her, and for you, returning to a familiar hobby will give you on-site inspection and comparisons of the "then" and "now" phases of your new life.

LEARNING SAFETY AGAIN

Here is a tool that applies to almost every hobby where power tools or mechanical devices of any kind are used in the project. When you were drinking, you became careless in the use of basic tools like safety goggles, gloves, or proper electrical connections. I have seen so many people who, while drinking, became so overconfident in their supposed mastery of a particular tool that they abandoned all the precautions and almost lost fingers over it.

In your new sobriety, you need to start again just as if you were picking up the machinery or tools for the first time. You may even feel a little scared about handling a large router or running stock through a jointer or table saw. Well, you should be leery about handling even the smallest soldering pencil or sewing machine in the same freewheeling manner that alcohol permitted you in the past. It may have been freewheeling, but it was also dangerous.

A good rule of thumb is to treat your hobby as if you didn't know very much about it and were trying to learn how to operate the particular tool for the first time. Another good method to remind you of safety procedures is to try to teach the use of the tool to someone else. In going over the basics you will want to show that person how to protect him or herself, and you will reinforce the importance of safety in your own mind.

You will not feel much joy in being sober if you seriously injure yourself by going back to the old habits you used when operating dangerous machinery while drinking. If you think your sewing machine is not dangerous, then think again. A lady told me that when she was an active drinker she got in the habit of making certain high-speed long-run stitches while watching her favorite television show. She would have her glass of vodka and the TV both close at hand. Once, during her operation of a fast row of sewing on her machine, she reached for her glass, did not take her foot off the treadle, and sewed several painful stitches into the edge of her index finger.

"It seemed to me," she said, "that I told myself to take my foot off the treadle, but thought at the same time that I could do the job with one hand and still get my vodka with the other. So why stop the machine?" The lady was afraid to go back to her machine for awhile, even in recovery, because she was frightened she would "do something else stupid."

Alcohol affects the brain and the motor functions. Your sobriety puts you in control once again of what you do and how you do it; therefore, remember that safety first is more important than ever. You need to think before you act, and then act with caution because you no longer have the crutch of alcohol to make you unconcerned about your mistakes. Those mistakes could cost you an eye or a limb. Your use of alcohol made you careless, and befuddled the basic thinking that helps us protect ourselves from danger. You will need to reinstill the basic regard for safety that you ignored in the past.

SHARING CRAFT GIFTS

Another part of the new importance of hobbies for you is to be able to share the fruits of your new-found sobriety with others. One of the best ways to gain this foothold on a long-lasting recovery is to put your hobby to good use, making gifts and giving them to family and friends.

This may seem a direct contradiction to my earlier caution to let holiday deadlines go by the wayside to remove pressure, but it's not—really. The beauty of making your gifts is that you can build a little storehouse of projects. You don't have to wait for a special day. In fact, it's a lot better if you don't. I've always liked the Lewis Carroll concept of celebrating an "un-Birthday." So will you. What's important for your recovery is for you to make your gifts and then give them away as you see fit, regardless of whether the occasion is Christmas, a birthday, a graduation, or just a good day to share your joy of sobriety. The recipients will be flattered that you remember them at times that are not traditional for gift-giving. You will get the benefits of receiving special attention at a time when it is not normally expected. While a Christmas gift you make is certainly appreciated, it may get lost in the pile of other lovely things under someone's tree. A gift that is specifically made and then delivered on your time schedule will do a lot to show yourself that you are making continuing progress in your recovery, and not just getting involved in seasonal sobriety.

I often recommend to people that they make a series of gifts to use for their Twelve Days of Christmas or as Hanukkah gifts, as we explored in Chapter Fifteen. You have all year to work on these little gifts, and then the added joy of giving them one day at a time. Try it with things like wood carving, candle making, knitting, and making stained glass. A recovering friend of mine dragged out his old toy soldier casting materials and spent many happy hours making new soldiers to give away on the Twelve Days. Now that he was sober, he could spend the necessary time and do the intricate painting and hand finishing that he had given up during his many years of active drinking. He told me of the great joy he felt hearing from nephews and other children who received these handcrafted articles. And his joy was twofold, because he had weeks of fun making the gifts *and* added days of fun giving them away.

Photographs you have taken, perhaps mounted on a piece of wood and decoupaged, can be worked on all year. Put them in your storehouse, and when a particular non-occasion occurs to you, send the gift. Enclose a card that says, "My joy in being sober needed to be shared with you. Hope you enjoy this remembrance of _____." You can think of other appropriate phrases or notes, but the point is to say them. Let the gift you have made and then shared speak out loud and clear for your sobriety.

FINISHING YOUR PROJECT

Here is one of the biggest changes that you are going to have to work on yourself. In your alcoholic days you started many, many projects, but chances are you didn't finish very many. I can't count the times I've heard people in group therapy tell about the projects that they always started and never finished. Of course, the difference now is that you can and will finish what you start.

In order to help you over this hurdle, I suggest that you limit yourself to only one project at a time. Now, this may seem foolish if the project is, for example, creative baking. Many women (and quite a few men) I know in recovery like to bake bread and give it for special occasions. Well, it certainly doesn't make sense to bake just one loaf of bread; I know that. What I do suggest is that you confine the project to meeting the needs of just one person. If it means that you are going to bake two or three Christmas loaves and some cookies for one particular person or family, then do that. Forget about trying to bake for six or seven different households.

Limit what you do until you have reestablished a solid track record for finishing what you start. Here again, your frustration levels can be held in check. You can utilize your "one-day-at-a-time" philosophy as "one project completed at a time."

It's perfectly natural to want to bite off more than you can chew. You feel so much better in recovery and you have more time to spend, so you fool yourself into thinking that you also have an unlimited energy bank from which to draw. That's not quite so. If you're not careful, you will find yourself starting a bunch of craft or hobby projects, and then burnout will strike. You will end up with a lot of half-done things sitting around, all of them making you angry.

Better to always hold the reins on your activities and use moderation in sobriety. A good tool for you to use to retrain yourself into finishing what you start is to go back and complete something you had started when you were actively alcoholic. Of course, you may very well make the decision that the project is no longer worthy of completion; in that case, destroy it and the memories that went with it, memories that were closely tied to your abuse of the chemical, alcohol. Make a fresh start.

A female client recently told me that she had gone back and totally torn out a large piece of crochet that she had started in her drinking days but never finished. Now she is starting all over and finding great joy and satisfaction in doing it right.

The "mistake box" in my workshop is further evidence of the good therapeutic value of this line of thinking. My unfinished projects found their way to the neighbors' fireplaces, so I can make new starts and, more important, new finishes.

Alcoholic thinking and behavior tend to make you believe that your judgment is invincible. Therefore, the alcoholic will continue to tackle much more than he can handle. Better to start and finish one small project and build a new base of confidence in your sober behavior patterns than to begin another whole mess of things that will go unfinished as well.

A recovering friend has been working for months on building his own house, a job he freely admits would have been impossible during his drinking days. At first, however, he had the same old habits which he had carried over from drinking to recovery—namely, he would hurry up and buy all the materials at once, then let everything sit there because the project became overwhelming. But he realized that he was back into the confetti thinking of his drinking days, so he stopped buying—no matter how good the bargains were—and began finishing what he had started. "It's amazing," he told me recently, "that house is really coming along, now that I'm not trying to be Superman with it."

It's kind of like the army phrase that appeared in so many mess tents worldwide during World War II (along with a lot of others that aren't printable). The slogan was, "Take all you want, but eat all you take."

Do all the projects you want in your recovery, but do them one at a time, and complete one before starting another. That's the way of sobriety.

HAVING HOBBY SPACE

I don't care how small a house, apartment, or room you have. It is essential that you have one little place where you can work on your hobby and not have to pick up after every time you work at it. If you are into model building or puzzle working, then you know the frustration of having to stop and clean up the mess. A lot of really great picture puzzles never get tackled because you haven't assigned a space where the thing can be left alone until you finish it.

Nothing is more discouraging than having to spend more time picking up and putting away than working on the hobby in the first place. This isn't always possible, of course, but wherever you can, assign yourself a working space that can remain undisturbed. The reasons for this are many, but for me, the idea of being able to sit down for fifteen minutes or so and work at my project, maybe while I'm waiting to go somewhere, or before I have to leave for our treatment center, is important. If there isn't a spot where I can sit down and draw a line or two, solder a part, drive a screw, or put a part into the wood clamps, I will soon lose interest in ever working on the project.

Look around your place and see where you can commandeer some unutilized corner or table top for a hobby spot. Of course, you may not want to leave out valuable coins or stamps, but models, ceramics, costume jewelry, and other craft projects can basically be left undisturbed. (However, small children in the house will dictate different security measures.)

One woman I know found a very unusual spot to work on her knitting, insuring that it would be left alone and she would not have to do much pick-up-and-put-away. Here's what Nancy did:

She had several toddlers in her house, and they had all used the playpen which was still in their room. But now that they were older and didn't always require her immediate attention, Nancy could put the boys in their room with their various books, toys, and other amusements, then climb into the playpen to knit. I thought it was the greatest thing I'd ever seen—she had her knitting in one easy-to-carry box, and all she had to do was haul that box into the playpen with her and spread out her materials. It was her space to work on her hobby, and I have laughed about it every time I hear of some client who feels trapped by her small children and can't find anyplace to work on her hobby. I'd be afraid to take a count of how many times I've passed along this unique tool that Nancy first brought to my attention.

So go to it. Find your own playpen and dare anyone to mess around with your hobby space.

HOW MUCH TO SPEND

If you are faced with the desire to start a new hobby but have been trudging around from store to store for days, you are perhaps feeling frightened by the cost of materials. The days of cheap leather, beads, balsa wood, lead, and glass are long gone, but here's one quick and easy way to help your spending. As best you can, add up the amount of money you were spending on your drinking habit.

Be honest. Count the times you stopped into the favorite bar and set up a round or two, left a tip, etc. Look in your checkbook (if you still have the old one) and see how many checks you wrote for liquor. Look back on credit card charges made at liquor stores or restaurants where the bar charges are broken out on the bill. Then remember that if you spend just half that amount on your new hobby, you will be in "fat city." It didn't seem like much when you were doing it, but you were probably spending an easy twenty dollars or more whenever you stopped at the bar or the liquor store. If you did this just twice a week, you can see how much money you can now afford to spend on a hobby. How much more fun it is to spend money on something that can help your long-term recovery rather than contribute to an early death.

Make your hobbies the kinds of things that speak openly of your new wellness.

Fine artwork that requires steady hands and a sound mind shouts out that you are gaining control of your life in sobriety. A neatly organized page of stamps, or cleanly typed and cleverly decorated set of recipe cards shows you and those around you that you are living a life of sober satisfaction. Before, the idea of hobbies was something that could possibly threaten your drinking time. Now, hobbies assume a new importance. They are not just a dreamed-up therapy, but a real solid method to make you feel good about yourself again and demonstrate to all your new joy in being sober. Go forth and create.

MORE JOY (An Update)

My woodworking shop continues to be a primary source of tension relief. There's just something about having to concentrate on running wood through a table saw or the way a router has to be held that makes the cares of the day, week, month and year just fade away.

Since I originally wrote this book, I have added another hobby—one I used to practice as a profession. I had let it drop, but now have picked up creative photography again. As the chapter says, it doesn't really matter what you do for a hobby. What continues to be important is that you celebrate your sobriety by using a new hobby or reviving an old one to demonstrate to yourself (as well as others) that you do make a difference.

It's wonderful to see the ceramics, oil paintings, model airplanes, cars and ships that clients create. They are always eager to keep working on some new project; as I have said before and want to emphasize again, they and you need to fill time that was once spent drinking, and there is no better way to do it than with hobbies.

It also doesn't matter whether anyone else likes your hobby or not. You are doing this for you, and that's what counts. Some of my clients have simply gotten back to assembling jigsaw picture puzzles. They will work for a half-hour or an hour at a time on one of those five-hundred- or five-thousand-piece jobbies. When it's done, many of them will glue the completed puzzle to a wood backing, then frame and hang their work of art. I think it's great—it shows perseverance and originality, even though many of these people have put themselves down by saying they don't "really have any talent."

One lady I worked with got the bright idea of taking old, heavy socks, forming animal or doll's heads, and painting and sewing on faces. She would then add dresses or costumes from scraps of cloth; suddenly she had a cottage industry going, selling her creations quicker than she could make them! She is still at it today, and—need I say?—still sober.

The role of hobbies in your life depends on you. You can continue to make few changes in the way you look at things, which really doesn't add much joy to your sobriety. Or you can decide to make the changes that are necessary to really savor being free from the slavery of alcohol.

When you take up a new hobby or pick up a long-forgotten one, you reclaim your place in your own self-esteem log book. The pleasure and satisfaction that you gain can hardly be measured, it's so complete. Take a look around you at people who are constantly busy doing things that give them pleasure. Do they look younger to you? If any of those people who can never find enough time to work on their hobby seem at all frustrated, it is only in a happy, wonderful sort of way.

How long ago was it that you promised yourself or someone else you would start that charcoal drawing, take those flower arrangement classes once a week, or learn how to tie flies? The hobbies are still there, more than you could ever count. They are crying out to you. I hope you heed their clarion call!

Be sober, be vigilant; because your adversary the devil,

as a roaring lion, walketh about seeking whom he may devour.

1 Peter (5:8) The Holy Bible

STAYING SOBER

So here we are, poised on the end of the diving board that is your new recovery. Shall we take the plunge? For the past nineteen chapters I have been sharing tools, methods, and strategies that help the newly sober person face and enjoy life without alcohol. This is the joy of being sober—to witness each day of your life as a new experience to be lived, not just tolerated; to know that you will be in control of yourself—what you say, what you do, and how you feel and react to what others do and say.

That's a new and wonderful experience, to know what's going on in this life and be a part of it. Remember when you were an observer, watching events through an alcoholic fog of uncaring and unknowing behavior? That's behind you now. The challenges ahead are those that will keep you sober, and keep you making your sobriety the number one priority in your life.

To do this, here is the final set of tools that I lay before you. Like all of the others, these tools can stay within the pages of this book and never find their way into your daily living pattern. Or they can be internalized and used as a regular part of your lifelong recovery program. I call them the Three "Rs" of Recovery:

1. Remember
2. Reinforce
3. Renew

That's easy enough, isn't it? As you go along in your recovery you will be able to add many more words that will trigger behavior modes to help you maintain and add to your sobriety. But for now, these are the basic Three "Rs" that I have used myself and with others in recovery.

REMEMBER

The first of the Three "Rs" is to remember. Remember how it was, and by remembering, compare that to how it is. There will be many instances in your daily life when you will observe other people and their behavior around drinking. The key is to remember that persons not afflicted with the disease of alcoholism can do things with alcohol that you can't. For openers, they can stop drinking. When someone says, "Have another?" the nonalcoholic can comfortably say, "No, thanks. I've had enough." Now, there's no way that you could respond like that. You are an alcoholic, and you will drink as long as there is anything to drink. Not now, of course, because you are sober and in recovery, but you can remember and share with someone how you used to behave.

Remembering is not an effort to keep you nailed to the cross which we spoke of in Chapter Five. It is a tool to make comparisons about how alcoholic behavior and sober behavior are different—how the two worlds that you have lived in are different and how you are enjoying the difference.

AA meetings are the best source of memory-sharing that you will be able to count on as long as you live. But you can also do this work with the significant other in your life, or with the companion you may be with when a particular incident occurs that causes you to think back on your past life.

Using the past can be painful, but growing is painful. Many times the very fact that you can remember an episode in which drinking was a particularly heavy disaster for you works to your advantage in recovery. The people around you who care about your recovery will often think of an episode and be afraid to share it, afraid that it might be too painful. You can encourage their telling you about the memory by saying, "It's okay. I'm strong enough to hear. In fact, I need to hear about my behavior so I can compare."

The thing that will amaze you is that you have been totally unaware of much of your past behavior. The alcoholic amnesia, the blackouts, may have wiped away many things that other people remember as clearly as if they just happened. Then you will be someplace and observe a particular behavior that will trigger a latent memory. Explore it. Make it work for you. It was a different person who acted the way you did when alcohol was the master in life and you were the slave. That's all changed now. It's part of the message of recovery to say, "It's okay to remember the past."

Always use the "R" of remembering in the context of a follow-up. If you are remembering a bad episode, ask for help from your companion who is remembering with you. Say something on the order of, "After that, what happened? What did I do?" When you have heard the entire memory, cite a recent experience where circumstances (a party, for example) were the same, but your behavior was different. This retelling will counteract the bad memory and replace it with new, positive behavior.

Everyone knows that it's easier to forgive than to forget, but you, the newly sober person, need to be willing to do both. You can forgive your behavior because alcohol was calling your every move. You can then begin the process of forgetting the pain by remembering the incident, talking about it, and sharing it with another.

Most people will need encouragement from you to do the memory work with you. They may see something that reminds them of how you were. They start to chuckle, or say, "Do you..." before stopping short, fearing that the membory will be too painful. You need to encourage them to go ahead and say what's on their mind. If it's about you and your past behavior, you need to know, because it will strengthen your recovery.

The need for you to remember will also help tie together many missing links in your past life that were conveniently submerged in booze. Sure, there will be some pain, maybe even some tears at remembering. But the self-therapy provided will outweigh a raft of "stuffing" that you may have been in the habit of doing.

Remembering just naturally leads us to the second "R":

REINFORCE

Whenever a client tells me that he has had a particularly moving experience in his new life, I urge him to recount the details so he can fix things firmly in his mind. Drinking prevented the good experiences that sober behavior allows.

To reinforce his sobriety, I then ask him how he would have acted when he was drinking in a similar circumstance, repeating the exact same set of details of the incident. Then, together, we explore how sober behavior far surpasses the old, alcoholic ways. You do the same every time you make comparisons. What you do is build in the good strokes, turn them into Warm Fuzzies for yourself, and then compare them to past behavior. Thus, you reinforce your desire to remain alcohol-free for the rest of your life.

When you achieve a particular accomplishment, you need to say, "Could I have done this if I were drinking?" It's always better to share out loud, to verbalize, but if there is no one around and you are some time away from a meeting or group therapy session where you can share with others, go ahead and ask yourself. This reinforcement works for you because the answers are mostly positive.

I recall a recovering person who used to take great pride in telling people, "I never got so drunk that I'd fall down." What this person had conveniently misfiled in his alcoholic memory bank was that he remembered just part of the story. While it was true that he didn't make a public spectacle of himself, his wife recalled incidents of his getting up in the middle of the night and taking horrendous falls. He would have great bruises on his arms and legs and not know where they came from.

Together, this couple began using the second "R" to reinforce his new, sober behavior. It became a game for them, one they openly shared with their friends. It went like this: he would see some poor fellow having to be helped up from the floor of a party or restaurant. Our recovering friend would start the process by saying, "Boy, that's one thing I never did when I was drinking." Then his wife would pick up her cue by saying, "No, Charlie, you sure didn't, but tell them what you did do." Charlie then began his reinforcement procedure by relating that he had been told that he would fall and stumble, hurting himself quite badly sometimes. His wife told me that Charlie would always add, "Thank God I don't have to do that anymore." And she would always add, "Nor explain where those awful bruises came from."

The reinforcement tool was deftly used when the couple would explain that Charlie's disease wiped out the memories of those incidents, and that seeing the person who had been helped from the floor only made their dual commitment to a new life of recovery and sobriety that much stronger.

It's a good tool, this second "R," and there are almost no limits on how it can be used. The person who could never drive himself home (thank God they didn't let him try), or the person who could not handle a particular task because of alcohol impairment can reinforce their new sobriety and their commitment to recovery every time they have the chance. Encourage others in your life to help you use the second "R." Give them every opportunity to hand out the strokes you need to hear, the positive results of your life without alcohol. Simple things like being able to thread a needle (you used to shake too badly to do it), hitting a tennis ball over the net, riding a bicycle, or mowing the lawn in a straight path are all simple little everyday tasks that many people take for granted, but you should never take anything for granted. You have had the help of many people and the God of your understanding to bring you to this path of recovery. Everything that other people take for granted is material you can appreciate for all it's worth. Use everyday challenges as methods to reinforce the difference between the good life and the dismal, depressing, frantic life of the sick alcoholic.

Reinforce you own good behavior patterns by repeating them. Don't try a task just once and then, knowing you can perform it, give it up. Do it consistently so that it will become firmly implanted. Your sobriety and recovery is enabling you to perform whatever the task may be.

You may drive people nuts for awhile, but keep telling them, "I need to hear that," or, "Thanks for telling me that. It's very important that I hear the differences in my life." Reinforce your program by visiting the hospitals and the detox wards on a more regular basis. See the other people who are just beginning their painful steps toward recovery. Remember where you were, then reinforce how far you have come.

When compliments are given you, accept them graciously, but always tie them into your recovery as added reinforcement for sobriety. "You've lost weight," says someone. You thank them and add, "That old booze was adding a lot of extra calories." Be open and forthright. The person you are reinforcing is yourself, and you need all the help you can get. When other people seem embarrassed to mention some facet of your past behavior, help them out and turn it into a reinforcement. "That's the way it was" is more to you than just the familiar sign-off used by Walter Cronkite. Be the first to acknowledge that was how it was, and quickly follow it with how it *is* in your life now. Don't let even one opportunity to reinforce yourself pass you by. As I suggested in Chapter Two, look at old photographs of yourself taken when you were drinking, then either look at a recent photograph or just hold the old photo up beside a mirror and note the difference.

No more puffy yellow eyes; they're nice and clear and white. No excess jowls that made you look like Miss Piggy even when you were starving yourself of everything except alcohol.

All of these positive reinforcements are necessary for you to maintain sobriety and continue to build your solid program of recovery.

RENEW

This last of my Three "Rs" is my favorite. Renew yourself in both spirit and body every chance you get.

We have already addressed the importance of spiritual activities for the recovering person. Your regular attendance and active use of the fellowship of AA is a proven method of continued sobriety. It's there for you to use as a renewal tool for both mind and spirit—all you have to do is make the effort to get there. Make the effort to call someone to get you to a meeting.

The "R" of renewal for your physical well-being is the most tangible evidence that you are beginning to be a new person. Your recovery is allowing you to feel again, to know the firm grip of a golf club in your hands, the pedals of a bike beneath your feet, the walks in the park, and the sting of snow on your lashes as you breathe in the fresh, clean air of a winter's day.

Every ounce of weight that comes off your body is another plus for the tool of renewal. You are being given the opportunity to build up the very thing (your body) that you spent so long tearing down. You know how food tastes in your sober state, how your energy levels build slowly but steadily until you actually get kind of antsy if you can't exercise.

Even if you are confined to a wheelchair or crutches, your life is better without alcohol. You must never give up on the fact that you have taken certain steps to intervene in the process that was destroying you far more than whatever tragedy had caused your disability.

For each of you—for every person who has taken the steps toward a life of recovery—there is the spectre of it all being wiped out with a return to the drinking arena that once was your life. It will require every support tool and every system of personal recovery that you can muster for the rest of your life to continue to enjoy the fruits of sobriety, but you can and will do it. The tools we have examined together within this book are there for you every time. There are others as well, and you will learn them as you wend your way along the sober path.

The joy of being sober is a personal joy. It is a breath of second life, and with your committed effort it can sustain you at times when you believe there is no hope, when the pressures of the disease threaten to flow over you like the swollen banks of a river.

If you are secure in the knowledge that to drink is to die, and that to remain sober is to truly live, then you have the very essence of life itself. No matter what befalls in the way of personal trials and tribulations, a return to alcohol is not the answer. Your personal program of recovery will gain strength with every shared moment with other recovering people, with every hand you extend to the other unfortunates who are afflicted with this disease.

This is not the end, but the start of your attempt to savor the real stuff of victory. And it is more than ever up to you to pick up your life and carry on with the resolve that you will never again turn to alcohol as an attempt to cope.

For you and for millions of others who have discovered it, there is a special joy in being sober. It is a joy I share gladly with you, no matter who you are. It is a force more positive than any kick received from champagne or any other alcoholic beverage.

You know it's there. Use it. Let it fly forth from you with great abandon. You earn it every day you draw breath. It is yours for the taking, this joy of being sober!

MORE JOY (An Update)

I cannot tell you the number of times that editors at publishing houses have come unglued because of my use of an exclamation mark. It seems that I just can't keep things under control—I have to put my excitement into my writing because I feel the joy of being sober so strongly. (Now, right there was a place I wanted to use an exclamation mark, but after eight or nine books, I'm getting better—and my editors are getting more tolerant.) What I'm trying to say ought to be obvious—there's just such a wonderful feeling in having your sobriety. It's such a precious gift that I am constantly amazed more people don't try it on a permanent basis.

It seems in every relapse case I deal with in practice, the person always believes that somehow they have "learned" to drink after a period of sobriety. There is absolutely no rationale for that, but then you know how "stinkin' thinkin'" can get a person in trouble.

When I see people who are still struggling with the denial of their disease, I try to encourage them to focus on how the three Rs of this chapter can help them cross over the line from failure to success. There's hardly a day that passes when I don't remember, reinforce and renew an experience that contributes to the solidity of my sobriety.

One thing I have come to really enjoy since I first wrote this book is hearing from readers of my work. I have received letters or phone calls from all over the country, and from several foreign countries. Each person wants to share some experience they have had around their sobriety or around the recovery program of someone close to them.

It is far more of an ego boost for a writer to hear from readers who like what they have read, but I assure you that I can handle criticism, too! What's important is that the reader took the time to drop a line because something I said between these covers made sense to him, made a difference in how she looks at things, or sparked the desire to either enter the world of sobriety or to try again.

My friends, the joy of being sober never ends. You can get it; you can keep it; and you can pass it along to a friend. If you would like to write to me, please do so at the following address:

Jack Mumey
Gateway Treatment Center
1250 South Parker Road, # 103
Denver, Colorado 80231

As before—now more than ten years ago—I have written these words with the hope that they will encourage someone somewhere who has not had the courage before to realize his or her potential to rejoin the human race and live the life that was intended—free, happy, loving, and, one day at a time, sober.

ABOUT THE AUTHOR

Jack Mumey is a nationally known author, workshop speaker, and lecturer. He is the author of seven books on alcoholism and relationships, including *Sex and Sobriety* (Simon & Schuster), *Loving an Alcoholic* (Bantam), *Secrets in the Family* (Contemporary), and *Age Different Relationships* with Cynthia Tinsley (Deaconess Press). Mumey holds state and national certifications as an alcohol counselor (CACIII, NCACII), and is a practicing hypnotherapist. He is the owner and president of Gateway Treatment Center in Denver, Colorado.